MW00899394

Can Mitt Romney Serve Two Masters?

The Mormon Church
Versus the Office of The Presidency
of the United States of America

Tricia Erickson

WestBow Press books may be ordered through booksellers or by contacting:

WestBow Press
A Division of Thomas Nelson
1663 Liberty Drive
Bloomington, IN 47403
www.westbowpress.com
1-(866) 928-1240

ISBN: 978-1-4497-1199-3 (sc)
ISBN: 978-1-4497-1200-6 (dj)
ISBN: 978-1-4497-1201-3 (e)

Library of Congress Control Number: 2011921677

Printed in the United States of America

WestBow Press rev. date: 5/31/2011

Contents

Introduction vii

Part 1 – Spiritual Portion 1

Chapter 1. Mormon History That, As a Presidential Candidate, Mitt Romney Does Not Want You to Know 3

Chapter 2. "The Blood Trail" 22

Chapter 3. Where Does Mitt Romney's Loyalty Lie? 31

Chapter 4. Mitt's Secretive Oaths, Allegiance, Covenants, Pledges to Death Penalties, and Commitments to the Mormon Church—And Its Bizarre Temple Rituals and Beliefs 43

Chapter 5. Mitt Will Try to Hide the Outrageous Racism Against the Black Race Taught Through His Church's Doctrine . 56

Chapter 6. Is the Mormon Church a Christian Denomination or a Cult? 68

Chapter 7. If Mitt Lives in Deception, Should We Not Question His Judgment to Discern the Truth in All Dominion of The Office Of The Presidency of the United States of America? 83

Part 2 – Political Portion 99

Chapter 8. The Mormon Church and Its Image Machine: A Clean-Cut Corporation 101

Chapter 9. Mormons In Politics 111

Chapter 10. Politics in the Family, Like Father, Like Son: George and Mitt Romney 123

Chapter 11. The White Horse: Salt Lake City and the Olympics 135

Chapter 12. Romney as Governor 147

Chapter 13. The 2008 Presidential Campaign: The Mormons, Mitt, and DeMoss 166

Chapter 14. Romney Reinvents Himself Yet Again 217

Conclusion 231

Introduction

(Note: I wrote this book in two parts. The first part, what I call the "Spiritual" part, is completely applicable to the second "Political" part of the book. However, if you are only interested in the political portion regarding Mitt Romney's political record, this book will be a tremendous resource for you.)

As a little girl, I recall my Mormon mother brushing my hair while getting her five kids ready for church. She said to me, "Pat (they called me Pat back then), you don't believe in our religion, do you?" This little Mormon bishop's daughter answered, "No, mommy, I don't." I couldn't have been more than nine years old, but when I think back on this, I thank the living God for the precious gift of discernment, even as a child. If God had not placed that wonderful spirit in me, I would not have written this book and I may have very well remained blinded to the truth and enslavement of my soul to the horrendously blasphemous lies of the well-masked cult of Mormonism.

I know this book will be a hard pill to swallow for some, including members of my own family who are still very much entrenched in the Mormon religion. I write this book with love for them, and with love for this great nation. In fact, when people are chastised for telling the politically incorrect truth, my response is that *it is a loving thing to tell the truth.* You see, when people are in the distorted state of mind of deception, I believe that if we choose to leave them there, it is a form of abandonment. I believe that if you love someone, you owe it to guide him or her into the truth in order that he or she can truly be set free. And you can almost take it to the bank that when lies are involved, the liar has something to gain, and it usually has to do with money or power.

When NPR fired Juan Williams regarding his comments about feeling uneasy when he sees people in Muslim garb on planes, his statement was actually forthcoming because most Americans truly feel the same way. However, they are not able to communicate this logical feeling, in light of 9–11, because the politically correct police will not allow it. Juan stated that political correctness could *"lead to some kind of paralysis, where you don't address reality."* What a profound statement!

In my humble opinion, I truly think we, as a nation, can no longer overlook the *reality* of any aspect of the background, character, belief system, and political truth that has formed the man or woman who will become the next president of the United States of America. There is too much at stake!

We have seen what can happen in the passion of it all. America voted, out of exhilarating emotion, for our current President Obama and his handlers banked on the fact that our media-driven generation would be drawn to the euphoria of *hope and change.*

The Obama 2008 campaign handlers put the bait out to the American people in great confidence that Obama could be presented in the nice pretty package of *the one we have all been waiting for.* His handlers understood that while Americans were distracted by elated feelings and excitement, Obama's actual credentials and experience would be bypassed. The American people took the bait and received the switch.

And here we are again with another Obama wrapped in Romney clothing. When you examine Romney's political history, the connected dots lead us to a very familiar smoke and mirror strategy. If Mitt looks presidential, speaks in an eloquent presidential tone, exudes confidence, and possesses the demeanor of capability, we can very well be led into the same 2008 result.

In addition, as Mitt Romney skirts around his religious beliefs, let me warn you that this is not another Kennedy Catholic moment. The Mormon religion is much more toxic to the control of the human mind, as you will see in part 1 of this book.

Please hear what I am saying. Mitt Romney's Mormonism, even as he makes great effort to distance himself from it, is a complete part of his DNA. What Mormon influence, if any, has escaped him, his massive liberal record makes up for it. Mitt is about as authentically conservative as Obama is authentically concerned with the well-being of our nation.

My hope is that this book will open your eyes to the importance of doing authentic diligence before we ever even think about voting with our hearts again. Our hearts are fickle, but the truth will set us free.

Matthew 6:24 (King James Version)

No man can serve two masters: for either he will hate the one, and love the other; or else he will hold to the one, and despise the other. Ye cannot serve God and mammon.

Part I

Spiritual Portion

Chapter 1

Mormon History That, As a Presidential Candidate, Mitt Romney Does Not Want You to Know

> I'm very proud of my faith, and it's the faith of my fathers, and I certainly believe that it is a, a faith—well, it's true, and I love my faith. And I'm not going to distance myself in any way from my faith! (Mitt Romney, *Meet the Press,* 2007)

In addition to the above interview, 2008 presidential candidate Mitt Romney affirmed to Greta Van Susteren that he would not be talking so much about the religion of Mormonism in his speech, but more about the plurality of faith in America. This is code for *there is so much to hide about the Mormon Church that I'll just dance around the Mormon issue by talking about faith in general.*

Mitt is a seasoned side-stepper and get-arounder (notice that I didn't mention that he is also a flip-flopper, which rhymes) who possesses the ability to posture and position himself to come across to the American people in a smooth and charming way.

In the 2008 election, Mitt's Kool-Aid was offered up to America in a slick, flowery speech about faith. When you think about it, in this tolerant era, the creed of tolerance is politically correct. Therefore, intolerance of Mitt's religion would be considered bigotry, right? Well, let's see … Mormons emphatically say and believe that The Church of Jesus Christ of Latter-day Saints, the Mormon Church, is the "one and only *true* church" on the face of this earth. Translated (no pun intended), that means all faiths other than the Mormon religion are false. Would this then not suggest that the Mormons are *not* tolerant of all faiths?

On the surface, you may pass over the above statement by Romney as just another Christian going on the record to establish his religious view, or *faith*; however, we must ask ourselves the following questions:

- What does his statement mean to you and me as it relates to Mitt Romney's ability to perform the duty of president of the United States if elected to office?
- What does his church (The Church of Jesus Christ of Latter-day Saints) teach, and as a professed Mormon, what does Mitt Romney believe?
- With Mitt as president, could this church's shady past affect *your* future?

To know the answers to such questions, we must first understand Mitt's church, its origin, its structure, and its teachings. I am not sharing this to bog you down in the history of it all, but it is important to illuminate the false teachings of this church that Mitt Romney believes in from its inception. These teachings were based upon the writings of a man named Joseph Smith.

In The Beginning: Joseph Smith and the Mormon Church

Joseph Smith was born on December 23, 1805, in Sharon, Vermont. He was the fifth child of Joseph Smith Sr. and Lucy Smith. The Smith family moved frequently around the New England area due to crop failure and disease during the era.

During the winter of 1815, young Joseph had an infection in his leg. The prognosis was not good and doctors suggested amputation. However, the Smith family refused and opted for a surgery that left Joseph with a long recovery and a lifetime limp.

Around 1816, after three years of crop failures in Norwich, Virginia, the Smith family was "warned out of town." Reasons for this are unknown. Perhaps, they were related to the family's financial difficulties. Joseph Smith Sr. moved alone to Palmyra, New York and his family soon followed. In Palmyra village, the father and his oldest sons took odd jobs and opened a "cake and beer shop." Because of the Smith children's necessity to help support the family, Joseph received minimal education.

In 1818, the family obtained a one-hundred-acre farm just outside Palmyra. Joseph Smith Sr. built a frame house on their new property; however, in 1825 the Smiths were unable to raise money for their final mortgage payment, and their creditor foreclosed on the property. In spite of this, the family was able to persuade a local Quaker, Lemuel Durfee, to buy the farm and rent it back to them.

As an adolescent, Joseph supplemented the family income through *treasure digging*. He was introduced to treasure digging by an itinerant magician and diviner who offered his services to the residents of Palmyra. The magician/diviner claimed he could not only locate ground water beneath the surface but buried Indian treasure as well. Some farmers believed the mystic's claims and hired him to find buried treasure on their land.

Joseph took great interest in the skills of the diviner and spent a great deal of time in his company attempting to learn from him and master his divining ability. One such ability was the use of magic stones, which the diviner peered into in order to discover the sites of buried treasure. This was done by placing the stones in a white stovepipe hat to envision the required information through reflections given off by the stone—this is an occult practice linked to witchcraft. However, no treasure was found, thus halting pay from additional farmers and sending the magician and con man on his way. But Joseph had spent enough time with the man to pick up some of his traits and acquired some magic stones of his own, so he went to work conning unsuspecting farmers in different areas. He had no greater success than his mentor did in finding treasure and soon charges were brought against Joseph for being an impostor.

He was also a fantasist. At the age of fourteen, Joseph claimed to experience a vision of two beings that appeared before him in flesh and bones. The Smith family had been to numerous churches and Joseph was seeking answers about God and religion. On his quest to seek the truth of which religion was the true religion, he went into the woods to pray and inquire of the Lord. According to Joseph Smith in his writings found in *Joseph Smith—History: Extracts from the History of Joseph Smith, The Prophet, Volume 1:*

> 16. I saw a pillar of light exactly over my head, above the brightness of the sun, which descended gradually until it fell upon me.

> 17. It no sooner appeared than I found myself delivered from the enemy which held me bound. When the light rested upon me I saw two Personages, whose brightness and glory defy all description, standing above me in the air. One of them spake unto me, calling me by name and said, pointing to the other—This is My Beloved Son. Hear Him!
>
> 18. My object in going to inquire of the Lord was to know which of all the sects was right, that I might know which to join. No sooner, therefore, did I get possession of myself, so as to be able to speak, than I asked the Personages who stood above me in the light, which of all the sects was right (for at this time it had never entered into my heart that all were wrong)—and which I should join.
>
> 19. *I was answered that I must join none of them, for they were all wrong; and the Personage who addressed me said that all their creeds were an abomination in his sight; that those professors were all corrupt;* that: "they draw near to me with their lips, but their hearts are far from me, they teach for doctrines the commandments of men, having a form of godliness, but they deny the power thereof."
>
> 20 *He again forbade me to join with any of them.*[1] [Emphasis added]

According to Smith's account, *all* creeds are an abomination to God, therefore the *only* church in the world that is legitimate is The Church of Jesus Christ of Latter-day Saints. This misconception by the Mormon Church still holds today.

In spite of the fact that Smith claimed to only hold a third-grade education while producing some of these writings in his teens, it should be reiterated here that The Church of Jesus Christ of Latter-day Saints (LDS) base its religious beliefs and doctrine largely upon *his* writings. In fact, Mormons place as much or more importance upon these writings than the Bible. So much so, that the first line in the introduction of The Book of Mormon states, "The Book of Mormon is a volume of holy scripture *comparable* to the Bible."[2]

Joseph Smith claimed to experience an additional encounter on September 21, 1823, with Moroni, "a glorified resurrected being."

According to Smith, Moroni possessed golden plates retaining the record of many ancient prophets; the record was an abridgment of the works of the prophets and seers that were recorded by a prophet historian named Mormon, who was the father of Moroni.

Smith further claimed that four years later, on September 22, 1827, Moroni delivered those plates to him and instructed him regarding transcribing the ancient record. Smith took with him a box that *allegedly* contained the golden plates.

His story continued that he began transcribing some of the characters that were engraved on the plates, in a language he described as "reformed Egyptian," although there is no archeological evidence that "reformed Egyptian" ever existed as a language. Smith further claimed that he used silver spectacles with lenses made of seer stones for translation. However, there are no witnesses of Smith using such spectacles for translation.

There are additional claims of him sitting at a table and often behind a curtain with the box (containing the plates) placed before him, while he used the same or similar method that he had previously used as a treasure hunter. This included gazing into the bottom of his hat at a seer stone while excluding all light so that he could allegedly see the translation reflecting off the stone.

Joseph Smith would not allow anyone to see the golden plates that he was supposedly transcribing. Furthermore, when asked by his father-in-law Isaac Hale to see the alleged plates, Joseph refused and a Mormon website reports him saying, "If anyone besides himself looked at the golden plates, it would mean instant death for the person."[3]

Yet, The Book of Mormon claims that eleven people witnessed the golden plates. Four of the witnesses included Jospeph Smith, his brother, their father, and Oliver Cowdery, the man who later helped scribe the translation. While there are eleven signatures included in The Book of Mormon testifying that these individuals actually witnessed the golden plates, beyond their testimony there is *no* proof!

Smith's translation of these supposed plates is now known as The Book of Mormon and according to the current Book of Mormon, Joseph Smith translated the golden plates *"by the gift and power of God."*[4] [Emphasis added]

During the time of the translation, Oliver Cowdery (1806–1850) acted as scribe to Joseph Smith and witness of The Book of Mormon (1829), he was second elder of the church (1830), assistant president of the church (1834), editor, and lawyer. Oliver Cowdery was next in authority to Joseph Smith in 1830.

According to Smith and Cowdery, "On May 15, 1829, John the Baptist appeared to them near Harmony, Pennsylvania, and bestowed the Aaronic Priesthood on them. This ordination gave the two men authority to baptize, and they immediately performed that ordinance for one another in the Susquehanna River. The Prophet Joseph Smith had received no previous revelations authorizing him to baptize; to perform that ordinance properly required specific authorization from God. The return of John to bestow the Aaronic Priesthood confirmed that divine authority had been lost from the earth and that a heavenly visitation was necessary to restore it."

> 69. Upon you my fellow servants, in the name of Messiah, I confer the Priesthood of Aaron, which holds the keys of the ministering of angels, and of the gospel of repentance, and of Baptism by immersion for the remission of sins; and this shall never be taken again from the earth until the sons of Levi do offer again an offering unto the Lord in Righteousness.
>
> 70. He said this Aaronic Priesthood had not the power of laying on hands for the gift of the Holy Ghost, but that this should be conferred on us hereafter; and he commanded us to go and be baptized, and gave us directions that I should baptize Oliver Cowdery, and that afterwards he should baptize me.
>
> 71. Accordingly we went and were baptized. I baptized him first, and afterwards he baptized me—after which I laid my hands upon his head and ordained him to the Aaronic Priesthood, and afterwards he laid his hands on me and ordained me to the same Priesthood—for so we were commanded.
>
> 72. The messenger who visited us on this occasion and conferred this Priesthood upon us, said that his name was John, the same that is called John the Baptist in the New Testament, and that he acted under the direction of Peter, James and John, who held the keys of the Priesthood of Melchizedek, which Priesthood, he said, would in due time be conferred on us, and that I should be called

> the first Elder of the Church, and he (Oliver Cowdery) the second. It was on the fifteenth day of May, 1829, that we were ordained under the hand of this messenger, and baptized.[5]

So according to this account, Smith claimed that he and Cowdery were baptized and also given authority to baptize by John the Baptist while Peter, James, and John who had the keys of the priesthood of Melchizedek watched.

Smith and Cowdery continued to translate the plates until The Book of Mormon was complete. Joseph Smith himself declared The Book of Mormon to be *"the most correct of any book on earth."*[6]

Yet, over *3,900* changes were made to the book since that statement was issued. The evidence that this is a misguided, fallacious, and arrogant statement is overwhelming.

In 1830, 5,000 copies of The Book of Mormon were printed. According to Smith, the golden plates were returned to heaven, leaving us no way to verify the existence of them or to validate the translation. It would be more believable if theses golden plates were available for inspection—there is no scientific evidence that proves they ever existed.

- How do we know that these plates ever existed?
- How can we be sure of their origin?
- How do we know that the supposed translation is correct?

Joseph Smith and the Mormon Church are asking us to place blind faith in his interpretation without a shred of evidence to back up any of his claims. Therefore, it is not unreasonable to question why God would leave historical and physical evidence of manuscripts of the Bible yet take away these plates. Christianity possesses proof of its text for every Scripture *except* the entire writings of Joseph Smith. This should be a red flag for those who are dedicated to this religion or considering becoming so.

Mormons believe The Book of Mormon is *another* testament of Jesus Christ, and that it is Holy Scripture comparable to the Bible. They use a combination of many books to establish doctrines and teaching of the LDS church including, The Book of Mormon, the Bible, *The Doctrine and Covenants* and *The Pearl of Great Price.* In addition to the aforementioned is

The Journal of Discourses. This is a twenty-six volume set of public sermons, discourses, lectures, etc. These are discourses that were delivered by the "Mormon Presidency," the "Mormon Twelve Apostles" and others officially sanctioned by Brigham Young and his two counselors. We will discuss the "Presidency" and the "Twelve" in chapter 2.

Fayette, New York

Smith claimed to have a mandate from God to open his church (that would be based upon his writings) and on April 6, 1830, he organized the first church at Fayette, New York. He opened under the name the Church of Christ. Four years later, on May 3 of 1834, the name was changed to The Church of Latter-day Saints. Then on April 26, 1838, the name changed to The Church of Jesus Christ of Latter-day Saints, also referred to as The Mormon Church, with the two names remaining to this day. While in Fayette, the church experienced growth and expanded to three small congregations.

In late January 1831, Joseph Smith and his wife Emma moved from New York to Kirtland, Ohio, and began a new church there. After being arrested on two different occasions in New York, Joseph thought that it was time to flee "the power of the enemy."

Kirtland, Ohio

The three small churches from New York migrated to Kirtland, Ohio. Kirtland was the second home of the church and it was not long until the congregation grew to one hundred people.

The church began its outreach from Kirtland and expanded in the direction of Missouri. Joseph taught that the Garden of Eden was located in Missouri and was called "Adam-ondi-Ahman." He further taught that the second coming of Christ would be to "Adam-ondi-Ahman." This is one of the two cities of Zion that Smith taught to be the New Jerusalem, located in Independence, Jackson County, Missouri, with the additional city of Zion as the city of Jerusalem in the land of Judah.

Construction of a new temple in Kirtland began in May 1833 and its dedication took place on March 27, 1836. The building came at a great sacrifice both physically and financially.

Times were tough in the 1830s and the community was having trouble keeping pace with the growth while debts mounted up for the church. Joseph Smith decided that opening a bank in November 1836 would alleviate some of the financial problems. He called this new bank the Kirtland Safety Society Bank. There was one major problem to his plan: the state of Ohio refused to grant him a charter.

Smith was infuriated, claiming that God told him that he was to open the bank and nothing could stop him from obeying the Lord. According to Smith, the license was denied because they were Mormon. Smith and his partner Sidney Rigdon opened the bank anyway.

They began printing bank notes that were unauthorized and all but worthless. While they boasted of having over $600,000 in coinage, accounts show they had about $60,000. Less than one month after opening the currency was trading for 12.5 cent per dollar.

Smith opened the bank to achieve a communal society where the members of the church would deed their property over to the church for the benefit of the community. The church would allow the members use of the land to make a living. The land was to be redistributed based on the size of a family and its need.[7]

This was the beginning of woes in Ohio and again Smith found himself on the wrong side of the law. He was arrested for violating state banking laws. A trial followed and he and Rigdon were both found guilty and fined $1,000.

Soon after, a warrant for the arrest of Smith and Rigdon was issued for bank fraud. These charges were more serious. Smith knew that if he and Rigdon were convicted, his dream of establishing his church would be squelched!

January 12, 1838, Smith and Rigdon fled Kirtland and moved to Caldwell County, Missouri, in hope of escaping the indictment and a return to prison.

Missouri 1831–1838

From 1831–1838 the Mormon Church was located in two primary locations: Kirtland, Ohio, and Independence, Missouri. After the failure of the bank in Kirtland and following the scandal that ensued, the Mormons migrated to Missouri as the church found another area to occupy.

The Mormons were not welcomed with open arms in Missouri either. Their reputation had found its way to the area before their arrival. From the beginning of their arrival in Missouri, the Mormons were looked upon as troublemakers. Fanning the flames and adding to the growing disdain was the teaching of Joseph Smith who called the locals (who were non-Mormons) "gentiles." The hostility worsened when he began to proclaim that Zion was to be built and that the current occupants would have to give up their homes and leave the area.

This teaching raised eyebrows of both the Missourians and the Mormons. The dissent of Mormons was intense and many left the church. Smith labeled the deserters apostates. Trying to hold the flock together while putting down the dissenters brought about a new organization known as the Danites. The Danites, also known as "Avenging Angels," were a military organization of secret police used to prevent dissention in the church. More fittingly, they were henchmen for the prophet, tasked to kill and torture for him.

Threats of legal action by the apostates prompted even harsher replies from both Rigdon and Smith, who declared that they "had been harassed to death, as it were, for seven or eight years, and they were determined to bear it no longer, for they would rather die than suffer such things." Joseph went as far to say "he did not intend in the future to have any process on him, and the officer who attempted it should die." As he put it, "any person who said a word against the heads of the Church, should be driven over these prairies as a chased deer by a pack of hounds."

To back up his threats, Joseph permitted the formation of a secret group of enforcers to "sustain church leaders without question." More bluntly they were organized "for the purpose of plundering and murdering enemies of the saints" They were called the Danites.[8]

Smith was trying to establish a theocratic state, which met opposition from the civil society already in place. Governor Lilburn Boggs issued an extermination order to defuse the situation and to shut down the church and its apparent effort to take over the territory. There were skirmishes between the Missourians and the Mormons. The Missourians prevailed and the Mormons again were forced to leave.

The Mormons had a history of being driven out of just about every place they tried to settle. While the Mormons proclaim *they* were persecuted and wrongfully run out of many towns, the truth is that they did most of the persecuting themselves and were often forced to leave a town for illegal acts and for trying to take the women as their polygamous wives.

On page 444 of *The History of the Church,* Joseph wrote that "he was obliged to flee" his persecutors just as the apostles and prophets of old were forced to do the same.

Nauvoo, Illinois

Nauvoo, Illinois, was the central gathering place for the Church of Jesus Christ of Latter-day Saints from 1839 to 1846. Joseph Smith, the founder of the church, purchased the site of the town of Commerce, located at the Mississippi River near Quincy. According to Smith, Nauvoo was a word that meant, "a beautiful location, a place of rest." Mormons moved to Nauvoo from all over the United States. The impact of the migration was felt almost immediately in that the population grew from a few thousand to close to 20,000 over the course of the next few years. The state legislature gave a charter to the city in 1840 permitting the city to form a militia and to organize its own municipal courts. Smith hoped that the Mormon militia would protect them from any further persecution.

Smith tried to create a capital city at Nauvoo for the church. A temple was constructed on a bluff that overlooked the city, a large hotel was constructed, and plans for a university were made.

He also became involved in politics in Nauvoo where he served as mayor of the city and was chosen to be lieutenant general of the militia.

Some of his most distinctive and controversial doctrines were revealed in Nauvoo. The practice of baptism for the dead was a ritual that, according to Smith, allowed those who were deceased to receive the benefits of the Mormon faith. (This practice still exists today and will be discussed in chapter 4.)

Joseph Smith also taught the principle of eternal plural marriage and instituted rituals that were available only to selected church members in the privacy of the temple. The doctrine of polygamy, allowing men to have multiple wives, was first practiced in Nauvoo and caused a rift in the church.

In fact, there are varying reports of Smith having thirty to forty wives, of which ten were already married to other men. Roughly a third of Smith's wives were teenagers, including two fourteen-year-old girls. It was taught that the practice of polygamy was upright because God ordained it through his prophets in order to build up a righteous community. The revelation also stated that these wives were sealed to these men throughout eternity and would remain married to them when they became gods in heaven.

Because opposition to the Mormons was growing in Nauvoo, a reformist movement was formed to oust them from local politics. The reformers pooled their resources to purchase a printing press and publish a newspaper that exposed Smith's false doctrine, which caused the church great concern. When Smith closed down the paper by destroying its press and burning the undistributed copies, non-Mormon citizens in the surrounding towns called for Smith's arrest.

Both Joseph and Hyrum Smith were arrested and held at the local jail for this crime. A local Mormon, Cyrus Wheelock, smuggled two pistols into their prison, giving one to each of the Smiths. On June 27, 1844, while the Smiths were awaiting trial, a lynching party invaded the jail. Both Smiths fired into the crowd, killing two men and wounding a third. During the shoot-out, both Joseph and Hyrum were shot and killed.

Were they murdered? Yes! Were they martyred as the LDS proclaim? No! This was an old-fashioned gunfight that ended in the death of Joseph Smith and his brother.

Brigham Young

"Brigham Young, who succeeded Smith as president of the church, remained in Nauvoo until opposition rose again. Young was operating a printing press and was engaged in counterfeiting. Government records indicate that Young along with apostle Willard Richards, John Taylor, Parley Pratt, Orson Hyde and others were involved in making counterfeit coinage."

"When US marshals reached Nauvoo in December of 1845 to arrest Young, he went into hiding in hopes of circumventing the law as Joseph had done so many times. Faced with the possibility of federal troops showing up, Young decided the exodus west could no longer wait. Young announced his response to the new threat on February 3, 1846, before a crowd at the newly finished temple. He did not try to explain away the counterfeiting charges, nor did declare that he would allow the courts to prove his innocence. Young simply stated that he would be taking his family west."[9]

On February 6, 1846, in the dead of winter and in cowardly fashion, the Mormons began to leave Nauvoo for the west. Shortly thereafter, the remainder of the saints followed and the temple was burned. Today Nauvoo has been restored as a tourist site and the reconstruction of the temple was completed in 2002.

Brigham Young the "Prophet"?

Brigham Young (June 1, 1801-August 29, 1877) was the second prophet and president of the Church of Jesus Christ of Latter-day Saints. Young is perhaps the most important person in LDS history after Joseph Smith Jr.

Young was born to a farming family in Vermont and worked as a traveling carpenter and blacksmith. He married his first wife in 1824 and lived with her until her death in 1833.

Young was a Methodist who converted to Mormonism after reading The Book of Mormon shortly after its publication in 1830. He officially joined the new church in 1832 and traveled to Canada as a missionary. After the death of his first wife in 1833, Young moved to Kirtland, Ohio, and joined many Mormons in establishing the community there.

In 1840 and 1841, Young traveled to England as a missionary and converted many people to The Church of Jesus Christ of Latter-day Saints. Many converts from England later moved to the United States to join Mormon communities. Young was among those who helped to establish the city of Nauvoo, Illinois, on the Mississippi River.

Joseph Smith appointed Young as president of the Quorum of the Twelve Apostles in 1841 and is generally considered second, only to Smith, in influence.

After Smith's death in 1844, several ambitious claimants campaigned for the role as prophet and leader of The Church of Jesus Christ of Latter-day Saints. Most members, including Smith's mother and brothers, considered Young to be Smith's most legitimate successor. However, a number of Mormons later rejected Young's leadership, including Joseph Smith's wife and children.

Westward

Brigham Young led the Mormons westward, outside of the jurisdiction and boundaries of the United States. Young's path led them through the Louisiana territory to just outside what is today Omaha, Nebraska, where they set up "Winter Quarters" for the duration of the winter. The flock built approximately 800 cabins in the area. This was intended to be a safe haven and a place to rest and gather strength before making the rest of the tour to the Salt Lake City area. However, during the winter 359 Mormons died due to illness and the lack of supplies.

Utah

Utah was the destination of Brigham Young and the migrating Mormons. At that time, Utah was still a part of Mexico and was located outside of the jurisdiction of the US marshals. Utah was also a remote place where Mormons could practice polygamy without restrictions from a government that opposed such practices. In fact, Brigham Young was the church's most notable polygamist, having twenty-seven known wives and fifty-six children. In 1856 he built The Lion House in Salt Lake City to accommodate his large family.

It wasn't until 1850 that Utah officially became a part of the United States of America, which brought a new conflict for the Mormons and the United States over the territory. The Mormons had already settled the Salt Lake City Basin when Young set up a theocratic government of which he was governor.

While in office, President James Buchanan, the fifteenth president of the United States, was attempting to establish government in the newly acquired region of Utah. When he encountered resistance from the Mormons and their militia, a war ensued over the territory between the Mormons and the United States government.

The Mormons had formed a militia that was set on defending the land and area they had settled into. President Buchanan sent Brigadier General

William Harney to subdue the Mormons into submission and end the uprising. Young refused to relinquish his position as governor until the end of his current term in 1854. When Young's term ended, he prepared the Mormons for war.

"Young, for all intents and purposes, had severed Utah's ties with the US government. The very next day he even held a strategy meeting with his top officer of the Nauvoo Legion, Lt. General Daniel Wells. Together they agreed that Mormon soldiers would "waylay our enemies, attack them from the ambush, stampede their animals, take the supply trains, cut off detachments and parties sent to canyons for wood or on other service." Thus began the Utah war of 1857/1858.[10]

Raids upon the dispatched US Army supply train by the Mormons forced Colonel Johnson and his troops to lay up at a base camp outside of Utah for the winter. Severe weather and minimal supplies caused the US troops to undergo tremendous hardship, with Brigham Young taunting the colonel all the while.

President Buchanan sent an unofficial liaison to Thomas Kane to negotiate with Young. Young initially refused the truce until President Buchanan offered a treaty with a full pardon for all of the former charges mounted up against both Young and the church members. Young accepted the deal and Alfred Cumming was appointed governor over the territory. The governor struggled against the church and its theocratic government. Cumming summed it up with the following statement:

> There is nothing to do. Alfred Cumming is the Governor of the territory, but Brigham Young is Governor of the people.[11]

Prior to this time and following it, the Mormon Church was involved in many acts of violence, some of them quite horrific. However, its retelling of these events is quite different from those outside the Mormon Church. The historic picture painted by the LDS of themselves is often poles apart from what actually happened. The Mormons' ill treatment of Native Americans is one example.

The Mormons wanted to convert Utah's Indians to Mormonism, believing that the so-called "*loathsome*" Indians would become a "*white and delightsome people*", *according to the* Book of Mormon 2 Nephi 5:21 23 and would be forgiven of the sins of their forefathers.

According to Mormon Church doctrine, the nature of the dark skin was a result of a curse from God. The reason for the curse was because the Lamanites *"had hardened their hearts against him (God)"* and the purpose was to punish them by making them "loathsome" unto God's people who had white skins.

However, according to historian Robert Carter, *"When the Ute failed to assimilate into Mormon culture, the answer was to exterminate them."*

In 1850 Mormon apostle George Albert Smith declared that the Indian people "have no right to their land" and he instructed the all-Mormon legislature to "extinguish all titles" and get them out of the way and onto reservations. This set the stage for the infamous Black Hawk War that would follow.[12]

February 28, 1849

The first so-called battle of what became known as the Black Hawk War began when a Mormon militia of forty-four men rode into the Utes' camp in the early morning hours.

On this dreadful day, seventeen men, women, and children were camped in teepees in the foothills above what is known today as Pleasant Grove.

Two of the Ute warriors, Kone and Blue Shirt, stepped from their teepee to find themselves surrounded by the Mormons. An argument ensued over missing horses that Brigham Young claimed were stolen.

Captain John Scott was the militia leader who opened fire. Kone was the first to be hit, with the top of his head being blown off. The Indians ran to a nearby ravine to take shelter from the onslaught that followed. The Utes were outmanned, and to make their plight worse they had one gun among them.

One of the warriors named Opecarry was unarmed and yet he was shot sixteen times. The Mormons killed all of the men. One young brave girl went to plea with the captain for the life of her brother and the women and children.

When the "battle" was over, there were twelve survivors of the attack. They were forced to leave their dead loved ones lying in the snow and were taken captive forty miles north to Salt Lake City where they were then forced to live with Mormon families. The twelve survivors of the brutal attack included nine women, two girls, and a twelve-year-old boy named Nooch, who was later known as Black Hawk.

"Mormon militia under the leadership of Captain John Scott left Salt Lake City in pursuit of a so-called 'Renegade Band of Indians' who, it was alleged, had taken horses from Brigham Young. According to reliable accounts Brigham Young gave the order to Captain Scott to find and punish the perpetrators."[13]

In 1850, a few months following the Battle Creek massacre, Nooch was forced to witness, again, the brutal killing of his relatives at Fort Utah. This followed a fierce two-day assault by Mormon militia and resulted in another seventy Indians being killed with fifty having their heads decapitated from their frozen bodies. The heads were piled into crates on a loading dock where Nooch had to look at them for two agonizing weeks. These events planted firmly in the mind of Nooch may have been the catalyst for what became known as the Black Hawk War.

The Circleville Utah Massacre

On April 21, 1866, during the Circleville, Utah, massacre, sixteen Paiute men, women, and children were murdered by way of their throats being slit.

As a result of the ongoing Black Hawk War, battles were raging and tensions were high in every direction. Officials of the Mormon Church ordered the Paiutes to be disarmed.

Although the group of Paiutes that remained camped in the Valley were friendly, the Mormons believed they were in constant danger and were afraid that at any moment "real trouble" could break out.

A message arrived from Fort Sanford relaying the story of a Paiute who was pretending to be friendly but then shot and killed a white militiaman stationed at the nearby fort.

The Circleville residents were warned to protect themselves against the neighboring Indians camped in the valley. The decision was made to arrest the Paiutes and bring them back to Circleville to be confined.

The men of the town surrounded the camp at night although no force was needed because James T.S. and Bishop William Jackson Allred had persuaded the Indians to come to a meeting at Circleville where they would have a letter read to them. All of the Indians, except one young warrior, agreed to go with them. The Indian warrior who refused to go began to shoot at the posse. The returning fire of the posse killed the young man and the remaining Indians were taken at gunpoint to Circleville. The letter was read to them and they were told that they were to be retained as prisoners. The twenty-six Indians were taken into custody and placed under guard in the meetinghouse.

The next evening some of the Indians were able to cut themselves loose from their bindings and make a break. Unfortunately, during the commotion two of the Indians trying to escape were shot and killed by the guard. The remaining captives were then taken to a potato cellar and imprisoned there while the decision was being made to kill all twenty-four of them. One by one the Paiute men, women, and children were led out of the cellar and one by one their throats were brutally sliced and their bodies thrust to the ground. Two boys and a girl around the age of seven decided to try to escape. So when the door was opened for the next victim, the three made a break, forcing their way past the guards and running for their lives. The guards fired several shots, but were only able to graze the ribs of one boy. The children were able to escape. Tragically, all of the Paiute males, five women, and two older children were killed that night.

The decimated lives of some 40,000 native *people caused by the Black Hawk War has simply been swept aside. Brigham Young's victory was perhaps a hollow one for, in order to fulfill his dream, he had to destroy a civilization. He complained it was "cheaper to feed them than to fight them" as he was spending millions in church funds equipping his private army to war against them. The truth regarding the history of the war has since been cloaked in brilliantly managed rhetoric to discredit the Ute* nation *in every conceivable way. The victors' accounts are saturated with ambiguities, omissions, platitudes, and half-truths, and they lead us to believe the fate of the Indian people was divine providence.*[14]

The Masking of the Truth

The historic events detailed above certainly do not look like the Mormonism that is portrayed by the LDS church on TV commercials and public service announcements today. It would seem logical to surmise from their history of violence and criminal activity that this is far from anything that Jesus Christ had in mind to represent Him and His father as the church.

It only seems logical to weigh the evidence against the Scriptures that can be verified and authenticated. While God does ask us to place our faith in Him, He gives historic evidence to verify His existence and the Bible. Manuscripts are available still today that verify the writings of the Bible and yet there is *not* one piece of empirical evidence that can validate the writings of Joseph Smith, which the doctrine of the Mormon Church is based upon. In addition to this, plagiarism seems to be the order of the writings since much was taken from all over the biblical text, from *A View of the Hebrews*, which was written by Ethan Smith (not related to Joseph Smith), and from various additional manuscripts and sources that were circulating at the time Smith's writings first appeared.

Why is it so important to have a perspective of Mormon origins and the history of the LDS church from a source other than the Mormon Church? Because, just as former Mormon Rocky Hulse so aptly states in his book *When Salt Lake City Calls*, "The Mormon Church sanitizes its history and rather than providing accurate information to its members and the public, only that which is 'faith promoting' is allowed to be printed."[15]

As someone who was born in to the indoctrination of Mormonism, my heart's desire in writing this book is to expose the falsehood of the Mormon Church so that many, including my loved ones, will be set free, as I have been. Moreover, so that the American people, including Christians, will know the truth about this counterfeit religion that many mistakenly assume is just *another* Christian doctrine. It behooves us all to hold this knowledge, especially in the instance that a long-standing, prominant, indoctrinated Mormon may very well be naively voted into White House.

As Jesus said in John 8:32, "And ye shall know the truth, and the truth shall make you free" (KJV).

Chapter 2

"The Blood Trail"

The church Mitt Romney supports looks like the perfect religion, doesn't it? After all, the LDS television ads portray it as a wholesome, caring, Christian doctrine. However, beyond the LDS facade of a loving, kind church that wants to serve Jesus in peace is a trail of blood and violence. The very historical doctrine the Mormons believe, sustain, and follow is violent and vengeful. It is not only unbiblical, but frankly it's dangerous. Such doctrines are the *doctrine of blood atonement* and the *law of vengeance.*

The doctrine taught by the Bible concerning the atoning blood of Jesus was and is to cover the sins of man; this biblical doctrine declares that the shedding of blood by our savior was *enough* to cover *all sin*, except for blasphemy against the Holy Spirit.

Contrary to the Bible, Mormon doctrine teaches that a man must shed his *own* blood to atone for certain sins committed by an individual. Beyond that, it is also the conclusion of *the blood doctrine* that you should love someone enough to shed their blood in order that their souls may be brought into right standing with God for eternity. This would include the shedding of the blood of a non-Mormon, or *gentile* as they call them. According to the blood doctrine taught by the church, if gentiles were murdered by a LDS church member their eternal souls would then be redeemed.

The following excerpt is from *The Journal of Discourses*, delivered by Mormon prophet Brigham Young:

> There are *sins* that men commit for which *they cannot receive forgiveness in this world, or in that which is to come,* and if they had

> their eyes open to see their true condition, they would be perfectly willing to have their blood spilt upon the ground, that the smoke thereof might ascend to heaven as an offering for their sins; and the smoking incense would atone for their sins, whereas, if such is not the case, they will stick to them and remain upon them in the spirit world.
>
> I know, when you hear my brethren telling about cutting people off from the earth, that you consider it is strong doctrine; but it is to save them, not to destroy them.
>
> I do know that there are sins committed, of such a nature that if the people did understand the doctrine of salvation, they would tremble because of their situation. And furthermore, I know that there are transgressors, who, if they knew themselves, and the only condition upon which they can obtain forgiveness, *would beg of their brethren to shed their blood*, that the smoke thereof might ascend to God as an offering to appease the wrath that is kindled against them, and that the law might have its course. I will say further; I have had men come to me and offer their lives to atone for their sins.
>
> It is true that the blood of the Son of God was shed for sins through the fall and those committed by men, yet men can commit sins which it can never remit. As it was in ancient days, so it is in our day; and though the principles are taught publicly from this stand, still the people do not understand them; yet the law is precisely the same. There are sins that can be atoned for by an offering upon an altar, as in ancient days; and there are sins that the blood of a lamb, of a calf, or of turtle doves, cannot remit, *but they must be atoned for by the blood of the man.* That is the reason why men talk to you as they do from this stand; they understand the doctrine and throw out a few words about it. You have been taught that doctrine, but you do not understand it.[16]

What are these "sins" that Mormons historically believe are *not* covered by the blood of Jesus, but only by the shedding of one's own blood?

1. Murder
2. Adultery and immorality
3. Stealing

4. Using the name of the Lord in vain
5. For not receiving the gospel
6. For marriage to an African
7. For covenant breaking
8. For apostasy
9. For lying
10. For counterfeiting
11. For condemning Joseph Smith or consenting to his death[17]

Yet, the Bible teaches something entirely different from this in Romans 3:23–25:

> For all have sinned and come short of the glory of God, being justified freely by his grace through redemption that is in Christ Jesus. Whom God has set forth to be a propitiation by his Blood through faith in his blood, to declare his righteousness for the remission of sins (KJV).

The Bible lets us know that the shedding of Christ's blood was *enough* to cleanse us from *every* sin that we commit with the exception of blaspheming the Holy Spirit for which Jesus taught there was no forgiveness.

> But Christ came as a high priest of good things to come, by greater and more perfect tabernacle (heavenly tabernacle) not made with hands, that is to say, not of this building; Neither by the blood of goats and calves, but by his own blood he entered once into the holy place, having obtained eternal redemption for us.
>
> For if the blood of bulls and goats, and the ashes of an heifer sprinkling the unclean, sanctifies to the purifying of flesh:
>
> How much more shall the blood of Christ, who through eternal Spirit offered himself to God, purge your conscience from dead works (sin) to serve the living God?" (Hebrews 9:11–14 KJV).
>
> And Colossians 1:13–14 reiterates.
>
> Who hath delivered us from the power of darkness, and hath translated us into the kingdom of his dear son: In whom we have redemption through *his blood*, even the forgiveness of sins (KJV). [Emphasis mine]

Ephesians 1:7 states, "In whom we have redemption through *his blood*, for the forgiveness of sins, according to the riches of his grace" (KJV). [Emphasis mine]

There are countless references to the blood of Jesus and the forgiveness of sins in the Bible with no verse suggesting the shedding of the blood of another human as a sacrifice.

Rather than a doctrine based upon peace, love, and forgiveness, the Mormon blood is necessary for the forgiveness of sins. Nor is the blood of a human necessary to appease God's wrath toward us. This Mormon teaching is in direct conflict with the word of God. God's wrath is turned away from us through the blood of the Lamb, the living Son of God. This Mormon doctrine is based on vengeance, retribution, lying, and the will of a man that justifies violence.

The following accounts are examples of the blood atonement doctrine taught and practiced by the Mormon Church.

9–11–1857

People from our generation can scarcely escape the horrific events of 9–11; however, it was not the first massacre to take place on this ominous date on innocent victims. On September 11, 1857, there was another historic event where the death of innocents occurred, known as the Mountain Meadow Massacre. The Mountain Meadow Massacre is a huge blight on the Mormon Church that cannot be explained away, winking at the historical evidence that implicates members of the church as blatant murderers. It shows an indictment against Young for having knowledge of and approving the massacre, which was an exercise of total injustice.

The event actually began with Parley Pratt, the great, great-grandfather of Mitt Romney and an apostle of the LDS church, who went to Arkansas on a mission trip. Pratt practiced plural marriage and had twelve wives. He had taken his tenth wife, Eleanor, under the Mormon teaching of polygamy. However, problems arose because Eleanor was already legally married to Hector McLean. McLean, the legal and jealous husband of Eleanor, was unwilling to accept this, tracked down Pratt, and killed him over the matter.

When news of Pratt's death reached Utah, it incited the Mormon people who already were at odds with the United States government. Shortly after this event, a group of roughly 200 settlers left Arkansas by way of wagon train to California to stay with their estimated 1,000 cattle. Some settlers split off from the party along the way, leaving 157 people in the Fancher-Baker party.

Completely unsubstantiated rumors that the Fancher-Baker party was involved in the assassination of Pratt, as well as the deaths of Hyrum and Joseph Smith, spread throughout the region and the Mormons were at fevered pitch. The Fancher-Baker party wagon trains arrived in Utah with around 800 cattle and were in need of replenishing their supplies. However, Brigham Young had given orders excluding the Mormons from doing business with outsiders. He also implemented martial law and allowed no passage through Utah without a permit. The problem was that he did not make that information public until four days after the massacre took place.

Cedar City, Utah, was the last town that the Fancher-Baker party would ever see. According to records, the party traveled through the area on or about September 3 or 4, only to find a less than friendly reception and their business denied.

The Mormons were following the orders of Brigham Young not to trade with the party or allow them to replenish their supplies, including water. After sending the party on its way, the massacre was planned by the Mormon people of Cedar City.

The day after being unwelcomed at Cedar City, the Fancher-Baker party found themselves in an ambush thirty-six miles outside the city in the Mountain Meadow. The Mormons disguised themselves to look like Indians for the purpose of framing the Paiutes, a local group of Native Americans, for the massacre.

The Fancher-Baker party was pinned down for the next five days, trapped with limited food and water. During the fifth day of the attack when the Fancher-Baker party was at its weakest, a Mormon bishop, John Doyle Lee, who was the adopted son of Brigham Young, rode out with William Bateman under a white flag of truce. They approached the party to discuss a conditional surrender and offer a way out. Lee told the party that if they surrendered their weapons and left their wagons and their cattle, they would be allowed to walk out of the situation unharmed. The

Fancher-Baker party agreed to the surrender and was placed in a single file line separating all of the women, men, and children.

Children under the age of eight years old were loaded into a wagon and taken away, while the wounded were loaded into a second wagon. As the captured party began to walk, the Mormon militia approached them from every side. The command was given by Major John H. Higbee for the Mormons *"to do their duty."* Then, in the most cowardly fashion, they shot the men and clubbed the women and children, killing the entire Fancher-Baker party with the exception of seventeen children who were under the age of eight.

Those seventeen children were distributed to different Mormon families. The reason for the sparing of the children was, again, a result of the Mormon doctrine; children below the age of eight are considered to be innocent and below the age of accountability.

"The unnecessary practice of baptizing babies and children who are under the age of accountability, which is eight years old. The Lord condemns infant baptism (Moroni 10–21). Children are born innocent and without sin. Satan has no power to tempt children until they begin to become accountable (D&C 29:46–47) so they have no need to repent or be baptized. Children should be baptized at the age of eight".[18]

Brigham Young was implicated in the massacre and believed to be complicit in the event. After the massacre, Young had a messenger go down and tell Lee to let the people have safe passage. It is believed by many that he was attempting to cover his tracks. It should be stated that many, including the heirs of both Young and the Fancher-Baker party, believed that Young had full knowledge of and even helped plan the massacre.

A question that arises is this: How do you persuade people who have lived non-violent lives to suddenly commit such a heinous act against people who were not guilty of anything worthy of a death penalty?

Even if the alleged incidents of taunting were true, there was no cause for the killings of these individuals by the Mormon militia. The answer to the above question is twofold:

1) They were acting under the law of vengeance, which stated, "You and each of you do solemnly promise and vow that you will pray, and never

cease to, importune high heaven to avenge the blood of the prophets on this nation, and that you will teach this to your children's children unto the third and fourth generation."[19]

2) They were following the prophet: In an address given in Salt Lake City on Nov. 8, 1857, then counselor to the first president Heber C. Kimball stated, "In regard to our situation and circumstances in these valleys, brethren, Wake Up, Wake up Ye elders of Israel and live to God and none else; and learn to do as you are told, both old and young; learn to do as you are told for the future ... Brother Brigham (Young) is my leader: he is my Prophet, my Seer, my Revelator; and whatever he says, that is for me to do; and it is not for me to question him one word, nor to question God a minute."[5]

In brief, whatever the prophet/seer (who at that time of the Mountain Meadow Massacre was Brigham Young) says—is to be done. And it's to be done *without* question. (It is important to note that this dangerous practice is still followed today and will be discussed in chapter 3.)

The nation demanded justice for the victims of the massacre in spite of Brigham Young and the church leaders attempt to obstruct justice. A decision was made to place the guilt of the entire event on John D. Lee, who was excommunicated from the church and tried for the heinous crimes.

A trial was held regarding the Mountain Meadow Massacre that ended in a deadlock vote from the jury. There were four Mormons and eight gentiles (non-Mormons) who made up the jury. The jury came back with a vote of eight guilty and four innocent. What a surprise!

Lying for the Lord!

There is a LDS church doctrine that declares that lying is permissible and in order *if* the truth either implicates the church or makes it *look* bad in any way. This is in spite of the fact that this practice directly contradicts the ninth commandment given by God not to lie: "Thou shalt not bear false witness against thy neighbor" (Exodus 20:16 KJV).

The ensuing trial from the Mountain Meadow Massacre was laden with deception and cover-up. It is a practice of Mormons not to answer direct questions that may implicate or demean the church in any way.

Mormons believe that they are not obligated to answer a specific question. In The Book of Mormon, the book of Alma records the following account in the eleventh chapter, verses 21–22.

> 21. And this Zeezrom began to question Amulek, saying: Will ye answer me a few questions which I shall ask you? Now Zeezrom was a man who was expert in the devices of the devil, that he might destroy that which was good; therefore, he said unto Amulek: Will ye answer the questions which I shall put unto you?
>
> 22 And Amulek said unto him: Yea, if it be according to the Spirit of the Lord, which is in me; for I shall say nothing which is contrary to the Spirit of the Lord.

This is a tactic that is taught to Mormons in order to avoid questions that may be undesirable to answer. Mormons are taught, instead, to answer questions that they believe *should* have been asked.

Accordingly, a mockery was made of the trial by concealing the truth under a litany of lies, and with a hung jury that could not return a verdict the proceedings were halted and a new trial was set.

The second trial was held in 1875, eighteen years after the massacre occurred, in front of a jury that was exclusively Mormon. During the interim, many crucial witnesses died and evidence was destroyed, including all correspondence between John D. Lee and Brigham Young.

In spite of this, the new jury found that John D. Lee was singlehandedly guilty of the massacre and was sentenced to death. According to reported findings, one man "acting alone" was able to subdue the entire Fancher-Baker party and committed the mass murders. It is hard to believe that *one man* could have halted, pinned down, and committed the entire massacre.

Sentenced to die at the scene of the crime, on March 13, 1877, Lee was executed by firing squad. Why was he shot by firing squad? *The blood atonement doctrine* allowed him to "shed his own blood" and cover his sins. In fact, until 2004, the state of Utah allowed capital punishment by firing squad in order that Mormons could "shed their own blood."

A year and a half after the massacre, the seventeen surviving children were recovered from the Mormons. Although, the Mormons claimed that they had to purchase them from the Indians, the children testified that they had never been with the Indians.

What is further outrageous is that the spoils from the massacre were found at Bishop Phillip Klingensmith's Cedar City Ward tithing room for the Mormons. These two things, along with the dying proclamation by John D. Lee that he was being sacrificed in a "*cowardly and dastardly manner,*" further implicate and incriminate the church and its leadership.

As recent as 1999, Gordon Hinckley denied any involvement by the LDS church. With the practice of "lying for the Lord" to protect the church from anything embarrassing or negative, it's completely believable that the LDS covered up or rewrote the history in its favor.

If the Mormons have nothing to hide concerning this gruesome event, why then did they purchase the killing fields where the Mountain Meadow Massacre took place and the victims are buried today? The further outrage is that the burial site is located on LDS private property where access is completely controlled!

Chapter 3

Where Does Mitt Romney's Loyalty Lie?

"Can He Pledge His Unconditional Allegiance to the USA without Having to Check with the Prophet, Seer, and Revelator of the Mormon Church?"

On December 6, 2007, Mitt Romney delivered his Faith In America speech to America. This speech was meant to smooth over any concerns that the American people might have regarding his Mormon *faith* influencing any decisions or judgment calls that he would make in the office of the presidency of the United States of America, if elected. In this famous speech, Mitt said "Let me assure you that no authorities of my church, or of any other church for that matter, will ever exert influence on presidential decisions. Their authority is theirs, within the province of church affairs, and it ends where the affairs of the nation begin."

Let me express to you in the simplest of terms that this statement was very likely a bold-faced lie. In spite of Mitt's promise that his faith and his presidency would remain separate, it is important for you to know that his belief is that the Mormon Church is the "one and only true church" and his *salvation* is the church and only comes through the *church*. Furthermore, as a male in Mormonism, he has direct priesthood authority from God by lineal descent.

The Mormon priesthood is made up, entirely, of males. Young Mormon males are ordained in the following offices: "deacon" at age twelve, "teacher" at age fourteen and "priest" at age sixteen. As a former ordained bishop in the Mormon Church, Mitt Romney is definitely a part of the priesthood and has been since an early age. Therefore, he has been, and continues to be, *bound* by the "Covenant of the Mormon Priesthood."

I agree with the statement Rocky Hulse makes in his book *When Salt Lake City Calls:* "Mormonism teaches that its 'Priesthood' has divine authority from God to conduct all aspects of Mormonism in this life and the life to come. This concept is paramount in understanding that the Mormon 'Priesthood' authority reaches beyond the grave; an aspect that leverages a very real controlling power over the living. As the controlling authority for the 'Church,' which is where salvation lies for the Mormon, allegiance to the 'Church' and its controlling authority (the Priesthood) cannot be underestimated."

In addition, Mitt Romney has been repetitively taught from childhood that the *prophets* of the Mormon Church are the mouthpieces of God to lead the "one and only true church," and that these prophets *cannot* lead the church astray. Therefore, it is every Mormon's duty to "follow the prophet"—no matter what; even if it leads to the death of innocent people as portrayed in earlier chapters.

"Do not think for yourself!"

Mormons are taught to follow the prophets/seers, church authorities, and brethren, and to do so without questioning or thinking on any alternative. They are taught that to question the prophet is an act of apostasy that could *negate* their *salvation and eternal future in the afterlife and with the church.* This action places their president/prophet in a position of authority that is never questioned, as he is believed to be infallible. Examples of this were previously demonstrated in the chapter 2 in the Mountain Meadow Massacre.

To thoroughly understand the above, we must examine the structure and doctrines of the LDS church. According to Mormon beliefs and the teaching of the LDS church, in order to obtain eternal status as a "god," there is no option but to follow the orders of the prophet as *his* word must take *precedence* over any other counsel. This would include the Joint Chiefs of Staff, if elected to the office of president of the United States of America. Allegiance must be to the Mormon Church and the prophets, making any other vow or oath secondary to the vows and covenants made to the church and the Mormon prophet.

According to Newsroom LDS, the organizational structure of the church is as follows:

The most senior apostle is the president of the church, and he selects two other apostles as counselors. These three function as the First Presidency, which is the highest governing body of the church. Twelve others form the Quorum of the Twelve—the second-highest governing body of the Church. Together, the First Presidency and the Twelve oversee the entire church. The president of the Quorum of the Twelve wields tremendous power as well the First Presidency.

These fifteen men are considered to be and revered as prophets and seers. They are known as the "Oracles of God."[21]

So to break it down, the president holds the highest position of the church. He is the "prophet" who elects two "counselors" to work with him and the three of them make up the First Presidency. The Quorum of the Twelve Apostles works directly under the First Presidency, but nevertheless also has a great deal of power. All of these men are known as prophets, seers, and revelators. In the Mormon Church, they are the "mouthpiece of God" and they require to be followed with blind obedience.

After the Quorum of the Twelve, the subsequent set of leaders are called the "Seventies," who assist the Twelve Apostles and serve in various locations throughout the world. There are currently eight quorums of the Seventy. Each quorum may have up to seventy members. Some seventies are assigned to headquarters administrative functions, but most live and work within a specific geographic region of the church.

The leader of a congregation is called a bishop, as Mitt Romney was a bishop. The bishop's administrative "parish" is called a ward. A group of wards form a stake and the leader of a stake is a stake president. Romney was also a stake president presiding over the Boston Stake, which included more than a dozen congregations in Massachusetts. "Stake" is not a term found in the New Testament, but is taken from Old Testament tent imagery in which the "tent," or church, is held up by supporting stakes.

Stake presidents and bishops are the leaders most commonly encountered by the broad membership of the church. These leaders are unsalaried and have a significant amount of local autonomy.

The substantial time and effort required to administer a stake or ward and meet the needs of the members is carried out by the members themselves. Most members are asked by local leaders to contribute in specific capacities.

Duties include local administrative, teaching, or service-oriented positions. These responsibilities are rotated from time to time. Bishops typically serve for about five years and stake presidents for about nine.[22]

The First Presidency and Quorum of the Twelve could very well be the Mormon presidential advisors and electing Mitt Romney could very well be a vote for these men. Unlike the Catholic Church, these are rules and rulers that cannot be ignored. When Mitt's Mormon faith is discussed in the media, the standard response is that John F. Kennedy had the same concerns posed to him regarding his presidency and John's answer was to assure the American people that the pope would not be running the country. He assured the American people that his religion and allegiance to the pope would remain separate from his office of the presidency. This simply is not the case with Mitt Romney—there is no separating the presidency from the church if you are a Mormon! A form of separation would be a direct act of disobedience and with that could come repercussions that most Mormons are simply not willing to face. Please hear what I am saying, I can assure the American public that this same assurance by Mitt Romney to the American people would not be the same. I can promise the American people that if Mitt Romney were to make the same commitment, it would be contrived, disingenuous, and not to be trusted.

It is important to understand the structure of the church in order to clearly interpret the doctrine associated with obedience to the prophets and seers. Although there are many authorities within the church, only the First Presidency/Prophet and the Quorum of the Twelve are considered to have the right, the power, and the authority to speak the mind and will of God to His people. There is a song that is taught to the Mormons from the time of their youth called "Follow the Prophet."

Follow the prophet,
Follow the prophet; don't go astray.
Follow the prophet …
Follow the prophet; he knows the way.
We can get direction all along our way,
If we heed the prophets—follow what they say.

A song, no doubt, that Mitt Romney, who grew up in the LDS church, is well familiar with.

In the Mormon book *The Doctrine and Covenants* states, "What I the Lord have spoken, and I excuse not myself; and though the heavens and the earth may pass away, my word shall not pass away, but shall be fulfilled, whether by mine own voice or the voice of my servants, it is the same."[23]

According to the doctrine of the church, the president/prophet of the church is the mouthpiece of God and high priest on the earth. He has all authority and is given sacred endowments, even as Joseph Smith supposedly possessed. The prophet has ongoing authority to change and supersede any other authority, including any former prophet or written word of the church.

Whatever the Prophet says goes ...

One example of the above is that when it was decided that John D. Lee would take the fall in the entirety for the Mountain Meadow Massacre, Brigham Young had him excommunicated from the church. Young stated "that under no circumstances should he be admitted as a member again."

However, after years of petitions from Lee's descendants, including his grandson Meritt L. Norton, the First Presidency and the Quorum of the Twelve restored his church membership and blessings. On May 9, 1961, Norton was *baptized on behalf of his dead grandfather* and apostle Ezra Taft Benson officiated in the *endowment and sealing ceremonies* at the Salt Lake Temple.

So, how was the previous order from Prophet Brigham Young overruled even though Mormon doctrine states that the prophet *"speaks for the Lord in everything"*?

It's simple really: the Mormon doctrine also states in chapter 5, fundamental 3 of *Fourteen Fundamentals in Following the Prophet,* that "*the living prophet is more important to us than a dead prophet.*"

So, which prophet was right and which was wrong? Who was actually hearing from the Lord? Shouldn't someone be asking these questions instead of blindly following someone just because he says, "Thus says the Lord"?

"That's ridiculous," you say. "I'd never follow a prophet or seer in such a manner."

Maybe not *willingly* my friend, but if you elect Mitt Romney as president of this nation, you will likely be following the prophet he follows because the decisions Mitt Romney will make for this country, in all likelihood, will be directly based upon the prophet and the teachings of his *faith.* Mitt's eternal future and exaltation to "god" status depends on it.

"More Powerful Than the Word of God"

To further demonstrate this teaching, President/Prophet Wilford Woodruff tells of an interesting incident that occurred in the days of the Prophet Joseph Smith:

> I will refer to a certain meeting I attended in the town of Kirtland in my early days. At that meeting some remarks were made that have been made here today, with regard to the living prophets and with regard to the written word of God. The same principle was presented, although not as extensively as it has been here, when a leading man in the Church got up and talked upon the subject, and said: 'You have got the word of God before you here in the Bible, Book of Mormon, and Doctrine and Covenants; you have the written word of God, and you who give revelations should give revelations according to those books, as what is written in those books is the word of God. We should confine ourselves to them.'
>
> When he concluded, Brother Joseph turned to Brother Brigham Young and said, 'Brother Brigham, I want you to go to the podium and tell us your views with regard to the living oracles and the written word of God.' Brother Brigham took the stand, and he took the Bible, and laid it down; he took The Book of Mormon, and laid it down; and he took the Book of Doctrine and Covenants, and laid it down before him, and he said: 'There is the written word of God to us, concerning the work of God from the beginning of the world, almost, to our day. And now,' said he, 'when compared with the living oracles those books are nothing to me; those books do not convey the word of God direct to us now, as do the words of a Prophet or a man bearing the Holy Priesthood in our day and generation. I would rather have the living oracles than all the writing in the books.' That was the course he pursued. When he was through, Brother Joseph said to the congregation, 'Brother

Brigham has told you the word of the Lord, and he has told you the truth.' [24]

According to this account, both Joseph Smith and Brigham Young taught that the words of the prophet and the oracles are more weighted than the Bible or even the writings in The Book of Mormon. If, in fact, you are a Mormon and you are trying to obtain eternal salvation and the status of becoming a god and ruling over your own planet/kingdom, you must follow the prophet no matter what, even if it defies logic or puts you or those whom you represent in harm's way.

There are fourteen teachings specific to the following of the prophet:

1. The prophet is the only man who speaks for the Lord in everything.
2. The living prophet is more vital to us than the standard works.
3. The living prophet is more important to us than a dead prophet.
4. The prophet will never lead the church astray.
5. The prophet is not required to have any particular earthly training or credentials to speak on any subject or act on any matter at any time.
6. The prophet does not have to say, "Thus saith the Lord," to give us Scripture.
7. The prophet tells us what we need to know, not always what we want to know.
8. The prophet is *not limited by men's reasoning.*
9. The prophet *can receive revelation on any matter, temporal or spiritual.*
10. The prophet *may advise on civic matters.*
11. The two groups who have the greatest difficulty in following the prophet are the proud who are learned and the proud who are rich.
12. The prophet will not necessarily be popular with the world or the worldly.

13. The prophet and his counselors make up the First Presidency—the highest quorum in the Church.

14. *The prophet and the presidency—the living prophet and the First Presidency—follow them and be blessed—reject them and suffer.*[25][Emphasis added]

The above teachings, coupled with the verse below, give a clear definition of what "reject them and suffer" means in the fourteenth teaching.

> And the arm of the Lord shall be revealed; and the day cometh that they who will not hear the voice of the Lord, neither the voice of his servants *neither give heed to the words of the prophets and apostles, shall be cut off from among the people.*[26]

To be "cut off from among the people" is an eternal punishment from which there is no relief or remedy. Mitt takes his faith and religion very seriously and has held the offices of missionary, missionary zone leader, assistant to the mission president (the highest position a missionary can hold), bishop, and stake president in the LDS church. And let's not forget that he was also a graduate of Brigham Young University. You cannot attain the "calling" from the Lord to serve as a Mormon bishop or stake president unless you are a thoroughly entrenched and obedient Mormon. Mitt Romney comes from a long lineage of Mormonism which spans no less than four generations; he is certainly deeply entrenched in the Mormon doctrine.

One can only conclude that to go against the prophet would be devastating for the individual and have eternal consequences, even for the president of the United States if he were a Mormon. After all, as president of the United States, Mitt would have less authority than that of the living prophet. He is therefore, no matter his position as a leader of this nation, subject to the prophet—to his orders and mandates. Even if those mandates go against this nation!

This is illustrated further by Spencer W. Kimball, who served as the twelfth president and prophet of the LDS church from 1973–1985. At the conclusion of the general conference in April 1978 he gave the following discourse:

> Now as we conclude this general conference, let us all give heed to what was said to us. Let us assume that the counsel given applies to

us, to me. *Let us hearken to those we sustain as prophets and seers, as well as the other brethren, as if our eternal life depends on it, because it does.*[27] [Emphasis added]

Continued reference to the importance of following the prophet and the strong implication of eminent judgment infers that a man's will is not his own. According to the following statements, thinking and judgment is not allowed for the average Mormon:

According to Ward Teacher's message, "Any Latter-day Saint who denounces or opposes, whether actively or otherwise, any plan or doctrine advocated by the prophets, seers, revelators of the church, is cultivating the spirit of apostasy. One cannot speak evil of the Lord's anointed ... and retain the Holy Spirit in his heart. This sort of game is Satan's favorite pastime, and he has practiced it to believing souls since Adam. He [Satan] wins a great victory when he can get members of the church to speak against their leaders and to do their own thinking."

"*When our leaders speak, the thinking has been done.* When they propose a plan—*it is God's plan.* When they point the way, there is no other which is safe. When they give directions, it should mark the end of controversy. God works in no other way. To think otherwise, without immediate repentance, may cost one his faith, may destroy his testimony, and leave him a stranger to the Kingdom of God."[28] [Emphasis added]

Further teachings are recorded in Mormon literature and lectures from an array of sources, including The Book of Mormon, *The Doctrine and Covenants*, *The Journal of Discourses* and countless LDS websites, making it hard to refute the fact that following is not only commanded, but to be done without any alternative. This mandatory doctrine makes it impossible for Mitt Romney or any other practicing Mormon to be able to act or pledge allegiance to any other entity or country ahead of his church.

He has been indoctrinated to believe that if the prophet speaks, it is God speaking; if the prophet has a plan—it is God's plan.

Disobedience to any of the commandments of "god" (those given by whatever prophet is in power) may result in being cut off, eternally, without any repentance here or in the life to come. It is this type of threat that keeps most Mormons inside the church walls, even after the light of truth has shown the error of their false doctrine. Threats of eternal consequences are not small, nor are they easily ignored after being thoroughly indoctrinated into the well-masked cult. The leaders of the church know the truth of their errant doctrine and history they have tried to cover through the use of media and teaching methods.

They prey on the minds of the simple and insist that blind faith is the only way to please God. Furthermore, questions by their members that could reveal the truth are discouraged.

> Then Jesus said to those Jews who believed him, "if you abide in my word, you are my disciples in deed and you shall *know the truth* and *the truth shall make you free"* (John 8: 31–32 KJV). [Emphasis mine]

The seeking of truth is discouraged by the leaders of the Mormon Church in order to keep their members psychologically enslaved. It should be noted that not everything that is true is truth. It may be true that someone made a statement for example, but that statement may be a lie. Therefore, we must seek truth and not just things that are true in order to be free. Furthermore, it is important to ask questions in order to be clear on topics as demonstrated that the Bible encourages questions.

James 1:5 states, "If any of you lack wisdom, let him ask God, that gives to all liberally and without reproach, and it will be given to him" (KJV).

This is contrary to what is taught by the Mormon Church where "the thinking has already been done." The Bible states the danger of this in Matthew 15:14: "They be blind leaders of the blind. And if the blind lead the blind, both shall fall into the ditch" (KJV).

The ongoing need for the prophet to be able to change and supersede everything prior, including all other writings, former prophets, and even the Bible, gives cause for concern. After all he's supposed to be speaking for God. If this is the case, it would mean that God changes His mind often. Several Scriptures in the Bible would have to be totally false in order for this to be valid.

"For I am the Lord, I change not" (Malachi 3:6 KJV).

"Jesus Christ is the same Yesterday, Today and Forever. Do not be carried about with various and strange doctrine. For it is good for the heart to be established by grace" (Hebrews 13:8–9 KJV).

The Scripture further admonishes us to be grounded in the doctrine of Jesus Christ, grounded in His grace, and grounded in *His* truth.

John wrote the final book in the Bible, sealing it as the complete word of God. No additional gospel is needed.

"For I testify to everyone who hears the words of the prophecy of this book; If anyone adds to these things, God will add to him the plagues that are written in this book: and if anyone takes away from the words of the book of this prophecy, God shall take away his part from the book of life, from the holy city, and from the things which are written in this book" (Revelation 22:18–19 KJV).

And Isaiah 46:9–10 states this:

> Remember the former things of old, For I am God, and there is *no other*; I am God, and there is none like me.
>
> Declaring the end from the beginning, and from the ancient times things that are not yet done. Saying my counsel shall stand and I will do all my pleasure (KJV). [Emphasis mine]

The above Scripture indicates two points:

1. That there is *no* other God. The word of God further conveys in Isaiah, "I am the LORD, and there is none else, there is no God beside me: I girded thee, though thou hast not known me: That they may know from the rising of the sun, and from the west, that there is none beside me. I am the LORD, and there is none else" (Isaiah 45:5–6 KJV).

In spite of what the Mormons teach about becoming gods and earning a place in heaven through works and obedience to the prophet/seer, there is only *one* way to God—and that is through His son Jesus. It is not through a prophet, church, seer, or a priest.

Jesus answered, "I am the way and the truth and the life. No one comes to the Father except through me" (John 14:6 NIV).

2. God already knows the end and therefore there would be no need for Him to have to make adjustments along the way. Alterations would make God a god who was unsure of who he is and what is happening. Mormon dogma is made up as the hierarchy of

> the church goes along, and allows for the continued adaptation of false doctrine in order to perpetuate the deception to future generations.

Unfortunately, following the prophet is not an option for a Mormon.

"And the arm of the Lord shall be revealed; and the day cometh that they who will not hear the voice of the Lord, neither the voice of his servants neither give heed to the words of the prophets and apostles, shall be cut *off* from among the people".[29] [Emphasis added]

Mitt Romney is entrenched in the Mormon Church and in spite of any claims he may make to the contrary, there is an extremely high and almost certain probability that his allegiance, if elected as president, would not be to the United States ... but to the prophet/seer/revelator and The Church of Jesus Christ of Latter-day Saints!

Chapter 4

Mitt's Secretive Oaths, Allegiance, Covenants, Pledges to Death Penalties, and Commitments to the Mormon Church—And Its Bizarre Temple Rituals and Beliefs

Mitt Romney is a long-standing, card-carrying, prominent "temple Mormon." Mormon temples are not places of worship. The temples are secretively closed to the public. Entrance into the Mormon temple is the utopia to strive for in Mormondom. Anyone who achieves "temple status" is by no means a casual Mormon. The primary mandate for a Mormon to be able to enter the temple is to be a consistent tithe payer of 10 percent of the gross of his income. No Mormon can enter without meeting this requirement.

The Mormon churches are completely different meeting places from the temples. The regular Sunday church weekly services are held in local church buildings known as chapels, meetinghouses, ward houses, or churches. The terms used for these buildings are interchangeable.

The Mormon temples, however, are closed on Sundays but open on weekdays, exclusively to card-carrying, temple-recommended Mormons. Closed to the public, only the most faithful followers of the prophet and the Mormon doctrine are allowed to enter. *The rituals in the temples—especially the "endowment"—are considered so sacred that Mormons are forbidden to discuss them outside the temple itself.*[30]

In fact, up until the 1990s, Mormon ritual participants were so sworn by oath to secrecy that if they revealed anything about these temple rituals, this act would be punishable by death. Here is the exact oath taken in the temple ceremony by participants:

"I will now explain the covenant and obligation of secrecy which are associated with this token, its name, sign and penalty, and which you will be required to take upon yourselves. If I were receiving my own Endowment today, and had been given the name of "John" as my New Name, I would repeat in my mind these words, after making the sign, at the same time representing the execution of the penalty: I, John, covenant that I will never reveal the First Token of the Aaronic Priesthood, with its accompanying name, sign, and penalty. Rather than do so, *I would suffer my life to be taken*."

Mitt Romney and his wife regularly attended and participated in these temple ceremonies and rituals that consist of secret handshakes, tokens, vows, death oaths, secret names, and scores of additional bizarre proceedings. There are many websites and books which accurately depict these secret temple ceremony rituals.

It is important for the reader to know that I am fully familiar with what I speak of. *You see, I personally experienced these secret ceremonies on my wedding day.*

Let me share my personal experience of what I endured in the endowment ceremony and sealing of my first marriage; though I'm not supposed to be alive to do so due to the outrageous oaths that a nineteen-year-old bride had to take and endure on what was supposed to be an enchanted day.

On the day of my wedding, I, my husband to be, my mother and father, and various relatives arrived at the Idaho Falls Mormon Temple. We all assembled on the front steps of the temple for wedding-day photographs. When it was time to go inside, most of our friends and relatives were left at the steps, as they were not allowed to go in and witness my wedding ceremony.

Once my future husband and I entered the lobby, I was instructed to walk through an entrance for only women. My fiancé, whom we'll refer to as Ted, was led through a separate entrance for men.

Once inside the temple, two "temple worker" women led me to a private locker room. One of the women pointed to a locker and instructed me to hang my beautiful white velvet wedding dress in it. I did as directed while looking around with curiosity. My parents had given no instruction or warning of what was about to take place because of the secretive nature of the temple.

As I stood by my locker, the women brought out a bowl of scented water and placed it on the ground at my feet.

"You need to remove all your clothing," a woman said. I was instructed, not asked. For a few seconds I wondered if they were serious.

They were! In spite of my embarrassment, questions, shock, and discomfort, I stripped down to my bra, panties, and slip. One of the ladies said again, "You will need to take everything completely off". My hands were trembling so badly I had some difficulty. The onlookers just watched with what seemed to me a bit of impatience.

As soon as I was completely stripped, the women began to wash my entire body from the bowl of water on the floor.

Though I felt very uncomfortable, and even violated, I didn't dare to speak up. After all, who was I? What did I know? Surely these people knew more than I. Besides, in Mormonism, it's drilled into one's head not to question, no matter how ridiculous things seem.

If this was not distressing enough, as they were washing my nude body they touched each breast, my navel, and one knee while praying. Lord only knows what whispering prayers they may have cursed me with.

I should state here that temple Mormons no longer have to be stripped down and be washed by strangers, though they still touch parts of the body with anointing oil. With the advent of the Internet, the secret ceremonies "came out" and became a PR problem for the church, forcing it to cover up many of its strange and occult practices.

Once they were finished with this washing ritual, one of the women left the room for a moment and returned with an item of clothing that she proudly held up for my inspection. The attire reminded me of long johns with short sleeves and was cut off at the knees. I recognized it because I had seen my Mormon-bishop father and mother in these bizarre garments since I was old enough to remember.

"Put these sacred temple garments on and wear them during the ceremony," one of the women said. "You are to wear them at all times. Only take them off to shower."

I took the special underwear and slipped into them quickly so that I would no longer be standing nude in front of these strangers. They may have thought them to be special, but I just found them peculiar.

The garments were one piece, made of a thin nylon type of a material, and had four markings on them: one over each breast, one at the navel, and another on one knee. These markings were located at the same places where they had touched my body and prayed over. There was an opening at the bottom that would enable me to go to the bathroom without taking them off.

The temple workers explained again how to use them. "Wear them at all times. Never take them off. Not even for marital relations. Only when you shower can they be removed and then replaced with a clean pair."

My mother bought me seven pairs so I would have one for every day of the week. *Mormons still practice the wearing of these special underwear, or "temple garments" as they are known.* This is why you will never see a temple Mormon wear sleeveless tops. These garments have a short sleeve that cannot be shown and since they reach the knees, you will most likely not see temple Mormon women wear shorts or short skirts. These garments are supposed to magically protect a person from all harm.

After the traumatic anguish of this intrusive process, I was finally allowed to put my wedding dress on and join Ted who was waiting for me in another small room where my wedding was to be held. Unfortunately, I can't recall every detail of the actual ceremony. I think I must have been in shock. However, I do remember that Ted and I kneeled facing one another on an altar that was equipped with kneeling benches.

A man, I don't really know who he was or what position he held, performed the wedding and sealing ceremony.

"I seal you together as husband and wife *for time and all eternity*," he proclaimed.

According to Mormon belief, this meant that upon passing on to our next life, we would live together as husband and wife, forever. We were "sealed" together. Not just "til death do us part," but forever! This phrase is embraced and used frequently in Mormon dogma.

After we were sealed, *for time and all eternity*, we were led out of this room and into an auditorium. In this auditorium, the men were separated from the women. The men sat on the right and the women sat across the aisle on the left. The only family allowed to attend my wedding ceremony were Mormons who had already been wed in the temple: my mother and father. *No one who had not been cleared to go through the Mormon temple was allowed to experience it in any way.* So this ruled out my brother, sisters, relatives, and all of our friends. In short, my wedding day was spent with about eighty peculiar strangers.

"Put these on", a temple worker instructed, as we were given silly-looking green leaf aprons to tie around our waists, representing the leaves that covered Adam and Eve. I was appalled that it had to be placed over my beautiful white velvet wedding gown. To make matters worse, we were given a green sash to place over our shoulders. So here I was, again I say, in my beautiful wedding gown with these silly green things tied over it.

The men wore what looked like Pillsbury Dough Boy chef hats and the women wore silly-looking veils.

We were being dressed for the endowment ritual, which represented scenes in the Garden of Eden. I can't express to you how utterly ridiculous I, and everyone else, looked in these clothes. Might I say again, *and over my beautiful wedding gown* on my wedding day?

A man and someone who was supposed to represent Lucifer came to the front of the auditorium.

"Please stand and repeat after me and do what I tell you to do," he ordered.

We all stood, as instructed, and began chanting the words he told us while making signs with our arms and hands.

"If you reveal any of these oaths and covenants you will pay with your life." The man said in a solemn voice, and I swallowed the lump in my throat. I can't remember all of the covenants and oaths because I was so stunned by it all.

I do, however, remember that the revealing of these secrets was demonstrated in the ceremony as being punishable by death. We were led to make signs that meant that if we ever spoke of the ceremony, we would be killed.

I, along with everyone else, followed the leader in making a sign with our thumbs that were drawn from the left ear across our necks to the right ear, symbolizing the slashing of our throats.

Next, we mimicked the motions of tearing our tongues out of our mouths. I wondered if they would really kill me. *Would I die if ever I spoke of these things? Is that why the whole temple thing was so hush-hush and my mom had not explained any of it to me?*

We then had to symbolize that we were holding a knife up in the air in our right hand, which we lowered and acted as if were cutting our hearts out of our chest. We then positioned the imaginary knife at our left lower abdominal area. While repeating the oaths led by the "puppet master" we were directed to symbolically and violently jerk the imaginary knife from its place at our lower left abdomen up and diagonally across our body to our right shoulder. This signified the slashing of our abdomens.

To make certain we understood the seriousness of the oath if we ever spoke of these secrets, we were told to raise our arms out to the side and bend forward, symbolic of our guts falling out on the ground. Over and over we repeated the words, "suffering our lives to death."

The entire ceremony continued with threatening, horrifying, and mind-controlling rituals.

I understand that in the present day, they make the same oaths with less violent orientation.

In her *New York Times* best seller *Secret Ceremonies,* Deborah Lake describes her first temple experience: "The actions that were going to guarantee my entrance at the gates [of heaven] would have nothing to do with love or charity or the other teachings of Christ that I'd been raised to believe God valued. In fact, I hadn't heard a single one of those words spoken today, the most primary day of religious instruction in my entire life. No, I was going to burst into heaven on the basis of mumbo-jumbo … The mysteries of life were fraternity rituals … Did all the white-suited glorifiers in the room unquestioningly accept a ritual of nutty gestures from the pseudo-occult as a sacrament? Those were the first moments when I viewed Mormonism with suspicion."[31]

After what seemed like hours of these absolutely outlandish dramas, instructions, and death oaths, I was given a secret name—Augusta—and told "Only your husband can know your name." *Great! Another secret.* I've since learned that many of the secret names are the same and in no way unique.

While both men and women are given secret names, the wife is not permitted to know her husband's given name. However, she has to confide to him her given secret name. The purpose for this is that only "he" has the power to summon the wife into heaven and this must be done by his calling her by the secret name given to her. This further demonstrates the power given to the "priesthood" (men) of the Mormon Church. Since, according to Mormon doctrine, men will become gods, they are in control of their wives' salvation. Not only does this give them complete authority over the women, but it negates the salvation of Jesus Christ, which is all the Bible plainly tells us is needed to enter heaven.

In other words, Ann Romney will not be allowed to enter the Celestial Kingdom unless Mitt calls her in by her secret name that only he knows, through the veil. Therefore, she cannot be saved by the grace of Jesus Christ—she will be saved by her Mormon husband and the Mormon religion. It's sad that most Mormon women are so caught up in this bizarre and blasphemous religion that they don't dare question the doctrine that mandates that the "man" has complete control over their eternal destiny, instead of the one and only God who created her.

To be even more frank, any woman who votes for Mitt Romney would be voting for a man who has been raised in a church where men are exalted to eternal godship and taught they have total control over their wives' salvation and destiny. *Even in the afterlife.* Now I ask you, what God-fearing Mormon wife is going to stand up against a husband who has the power to deny her the attainment of the highest degree of glory in heaven? In my humble opinion, a vote for any man that follows these beliefs would be a vote *against* women. Of course, the church propagandizes to have the highest respect for women. But hello! If the "man" has control over the woman's eternal destiny, this does not demonstrate respect. It demonstrates ultimate control over her.

Works, Not Faith, Determine Which Heaven a Mormon May Attain

Mormonism teaches that there are three degrees of glory (heavens). If one accomplishes enough good works in the Mormon Church, he can attain a place in the highest degree of heaven which is called the Celestial Kingdom. This is the only heaven where God resides. There, the "perfect Mormons" who have been obedient to the church and to the prophet, as well as have earned their way to heaven by good works, will become gods of their own heavenly kingdoms or planets. They will populate their planets by having eternal sex and bearing spirit children in order to build their kingdom for which they will reign over for *"time and all eternity."*

It is important to repeat that the female/wife will *not* be able to enter in to the Celestial Kingdom unless her husband calls her in to heaven. If he does not call her by her secret name, she will remain in the lower Mormon heavens or "degrees of glory" and will never be able to attain entrance into the celestial kingdom. As a further consequence, she will probably be separated from her earthly children in this imaginary hereafter as well. Again, this gives the male complete control over the wife's eternal destiny.

Upon death, if enough good works were not achieved, but the Mormon lived an adequate, although not exceptional life, the reward would be entrance into the Terrestrial Kingdom. This "second degree of glory" kingdom isn't as great as the Celestial Kingdom, but it's not too bad either. Plus, there's the possibility of earning your way out of there and moving up a notch to the third degree of glory/Celestial Kingdom after a period of time.

If a person performs really poorly and does not perform enough good works, he will end up in the "first degree of glory," the Telestial Kingdom. This is not a place of torment like hell. In fact, Mormons rarely speak of hell because they have their own system of glory set up. Their eternal system is one based largely on works (or deeds). This is completely contrary to the Bible, which proclaims in Titus 3 verses 5–7:

> *Not by works* of righteousness which we have done, *but according to His mercy He saved us*, through the washing of regeneration and renewing of the Holy Spirit, whom He poured out on us abundantly through Jesus Christ our Savior, that having been

justified by His grace we should become heirs according to the hope of eternal life" (NKJV). [Emphasis mine]

According to this Scripture, our salvation and entrance into heaven are based ***solely*** upon the unmerited, undeserving favor and grace of Jesus Christ and not upon our works. Ephesians further confirms this truth: "For by grace you have been saved through faith, and that not of yourselves; it is the gift of God, not of works, lest anyone should boast" (Ephesians 2:8–9 NKJV).

Baptism for the Dead

It is important for the readers to know enough about this well-masked cult to come away from this book protected by the truth. For brevity's sake I'll spare you from going further into all of the oaths and rituals. There are many books and websites that describe these practices, in detail, which I would urge the reader to do further study.

However, I will include the baptism for the dead. Inside Mormon temples are large baptismal fonts which are spacious enough for several people to stand waist-deep in water. These baptismal fonts are very elaborate with sculptured oxen at the base holding up the huge bowl. It is here that baptisms for the dead are performed. Of course dead people are not actually immersed into the water—it is done by proxy.

When I was a teenager, my bishop dad made me go through this ritual proxy for the dead. I waited in line with around twenty other teenagers until it was my turn to be baptized in the name of a deceased person. The proxies are usually adolescents dressed in white (everyone is dressed completely in white in the temple), who are immersed into the water by the officiators reciting a short baptismal prayer:

> Having authority given me of Jesus Christ, I baptize you for and in behalf of (the dead person's name goes here), who is dead, in the name of the Father, and of the Son, and of the Holy Ghost. Amen.

The name of the dead person is read from a list to the officiator just before the immersion. One proxy may be baptized quickly in succession for ten or fifteen dead people. After the baptisms, two other officiators confirm the newly baptized dead persons as members of the Mormon Church and confer upon them the gift of the Holy Ghost by placing their hands upon the head of each proxy, with a similar short pronouncement. Hundreds of such baptisms and confirmations can be performed in a few hours multiplied by every Mormon temple across the world. It is an efficient, production-line operation.

Mormons wholeheartedly believe that they gain entrance into heaven for the deceased who have not *entered into the gate of Mormon baptism* by participating in this ritual. The Mormon book *The Doctrine and Covenants* states that *God has ordained baptism for the dead as* the *means whereby all his worthy children can become heirs of salvation in his kingdom. For them a just God has ordained baptism for the dead, a vicarious-proxy labor.*[32] [Emphasis mine]

Mark 16:16 says, "He that *believeth* and is baptized shall be saved; but he that believeth not shall be damned" (KJV).

While the Bible does instruct us to be baptized, it also tells us to *believe.* Our salvation is dependent upon our belief in the only begotten son of God, Jesus Christ.

The following is just such an example of this bizarre ritual of baptizing the dead, which is provided by Helen Radkey:

> Oral Roberts was "posthumously" baptized by Mormons when he was alive? © Copyright 2009, Helen Radkey, December 19, 2009
>
> Granville Oral Roberts (January 24, 1918-December 15, 2009), famous television evangelist, and one of America's most well-known preachers, was probably baptized into the Mormon faith on May 19, 2009, without his knowledge, while he was still living.
>
> Information about the pre-death LDS temple rites for Oral Roberts first appeared on this website: http://famousdeadmormons/com/ at 9:17 PM (MST) on December 17, 2009[33]
>
> From the new FamilySearch online, here are the details of the LDS temple rituals that were performed on behalf of Oral Roberts almost seven months prior to his death:
>
> Individual Ordinances:
>
> **Baptism** Completed 19 May, 2009, Mesa Arizona Temple

Confirmation Completed 19 May, 2009, Mesa Arizona Temple

Initiatory Completed 19 May, 2009, Mesa Arizona Temple

Endowment Completed 29 August, 2009, Mesa Arizona Temple

Sealing to Parents Completed 13 October, 2009, Mesa Arizona Temple

My copy of the telltale Mormon entry that reveals the LDS rites for Roberts was obtained at 9:11 AM (MST) on December 18, 2009. By around 10:00 AM, the same day, that record had disappeared from the new FamilySearch, which requires a log-in to access. It appears that Mormons scrambled to hide the evidence of their rituals for Oral Roberts.

Why would Mormons have the audacity to baptize Oral Roberts? Because they believe the Mormon Church is the only true and living church on the face of the earth one which Oral Roberts was not a part of or baptized in. Therefore, he must be baptized by proxy so that he can enter into heaven. The fact that the record of this ritual disappeared in quick order is further proof of the deceit and subterfuge that the Mormon Church uses to hide its actions.

As a member of the priesthood and an ordained bishop in the Mormon Church, Mitt has participated in numerous such rituals, handshakes, and oaths. He has willingly and repeatedly participated in the endowment ceremony of the Mormon Church. In this endowment ceremony, four different "laws" are presented and secret oaths are sworn that bind the Mormon to those laws by covenant.

The fourth law, "The Law of Consecration" is the one that should most concern you as an American citizen. In this covenant and oath, Mitt and all Mormons swear to "to consecrate yourselves, your time, talents, and everything with which the Lord has blessed you, or with which he may bless you, to the Church of Jesus Christ of Latter-day Saints, for the building up of the Kingdom of God on the earth and for the establishment of Zion."[34]

Do you understand this implication regarding the office of the presidency of the United States?

This oath places a Mormon, Mitt Romney, in an uncompromising position of submission and compliance to the Mormon Church and its power, and Mormons who have been born into the Church, *as Mitt Romney was,* have had years of indoctrination, or brainwashing if you will, to believe that they simply cannot not disobey the oaths, covenants, or church teachings. To do so would be detrimental to their soul to the point of being "cut off." Being "cut off" to a Mormon means that he or she will not become a god in the celestial kingdom which is the loss of his or her status in heaven; to Christians it would be likened to going to hell.

Do not underestimate the power that is placed over the members of the Mormon Church by its leaders who are believed by Mormons to be God's oracles. Therefore, whatever God's oracle (mouthpiece) says to do, *must* be done … even by a Mormon president of the United States. Mitt's very life is staked on it.

In his book *When Salt Lake City Calls,* Rocky Hulse asks a legitimate question: When Salt Lake City calls, what will a member of the Mormon Church do?

His answer is frightening:

> The religion of Mormonism places a Mormon in servitude to its human leadership. This bondage is real, it is expressed in its doctrinal passages, is reinforced twice yearly by the sustaining vote of the leadership, and obedience to it is required for a member to be considered in "good standing" and to have the expectation to go on to exaltation (Godhood) in the next life.[35]

It is impossible for a Mormon to give true allegiance to his country, or to any earthy government for that matter, due to the deep misguided beliefs, oaths, covenants, and wholehearted allegiance to the false religion of the Mormon Church. There *is* a conflict between Mormonism and the public trust.

A book adhered to by Mormons is *The Journal of Discourses.* This book instructs Mormons to do this:

> Wake up, Ye Elders of Israel, and Live to God and none else; and learn to do as you are told … But if you are told by your leader

to do a thing, do it. None of your business whether it is right or wrong.[36]

Can Mitt Romney serve two masters?

Luke 16:13 in the Bible plainly states that he cannot.

No servant can serve two masters; for either he will hate the one and love the other, or else he will be loyal to the one and despise the other (NKJV).

Chapter 5

Mitt Will Try to Hide the Outrageous Racism Against the Black Race Taught Through His Church's Doctrine

When I was a little girl around five years of age, I distinctly remember riding through what was called the "Negro section" of Wilmington, North Carolina, in my Mormon bishop dad's Cadillac that had the pointy fins on the back. My dad would look at the black Americans on the sidewalks and say, over and over in disgust, "Look at that nigger!" As a tiny little girl, there was something that stuck in my gut that I just knew was very wrong. I remember saying, "Daddy, they are people like us!" He got very angry at me and screamed at me, "They are niggers!" I will never forget how horrible it made a tiny little girl feel that her father would be so angry and disgusted at people who were not white. I knew, no matter what he said, that this was very, very, very wrong. Now, as a grown-up woman, I understand where his roots of prejudice came from.

Though Mitt Romney will not want to address this subject, racism is quietly alive and well in the Mormon Church and very much a part of Mormon culture. The LDS church teaches that African-American people are cursed by God because of their lives in what is known as the "pre-existence before their mortal state."

In this chapter we will examine historical evidence and writings within Mormon literature propagating racism, which cannot be refuted or denied. *Starting with The Book of Mormon.*

The following quote is found in The Book of Moses in The Book of Mormon.

"And Enoch also beheld the residue of the people which were the sons of Adam; and they were a mixture of all the seed of Adam save it was the seed of Cain, *for the seed of Cain were black*, and had not place among them."[37] [Emphasis added]

The book of Genesis found in the Bible describes a historical event that took place between two brothers named Cain and Abel. Cain was jealous of Abel and took his life. Genesis 4:15 states that God placed a mark on Cain in order that others who saw him could identify him. The Bible is silent on what the "mark" was or is; however, the Mormons have concluded and teach that the "mark" was and is black skin. There is no evidence, scientific or otherwise, to support their claims. The above reference *supposes* that "mark" to be the curse of the black skin of African descendants placed upon them by God.

"Now perhaps you will have a partial answer to some of your questions as to why, if God is a just Father, that *some of his children are born of an enlightened race* and in a time when the Gospel is upon the earth, while others are born of a heathen parentage in a benighted, backward country; and still *others are born to parents who have the mark of a black skin with which the seed of Cain were cursed and whose descendants were to be denied the rights of the priesthood of God.*"[38] [Emphasis added]

To understand the driving force behind this racist view of the LDS church, you must understand their belief of where it all begins. Mormons believe and teach that God is in heaven with his spiritual wives having spirit babies throughout eternity and that we lived with God in a spiritual state prior to being born into this world. How well you lived in your pre-mortal state, and your valor, determined where you would reside in the present state. If, in your pre-mortal state, you were cowardly and displeasing, then you would be placed in a body with *dark skin* to identify that you were cursed by God.

This is taught by the leadership of the Mormon Church and is included in its doctrinal notes and books. The following, by Bruce Redd McConkie, apostle of the Mormon Church, in *Mormon Doctrine* is further evidence:

"In the pre-existent eternity various degrees of valiance and devotion to the truth were exhibited by different groups of our Father's spirit offspring, some were more valiant than others. *Those who were less valiant in pre-existence and who thereby had certain spiritual restrictions imposed upon them during mortality are known to us as the negroes.* Such spirits are sent to earth through the lineage of Cain, the mark put upon him for his rebellion against God and his murder of Abel being a black skin… *Negroes in this life are denied the priesthood;* under no circumstances can they hold this delegation of authority from the Almighty. *The present status of the negro rests purely and simply on the foundation of pre-existence. The negroes are not equal with other races where the receipt of certain spiritual blessings are concerned, particularly the priesthood and the temple blessings that flow there from,* but this inequality is not of man's origin. It is the Lord's doing, is based on his eternal laws of justice, and grows out of the lack of spiritual valiance of those concerned in their first estate."[39] [Emphasis added]

McConkie (July 29, 1915-April 19, 1985) was a member of the Quorum of the Twelve Apostles of The Church of Jesus Christ of Latter-day Saints from 1972 until his death. McConkie was a member of the First Council of the Seventy of the LDS church from 1946 until his calling to the Quorum of the Twelve Apostles.

He was also a Mormon prophet and seer, as we discussed in chapter 3. Mormons are taught to follow the words of the prophets and seers as if God himself were speaking. So, to a Mormon, if the prophet says that African-Americans are cursed, then they are cursed!

Since the opinion and doctrines of the church are formed and based upon the teaching of the pre-existence, considering that God has passed judgment on the Africans and Native Americans, the segregation and discrimination cannot be ignored. While the LDS church has more recently tried to follow a more politically correct agenda, its history is replete with contrary evidence. The Book of Mormon accuses God of cursing Africans and Native Americans in the following passages of The Second Book of Nephi, chapter 5:

> 21. And he had caused the cursing to come upon them, yea, even a sore cursing, because of their iniquity. For behold, they had hardened their hearts against him, that they had become like unto a flint; wherefore, as they were white, and exceedingly fair and delightsome, that they might not be enticing unto my people the Lord God did cause a skin of blackness to come upon them. 22. And thus saith the Lord God: I will cause that they shall be loathesome unto thy people, save they shall repent of

their iniquities. 23. And cursed shall be the seed of him that mixeth with their seed; for they shall be cursed even with the same cursing. And the Lord spake it, and it was done.

In *The Journal of Discourses*, Brigham Young adds emphasis in the following statement:

Classes of the human family that are black uncouth uncomely disagreeable and low in their habits wild and seemingly deprived of nearly all the blessings of the intelligence that is generally bestowed upon mankind the first man that committed the odious crime of killing one of his brethren will be cursed the longest of any one of the children of Adam. Cain slew his brother. Cain might have been killed and that would have put a termination to that line of human beings this was not to be and *the lord put a mark upon him which is the flat nose and black skin* trace mankind down to after the flood and then another curse is pronounced upon the same race that they should be the 11 servant of servants and they will be until that curse is removed and the abolitionists cannot help it nor in the least alter that decree how long is that race *to endure the dreadful curse that is upon them that curse will remain upon them.*[40]

Shall I tell you the law of God in regard to the African race? If the *white man* who belongs to the *chosen seed* mixes his blood with *the seed of Cain* the penalty under the law of God is *death on the spot.*[41] (Emphasis added)

In other words, the uniting of an African-American to a Caucasian is punishable by death. On the spot! In fact, it is listed as number 6 on the list of eleven sins that are not covered by the blood of Jesus. See chapter 2 in this book.

It is impossible to read any of the above references and conclude that the Mormon Church has been anything less than racist. Weighing the evidence found in the books the Mormon Church uses to establish teachings makes it impossible to conclude that the LDS church suddenly changed its view of the Native American or the African-Americans.

If you teach that The Book of Mormon is the most perfectly written book ever, if you base a teaching for the last 150 years that God has cursed a race of people since the original family of the Bible, how can you suddenly change that teaching? Did this book that is *perfect* change or did God? It is ludicrous and naive to believe that suddenly the LDS church had a new revelation.

McConkie insinuates that Cain was an associate of Lucifer and is the father of the Negros.

"Though he was a rebel and *an associate of Lucifer in pre-existence*, and though he was a liar from the beginning whose name was Perdition, Cain managed to attain the privilege of the mortal. Under Adam's tutelage, he began in this life to serve God … he came out in open rebellion, fought God, worshiped Lucifer, and slew Abel … As a result of his rebellion, Cain was cursed with a dark skin; he became the father of the Negroes, and those spirits who *are not worthy* to receive the priesthood are born through his lineage. He became the first mortal to be cursed as a son of perdition. As a result of his mortal birth he is assured of a tangible body of flesh and bones in eternity, a fact which will enable him to *rule* over Satan."[42] (Emphasis added)

McConkie in the above statement takes this a step farther into consorting with and worshiping of Satan. Satan is God's eternal enemy; therefore, according to LDS' third prophet, John Taylor, Cain was the original Satanist who somehow found his way into the human race as the father of the damned.

"After the flood we are told that the curse that had been pronounced upon Cain was continued through Ham's wife, as he had married a wife of that seed. And why did it pass through the flood? Because *it was necessary that the devil should have a representation upon the earth as well as God.*"[43]

These are not things I'm making up, but are actual teachings in the *Mormon Doctrine.* These are actual statements handed down by *their* prophets; the same prophets they follow above all else. Mormons have been indoctrinated to believe that anyone with black skin is of a lower class. Furthermore, blacks are called uncouth, uncomely, and deprived of intelligence as you'll plainly read in the following passage by Brigham Young:

> You see some classes of the human family that are *black, uncouth, uncomely, disagreeable and low* in their habits, *wild*, and seemingly *deprived of nearly all the blessings of the intelligence* that is generally bestowed upon mankind. The first man that committed the odious

> crime of killing one of his brethren will be cursed the longest of any one of the children of Adam. Cain slew his brother. Cain might have been killed, and *that would have put a termination to that line of human beings.* This was not to be, and the Lord put *a mark* upon him, which is *the flat nose and black skin.* Trace mankind down to after the flood, and then another curse is pronounced upon the same race—that they should be the "servants of servants" and they will be, until that curse is removed; and the Abolitionists cannot help it, nor in the least alter that decree."[44] (Emphasis added)

Since the Bible teaches about a flood that totally annihilated the outside population with the exception of the immediate family of Noah, it is necessary to perpetuate the continuation of the curse. Mormons explain it by saying that one of Noah's son's wives was contaminated and therefore their children are Africans today.

> A special problem exists with respect to blacks because they may not now receive the Priesthood. Some Members of the Church would justify their own un-Christian discrimination against blacks because of that rule with respect to the Priesthood, but while *this restriction has been imposed by the Lord*, it is not for us to add burdens upon the shoulders of our black brethren. They who have received Christ in faith though authoritative baptism are heirs to the Celestial Kingdom along with men of other races.[45](Emphases added)

By laying this at the feet of God, they are able to escape the guilt associated with the sin of prejudice. One of the main ways Mormons deal with the issue is to say, "That was in the past, let's move on."

The problem is that the doctrine of Cain's curse is still taught as doctrine today. Additionally, the Church has in no way formally refuted or apologized for the statements from Joseph Smith all the way back through the beginning of the church, including those made by other church presidents and leaders.

Mormon Racism Still Exists Today!

In January, 2010, Harry Reid, the Senate majority leader, came under fire for his comments concerning Barak Obama in the book *Game Change* by John Heilemann and Mark Halperin. In this book, Reid stated that he "*believed that the country was ready to embrace a black presidential candidate, especially one such as Obama—a 'light-skinned' African American with no Negro dialect, unless he wanted to have one.*" Newscasters from every major network jumped on the story; some came to defend his racist statements as poor judgment, while others were concerned about this politically incorrect statement. Few, if any, brought to light that Reid is a *Mormon* and the doctrine of his church predisposed him to his prejudice attitude.

The Book of Mormon states in Alma 3:6–9 the following:

> 6. *And the skins of the Lamanites were dark, according to the mark which was set upon their fathers, which was a curse upon them because of their transgression* and their rebellion against their brethren, who consisted of Nephi, Jacob, and Joseph, and Sam, who were just and holy men. 7. And their brethren sought to destroy them, therefore they were cursed; *and the Lord God set a mark upon them,* yea, upon Laman and Lemuel, and also the sons of Ishmael, and Ishmaelitish women. 8. And this was done that their seed might be distinguished from the seed of their brethren, that thereby the Lord God might preserve his people, that they might not mix and believe in incorrect traditions which would prove their destruction. 9. *And it came to pass that whosoever did mingle his seed with that of the Lamanites did bring the same curse upon his seed.*[46]

The above text references a second type of prejudice that we have yet to discuss, which is prejudice against Lamanites. According to *Mormon Doctrine,* Lamanites are Native Americans. While Lamanites are considered somewhat a better class of those who were cursed, the Native Americans (Lamanites) are still looked at as being inferior. Not only are they believed to be inferior, but anyone who intermarries or mingles with them is cursed as well, according to Mormon teaching.

These horrible, prejudicial beliefs are reiterated again and again in The Book of Mormon, found in the books of Alma, Mormon, and Nephi as quoted below, directly from their teachings:

Alma 3:6 "And the skins of the Lamanites were dark, according to the mark which was set upon their fathers, which was a curse upon them because of their transgression and their rebellion against their brethren, who consisted of Nephi, Jacob, and Joseph, and Sam, who were just and holy men"[47]

Mormon 5:15 "And also that the seed of this people may more fully believe his gospel, which shall go forth unto them from the Gentiles; for this people shall be scattered, and shall became a dark, a filthy, and a loathsome people, beyond the description of that which ever hath been amongst us, yea, even that which hath been among the Lamanites, and this because of their unbelief and idolatry."[48]

According to The Book of Mormon, dark skin is always associated with sinners who God has cursed. The following passage claims that even those who were white at one time had their skins darkened because of their sins.

> And he had caused the cursing to come upon them, yea, even a sore cursing, because of their iniquity. For behold, they had hardened their hearts against him, that they had become like unto a flint; *wherefore, as they were white, and exceedingly fair and delightsome, that they might not be enticing unto my people the Lord God did cause a skin of blackness to come upon them*[49]

If you study the history of our nation, you will find that when the Mormons moved into the Salt Lake City Basin in 1847, the population of Native Americans was estimated to be around 70,000 and was reduced to 2,300. Accordingly, the census in 1909 demonstrated that Lamanites (the Indian population) were viewed as little more than animals.

War records can account for only a fraction of the Indian deaths that were due to battles. A few accounts testify to the poisoning of food, water, and germ warfare. Brigham Young is quoted as saying, "You can get rid of more Indians with a sack of flour, than a keg of powder." *Just how many did he get rid of?*

Brigham Young acknowledged an alarming rate of decrease of the Indian population. He was pleased when he was quoted in a Denver newspaper saying: "Just three out of three hundred Indians remain from the time we first arrived in the valley."[50]

Mitt's Claims

Mitt claims that the day the church changed its view, allowing African-Americans into the *Priesthood* (of the Mormon Church), he pulled his car over and wept. No one was there to validate his story.

Mitt additionally claims that his father George W. Romney marched with Dr. Martin Luther King Jr. However, the *Boston Phoenix* reported in a December, 2007, "Talking Politics" article by David S. Bernstein that "A spokesperson for Mitt Romney now tells the *Boston Phoenix* that George W. Romney and Martin Luther King Jr. marched together in June, 1963—although possibly not on the same day or in the same city."

The senior Romney, according to written source material provided by the campaign, made a "surprise" appearance at a small march in Grosse Pointe, Michigan, in late June—several days after King led a much larger march in Detroit. Romney spokesperson Eric Fehrnstrom suggests that these two were part of the same "series" of events, co-sponsored by King and the NAACP, and is thus consistent with Romney's claim that "I saw my father march with Martin Luther King."[51]

In other words, Mitt's statement that his father and Martin Luther King marched "together" could very well mean marching on different days and in different cities! According to the *Boston Phoenix,* Mitt's campaign then said that a 1972 book about Detroit mentions that Mitt's father "was among the prominent whites marching with Reverend King" in the Freedom March. Nevertheless, reports were contrary to that account as well.

Numerous contemporaneous and historical accounts say that Romney did not participate in the Detroit Freedom March, because it was held on the Sabbath. The *New York Times*, for example, wrote the next day that "Gov. George Romney, who is Mormon and does not make public appearances on Sundays, issued a special proclamation."

The Romney campaign also provided one account, from a 1987 book about Detroit, that places George Romney at the march in Grosse Pointe later the same month. A Grosse Pointe historian has told the *Phoenix* that *Romney did not participate in that 1963 Grosse Pointe event.*

King did not participate in the Grosse Pointe event, but Fehrnstrom argues that King's Freedom March in Detroit and the Grosse Pointe march later that month *were part of the same "series" of marches* co-sponsored by King and the NAACP.[52](Emphasis added)

It would seem that though George W. Romney and Martin Luther King Jr. may have participated in the same series or marches, they did not actually march "together." Given the level of prejudice George Romney was exposed to—as well as willingly participated in as a member of the Mormon Church—and the era in which he lived, it is highly unlikely he marched at all.

This is just another attempt by Romney to avert blame and guilt associated with his church. Another presidential candidate, John Kerry, became known as a flip-flopper because he continued to vacillate on issues during his campaign in 2004.

This type of "smoke and mirrors" politics is what Mitt Romney brings to the table. He has been and is associated with the Mormon Church that not only has taught prejudice, but has also practiced it throughout its existence.

When a foundation of a building is defective, the whole building, though it may seem beautiful from the outside, is in danger of collapsing and destroying all who are inside. This is a depiction of the LDS church that may one day fall and crush all those who have sought safety inside of it.

In my humble opinion, it would be quite perplexing to see an African-American or a Native American vote for a Mormon to be placed in the White House. If such a vote of support for Mitt Romney took place, it would most certainly be enacted from a lack of factual knowledge surrounding Mitt Romney's theologically based beliefs.

A Total Disdain for Jews

Deeper in this vein of prejudice, we come to the Jewish nation; in the following passage Mormon prophet Brigham Young describes his view of the Jews:

> I would rather undertake to convert five thousand Lamanites [Native Americans], than to convert one of those poor *miserable creatures [Jews] whose fathers killed the savior* ... Yes, I would rather undertake to *convert the devil himself*, if it were possible ... I would say, *leave them, and come home, the lord does not require you to stay there, for they must suffer and be damned ... [l]eave them to live and die in their sins and ignorance ... [t]hey take pleasure in their wickedness ...* [53] (Emphasis added)

Jews are clearly held in low regard by one of the former prophets and seers of the Mormon Church. Brigham Young said that his word was to be upheld as Scripture; therefore we can see the dangers in the words of a man who clearly had a heart filled with hate. Yet, in 1 John 4:20–21, the Bible plainly states that we cannot love God if we hate others.

> If someone says, "I love God," *and hates his brother, he is a liar;* for he who does not love his brother whom he has seen, how can he love God whom he has not seen? *And this commandment we have from Him: that he who loves God must love his brother also"* (NKJV). [Emphasis added]

The Bible also tells us to consider our words carefully. Proverbs 18:21 says, "Death and life are in the power of the tongue, and those who love it will eat its fruit" (NKJV).

Death has been on the tongue of the Mormon Church with no reservation about the destructive nature of its teachings. The Lamanites (Native Americans) have paid a particularly high price with the slaughter of thousands that drove them to the edge of extinction.

When you have no respect for the sanctity of life outside of your own race or religion, you can justify any behavior—even murder of the innocent. The most disturbing matter of all is when men believe they are acting on behalf of and under the authority of God.

James 1:19–20 states, "So then, my beloved brethren, let every man be swift to hear, slow to speak, slow to wrath; for the wrath of man does not produce the righteousness of God" (NKJV).

The practice of being slow to speak would be a benefit for everyone. It would have been of particular benefit with some of the statements of the Mormon Church throughout its existence. At a minimum, an apology along with a proclamation distancing itself from the aforementioned doctrine would be in order. It is not likely that such a sincere statement will ever come forth from the LDS church and its leadership.

James 2:1–4 says, "My brethren, do not hold the faith of our Lord Jesus Christ, the Lord of glory, with partiality. For if there should come into your assembly a man with gold rings, in fine apparel, and there should also come in a poor man in filthy clothes, and you pay attention to the one wearing the fine clothes and say to him, "You sit here in a good place," and say to the poor man, 'You stand there,' or, 'Sit here at my footstool,' have you not shown partiality among yourselves, and become judges with evil thoughts?" (NKJV).

James condemns the acts of *prejudice* or partiality in the above Scriptures. He says that it is evil to set oneself up as a judge based on wealth, class, and race. Instead, true Christianity is blind when it comes to the color of man; Christ died for all, not just the Mormon.

Perhaps the most quoted verse from the Bible is John 3:16: "For God so loved the world that He gave His only begotten Son, that *whoever* believes in Him should not perish but have everlasting life (NKJV). [Emphasis added]

The word *whoever*, in this Scripture, implies everyone, not just one particular race of people. To place any other stipulation on this verse would weaken it and change the meaning of it. Doing so, the message of hope would be lost and we would all have our eternal hope snatched from us.

No matter how they dispute it, sugarcoat it, or mask it, prejudice exists in the Mormon Church. Prejudice and racism are ugly and should not be perpetuated in a home, a house of worship, and certainly *not* from the White House.

Chapter 6

Is the Mormon Church a Christian Denomination or a Cult?

"I'm a little tired about this constant back and forth about Governor Romney's faith—personal faith. It is the Church of Jesus Christ of Latter-day Saints. I mean Presbyterians disagree with Methodist, disagree with Catholics, disagree with LDS. It seems that the bigger issue is the value system, in spite of these doctrinal differences."

Sean Hannity on *Hannity & Colmes* made the above statement on February 5, 2008, in connection with Mitt Romney's run for the presidency.[54]

Like Hannity, many people seem to be confused about what Mitt Romney actually believes—what Mormons believe. After all, as Sean put it, they are "the Church *of Jesus Christ* of Latter-day Saints." Sean made it seem so innocent, but this church is anything but innocent. By the use of the name "Jesus Christ," it shills to cover its hidden beliefs and doctrines to the non-discerning public.

It is important to delve below the surface to examine these doctrinal differences and determine if the Mormon Church is truly a church of Jesus Christ, or a counterfeit gospel made up by "mortal men." Are Mormons a Christian denomination or something else—a cult, perhaps?

To define this clearly, we must first differentiate between a Christian church and a cult. The Christian church is totally indoctrinated in its belief in Jesus Christ and the work that took place at Calvary on the cross; furthermore, salvation is obtained simply by faith in Christ, not through any type of works. Christianity teaches of an eternal heaven and eternal hell, that Jesus was born through the miraculous birth of a virgin, that he died on the cross, was buried for three days, was resurrected, and that his blood atones for all sin except for blaspheming against the Holy Ghost, for which there is no forgiveness.

On the other hand, a *cult* is a particular system of religious worship, especially with reference to its rites and ceremonies; a group or false sect bound together by veneration of the same thing, person, ideal, etc.; a religion or sect considered to be unorthodox, or extremist, with members often living outside of conventional society under the direction of a charismatic leader; the members of such a religion or sect.[55]

Like other cults, Mormonism can be very deceptive. Jesus warns of this in His word: "And Jesus answered and said to them: "Take heed that no one deceives you. For many will come in *My* name, saying, 'I am the Christ,' *and will deceive many*" (Matthew 24:4–5 NKJV) .

It is this very deception that I'm concerned about. If there are only a few remote differences between what Mormons believe and practice, and what Christians believe, then maybe Sean has a point. However, the evidence substantiates something entirely poles apart. While there are many doctrinal differences (more than can be covered in one chapter), we will concentrate on a few key distinctions by comparing Mormonism to the Eight Essentials of Christianity. Watchman Fellowship uses the following list to gauge how various religious groups compare with the essential fundamentals of Christianity, as defined in the Bible:

- The sufficiency of Scripture
- Deity of Christ
- The Trinity
- Bodily resurrection
- The virgin birth
- Salvation by grace
- Universality of sin
- The atonement

Rocky Hulse states in his book *When Salt Lake City Calls,* "When these essential fundamentals are compared to Catholic, Protestant, and most nondenominational Christian Churches, with few exceptions they all agree on the basic tenets of Christianity. Using this doctrinal comparison list, it is possible to identify various religious sects without any bigotry or bias."

It is without bigotry or bias that I am writing this—but with a desire to shine the light of truth on Mormonism. The previous chapters illustrate that the actions and beliefs of Mormons closely resemble the above definition of a cult. By delving farther into their doctrine, this chapter will further highlight this reality.

Mormonism versus Christianity

The Christian Church uses the Bible as the sole divine revelation and believes that it is good for doctrine and is a completed work not to be tampered with. The Bible is the basis upon which Christianity is built.

2 Timothy 3:16 states that "All Scripture [is] given by inspiration of God, and [is] profitable for doctrine, for reproof, for correction, for instruction in righteousness."

And Revelations 22:18 says, "For I testify to everyone who hears the words of the prophecy of this book: If anyone adds to these things, God will add to him the plagues that are written in this book."

Revelations 22:19 says, "And if anyone takes away from the words of the book of this prophecy, God shall take away his part from the Book of Life, from the holy city, and from the things which are written in this book" (NKJV).

In spite of the clarity in these Scriptures, Mormons believe all religious authority is based upon sacred texts equally, and in continuing revelations through the use of their prophets and seers. Sacred texts include, but are not limited to, the Bible and the following Mormon doctrinal books: The Book of Mormon, *The Doctrine and Covenants, the Pearl of Great Price* and anything written or voiced by the First Presidency (Prophets) and the counsel of Twelve Apostles. Contrary to Revelations 22:18-19 (stated above), Mormons believe in the continuation of adding to and taking away from the words of the Bible. Thus they follow The Book of Mormon, *another* testament of Jesus Christ. This leads to the first fundamental difference between Mormons and Christians.

I. Sufficiency of Scriptures

Christianity: Christians believe Matthew 24:35, which states, "Heaven and earth will pass away, but My words will by no means pass away."

As well as, Isaiah 40:8: "The grass withers, the flower fades, but the word of our God stands forever."

And, 1 Peter 1:23 confirms that God's word is eternal: For you have been born again, not of perishable seed, but of imperishable, through the living and enduring *word* of *God.* (Emphasis added)

Mormonism: Joseph Smith doubted the validity of the word of God and did not believe it could be trusted, claiming; "Ignorant translators, careless transcribers, or designing and corrupt priests have committed many errors." [56]

In the Mormon's revised *Articles of Faith,* number 8, Smith allows for more doubt regarding the validity of the Bible while supporting the validity of The Book of Mormon: "We believe the Bible to be the word of God *as far as it is translated correctly;* we also believe The Book of Mormon *to be the word of God."* [57]

Isn't it amazing that, in Mormonism, the Holy Bible's correct translation is doubted while The Book of Mormon is believed to *be* the word of God? What's even more astounding is that the Mormons have made *thousands* of additions, corrections, changes, and deletions to their Book of Mormon, *Doctrine and Covenants,* and *the Pearl of Great Price,* while pretending that these massive alterations have never occurred.

II. The Deity of Christ

Christianity: Christians believe, according to the word of God, that Jesus came to earth as God in the flesh — that He is God incarnate.

John 1:1–2 states, "In the beginning was the Word, and the Word was with God, and the Word was God. He was in the beginning with God."

John 1:14 continues: "And the Word became flesh and dwelt among us, and we beheld His glory, *the glory as of the only begotten of the Father,* full of grace and truth." (Emphasis added)

Mormonism: Mormon doctrine plainly contradicts this with its teachings in *The Gospel Through the Ages,* which states that Jesus is man's older brother.

> Jesus is man's spiritual brother. We dwelt with him in the spirit world as members of that large society of eternal intelligences, which included Heavenly Parents and all the personages of who have become mortal beings upon this earth or who ever shall come here to dwell. In that spirit-creation, when we became children of God, Jesus was the "first born," and so He is our eldest brother. [58]

Furthermore, according to their *Doctrines of Salvation,* they believe that Jesus is merely "a God" —not God incarnate. "Although he was a God, even the Son of God, with power and authority to create this earth and other earths, yet there was something lacking which he did not receive until after his resurrection." (Emphasis added). [59]

III. The Trinity

Christianity: Christians believe in the Trinity, namely the Father, the Son and the Holy Spirit—are three persons in one being. First, is God the Father who does not have a body; Jesus Christ, the Son of God, also known as the word of God who became flesh and blood with a physical body, is the second person of the Trinity; Holy Spirit, the third person of the Trinity, is a spirit being who is a separate being from God and Jesus, who has no body and is not confined to a limited physical location.

Scripture tells us in 1 John 5:7, "For there are three that bear record in heaven, the Father, the Word, and the Holy Ghost: and these three are one."

And again, John explains that the word was with God in the beginning and became flesh (the Son of God) and lived among us.

> In the beginning was the Word, and the Word was with God, and the Word was God. He was in the beginning with God. (John 1:1–2)

> And the Word became flesh and dwelt among us, and we beheld His glory, the glory as of the only begotten of the Father, full of grace and truth (John 1:14).

Mormonism: Mormons reject the Trinity and believe that the Father, Son, and Holy Spirit are three distinct beings (gods) who are one in *purpose.* Within this belief, they also hold to two additional and vastly opposing views to Christianity: the belief in many Gods and the belief that God the Father is an exalted man with a body of flesh and bones who once lived on another planet in another galaxy.

Let's look at these two contrasting views:

1. **Christianity Believes in One God while Mormons Believe in Many.**

   The following is a list of Scriptures from the Bible that declare there to be only one God:

Deuteronomy 6: 4: "Hear, O Israel: The LORD our God, the LORD is one!" (NKJV).

Isaiah 43:10: "'You are My witnesses,' says the LORD, 'And My servant whom I have chosen, That you may know and believe Me And understand that I am He. Before Me there was no God formed, Nor shall there be after Me'" (NKJV).

Isaiah 45:5: "I am the LORD, and there is *no other; There is no God besides Me.* I will gird you, though you have not known Me" (NKJV). [Emphasis added]

Isaiah 46:9: "Remember the former things of old, For I am God, and *there is no other;* I am God, and there is none like Me" (NKJV). [Emphasis added]

1 Timothy 2:5 "For there is *one* God and *one* Mediator between God and men, the Man Christ Jesus" (NKJV). [Emphasis added]

2. **Mormons believe the following concerning multiple gods:**

   Joseph Smith said in *Discourses of the Prophet Joseph Smith* on page 35:

"I wish to declare I have always and in all congregations when I have preached on the subject of the Deity, *it has been the plurality of Gods.* It has been preached by the elders for fifteen years." [Emphasis added]

Brigham Young, the second president of the LDS church, once stated this:

How many Gods there are, I do not know. But there never was a time when there were not Gods and worlds, and when men were not passing through the same ordeals that we are now passing through. That course has been from all eternity, and it is and will be to all eternity. You cannot comprehend this; but when you can, it will be to you a matter of great consolation.[60]

The Bible is most explicit in stating that God is not a man.

Numbers 23:19: "God is not a man, that He should lie, nor a son of man, that He should repent" (NKJV).

1 Samuel 15:29: "And also the Strength of Israel will not lie nor relent. For He is not a man, that He should relent" (NKJV).

Hosea 11:9: "I will not execute the fierceness of My anger; I will not again destroy Ephraim. For I am God, and not man, The Holy One in your midst" (NKJV).

Joseph Smith, the founder of the Church of Jesus Christ of Latter-day Saints, was cited in both the *Teachings of the Prophet Joseph Smith* and also in *Gospel Principles* as saying,

We have imagined and *supposed* that God was God from all eternity. *I will refute that idea,* and take away the veil, so that you may see. These are incomprehensible ideas to some, but they are simple. It is the first principle of the Gospel to know for a certainty the Character of God, and to know that we may converse with him as one man converses with another, and that he was once a man like us. [Emphasis added] [61]

In contrast to this, Psalm 90:2 states, "Before the mountains were brought forth, or ever you have formed the earth and the world, *even from everlasting to everlasting, you are God."* [Emphasis added]

According to Joseph Smith, God is a glorified, perfected human being with a body of flesh and bones.

His teachings as follows are recorded in both the *Teachings of the Prophet Joseph Smith* and *Achieving a Celestial Marriage:*

God himself was once as we are now, and is an exalted man, and sits enthroned in yonder heavens! That is the great secret, if the veil were rent today, and the great God who holds this world in its orbit, and who upholds all worlds and all things by his power, was to make himself visible,—I say, if you were to see him today, you would see him like a man in form—like yourselves in all the person, image, and very form as a man; for Adam was created in the very fashion, image and likeness of God, and received instruction from, and walked, talked and conversed with him, as one man talks and communes with another.[62]

Mormons are taught and teach that God the Father is an exalted man (a man who has progressed to godhood) with a body of flesh and bones. These beliefs are included in *Teachings of Joseph Smith* on page 346: "God himself was once as we are now, and is an exalted man…I say, if you were to see him today, you would see him like a man in a form-like yourselves in all the person, image, and very form as a man."[63]

And again in the Mormon book, *Doctrine and Covenants,* 130:22: "The Father (God) has a body of flesh and bones as tangible as man's; the Son also." [Emphasis added]

IV. Bodily Resurrection

Christianity: Belief in the resurrection and heaven and hell is a basis for Christianity found in John 11:25: "Jesus said to her, 'I am the resurrection and the life. He who believes in Me, though he may die, he shall live.'"

Accompanied by this belief, God states that not only will there be a resurrection but those who believe in Christ as their personal Lord and Savior and accept the work He did for them at Calvary will live forever with Him in heaven, while those who do not will spend an eternity in hell.

Biblical Scripture bears this out in John 6:40: "And this is the will of Him who sent Me, that *everyone who sees the Son and believes in Him may have everlasting life; and I will raise him up at the last day."* (Emphasis added)

And again in Matthew 25:46: "And these will go away into everlasting punishment, *but the righteous into eternal life.*" (Emphasis added)

Psalm 9:17: "The wicked shall be turned into *hell,* And all the nations that forget God." (Emphasis added)

Mormonism: Regardless of the above Scripture, though Mormons believe in being resurrected from the dead, their doctrine contradicts that they will spend an eternity in heaven or hell. Mormon doctrine also directly contradicts the Bible with the teaching that hell only exists prior to the resurrection and then is abolished. This is stated on page 349 in *Mormon Doctrine; "Hell will have an end."*

As stated in chapter 4 of this book, Mormons believe in three levels of heaven or "kingdoms of glory where the resurrected will reside: the Celestial Kingdom, the Terrestrial Kingdom, and the Telestial Kingdom.

> According to the Mormon book *The Doctrine and Covenants* Section 76:
>
> Contrary to the views found in the uninspired teachings and creeds of modern Christendom, there are in eternity *kingdoms of glory* to which all resurrected persons *except the sons of perdition* will eventually go. These are named; celestial, terrestrial and telestial—the glory of each being beyond mortal comprehension.

Who are the *sons of perdition* that do not get to go to one of the three *kingdoms of glory?* Anyone who walks away from the Mormon Church! Mormons are repetitively taught that people who leave the Mormon Church are apostates and they will be cast into outer darkness with Satan and the demons.

Mormon Doctrine states, "Their destiny, following their resurrection, is to be cast out with the devil and his angels, to inherit the same kingdom in a state where 'their worm dieth not, and the fire is not quenched.'" [64]

It is this type of *cultish* mind control induced by fear that keeps many people bound to the Mormon Church. Members of the Mormon Church are afraid that if they leave, they will literally be cast into outer darkness.

V. The Virgin Birth

Christianity: "Then the angel said to her, "'Do not be afraid, Mary, for you have found favor with God. And behold, you will conceive in your womb and bring forth a Son, and shall call His name JESUS. He will be great, and will be called the Son of the Highest; and the Lord God will give Him the throne of His father David. And He will reign over the house of Jacob forever, and of His kingdom there will be no end." Then Mary said to the angel, "How can this be, since I do not know a man?" And the angel answered and said to her, "The Holy Spirit will come upon you, and the power of the Highest will overshadow you; therefore, also, that Holy One who is to be born will be called the Son of God" (Luke 1:30–35).

The above Scripture is key to what Christians believe as it relates to the birth of Jesus, which is that He was born of a Virgin named Mary who conceived the Son of God by the overshadowing of the Holy Spirit. This fulfills prophecy concerning the virgin birth of the Savior found in Isaiah chapter 7, verse 14.

Matthew 1:20 further confirms this: "But while he thought about these things, behold, an angel of the Lord appeared to him in a dream, saying, 'Joseph, son of David, do not be afraid to take to you Mary your wife, *for that which is conceived in her is of the Holy Spirit.*" (Emphasis added)

Mormonism: Once again Mormon doctrine completely contradicts Christian doctrine and the Bible.

In *The Journal of Discourses,* Brigham Young states, "I have given you a few leading items upon this subject, but a great deal more remains to be told. Now remember from this time forth and forever, that Jesus Christ was not begotten by the Holy Ghost." [65]

Mormon prophet Joseph Fielding Smith agrees with this statement by Young in the *Doctrines of Salvation:* "They tell us The Book of Mormon states that Jesus was begotten of the Holy Ghost. I challenge that statement. The Book of Mormon teaches *no such thing! Neither does the Bible.*"[66](Emphasis added)

Furthermore, Mormons teach that Christ was conceived through a physical, sexual, and mortal encounter between God, himself, and Mary, furthered by the belief as stated earlier that God is a man of flesh and bones!

Mormon's also believe God has wives and spirit babies!

Mormons believe that God has wives and spirit babies and those spirit children are placed into humans as they are born into this realm.

Nowhere does Scripture even hint at the existence of an eternal mother, yet Mormon doctrine teaches that God the Father has a wife, through whom he procreates spirit children:

"Implicit in the Christian verity that all men are the spirit children of an Eternal Father is the usually unspoken truth that *they are also the offspring of an Eternal Mother.* An exalted and glorified Man of Holiness (The Mormon Book: The Pearl of Great Price, Moses 6:57) could not be a Father unless a Woman of like glory, perfection, and holiness was associated with him as a Mother." [67] (Emphasis added)

Yet, not a single verse in the Bible even remotely suggests that God has a wife, but Isaiah explicitly says that the Lord made all things by Himself:

> Thus says the LORD, your Redeemer, And He who formed you from the womb: "I am the LORD, who makes all things, Who stretches out the heavens all alone, Who spreads abroad the earth by Myself" (Isaiah 44:24 NJV).
>
> Acts states, "God, who made the world and everything in it, since He is Lord of heaven and earth, does not dwell in temples made with hands. Nor is He worshiped with men's hands, as though He needed anything, since He gives to all life, breath, and all things" (Acts 17:24–25 NKJV).

VI. The Doctrine of Salvation (Salvation by Grace)

Christianity: Christians believe that only those who *accept* Jesus' sacrifice on the cross and surrender themselves to Him will receive the benefit of Jesus' death and resurrection, which is forgiveness of sins and an eternity in heaven. It comes by faith in the act of grace completed on the cross of Calvary.

Romans 10:9 states, "That if you confess with your mouth the Lord Jesus and believe in your heart that God has raised Him from the dead, you will be saved." (NKJV)

"To Him all the prophets witness that, through His name, whoever believes in Him will receive remission of sins" (Acts 10:43). [Emphasis added]

Eternal life "in Christ," and not just simply eternal existence through resurrection, is the gift offered by God to humanity!

Romans 6:23–24 affirms this: "For the wages of sin is death, but the gift of God is eternal life in Christ Jesus our Lord."

Ephesians 2:8–9 explains this gift is obtainable only by grace through faith: "For by grace you have been saved through faith, and that not of yourselves; it is the gift of God, not of works, lest anyone should boast."

Romans 11:6 confirms that salvation is a gift of grace and not of works with, *"And if by grace, then it is no longer of works*; otherwise grace is no longer grace. But if it is of works, it is no longer grace; otherwise work is no longer work." (Emphasis added)

Christians believe that Jesus' death serves to reconcile all believers to God. In dying, Jesus broke down the wall of separation between God and man.

Mormonism: Mormons believe that salvation by grace and faith in Jesus alone is a false teaching. *The Mormon Doctrine* states as much:

"However, *one of the untrue doctrines found in modern Christendom is the concept that man can gain salvation by grace alone and without obedience.* This soul-destroying doctrine has the obvious effect of lessening the determination of an individual to conform to all of the laws and ordinances of the gospel, *such conformity being essential* if the sought for reward is in reality to be gained."[68]

There's a litany of rituals, laws, works, and rules in Mormonism which must be performed in order to obtain salvation to achieve entrance into one of the fictional three levels of eternal reward. Again this contradicts Christianity and falls more in line with *cult* practices.

VII. Universality of Sin

Christianity: At the heart of Christianity is the belief that all men are born sinners (or with a sinful nature) due to the fall of Adam and Eve in the Garden of Eden. Sin entered the world through Adam and because of this every man and woman, thereafter, is born into sin.

Romans 5:12 states, "Therefore, just as through one man sin entered the world, and death through sin, and thus death spread to all men, because all sinned."

Romans 3:23 further illustrates, "for *all* have *sinned* and fall short of the glory of God." (Emphasis added)

Anyone claiming to be without sin or having never sinned believes a lie and lives in deception.

"If we say that we have no sin, we deceive ourselves, and the truth is not in us" (John 1:8).

Mormonism: Mormons hold the opposing belief that you should rejoice over the fall of man. Their belief is that death and sin came through the fall of Adam and Eve. But their deed was not actually a "sin." It was really a blessing because it enabled man to continue progressing on toward eternal life.

"They (the Christian world) have been long taught that Adam and Eve were great transgressors …We, the children of Adam, should rejoice with them, that through their fall and the atonement of Jesus Christ, the way of eternal life has been opened up to us."[69]

However, rejoicing is hardly the proper response to Adam's sin. Because of that sin, both Adam and Eve died spiritually and their physical bodies began to deteriorate. Eve had a curse placed on her by God in which she would have increased pain and sorrow in childbearing. Adam was also cursed and required to work in order to eat; all of creation was cursed as a result of sin. Adam and Eve were thrown out of the garden forever, and the entire human race was to be born into sin, thereby living as children of God's wrath by nature. To rejoice in the fall of man is to embrace Satan's lie. Satan deceived Eve by convincing her that sin was good and would bring her knowledge and reward.

Mormonism continues embracing this lie by teaching that it was in God's plan for Adam and Eve to sin and He, in fact, designed it. In *The Journal of Discourses*, 10:312, Brigham Young says, "He (GOD) had designed that they should." (Emphasis added)

VIII. The Atonement

Christianity: "For God so loved the world that He gave His only begotten Son, that whoever believes in Him should not perish but have everlasting life. For God did not send His Son into the world to condemn the world, but that the world through Him might be saved" (John 3:16–17 NKJV).

Christians hold fast to the very familiar verse above and the belief that Jesus paid for their sins on the cross of Calvary. He gave his own life and whoever accepts this sacrifice and believes in Him is saved.

It is the shedding of the Savior's blood that washes away our guilt and puts us in right standing with the heavenly Father. It is His atoning blood that justifies us—it is through His blood that we are made righteous, as found in 2 Corinthians 5:21: "For He made Him who knew no sin to be sin for us, that we might become the righteousness of God in Him."

Scripture is very clear that Jesus' sacrifice paid for *all* sins—not just some sins. In fact, 1 John 1:7 says that the blood of Jesus Christ His Son cleanses us from *all* sin.

Mormonism: In direct contrast to Christianity, Mormonism has a foundational belief that Jesus' blood does not cover all sin. This was addressed in earlier chapters when recounting the story of the Mountain Meadow Massacre and the trial of John D. Lee, which dealt with the Blood Atonement—the shedding of one's blood to atone for sin.

As recounted earlier, there are eleven sins the *Mormon Doctrine* states as being so grievous the transgressors are placed beyond the power of atonement of Christ.[70] The blood of Jesus does not cover these sins, even if the person repents!

According to Joseph Smith in *Doctrines of Salvation,* 1:134: "But many may commit certain grievous sins—according to his light and knowledge—that will place him beyond the reach of the atoning blood of Christ. If then he would be saved he must make sacrifice of his own life to atone—so far as in his power lies—for that sin, for the *blood of Christ alone under certain circumstances will not avail."* (Emphasis added)

This teaching is ludicrous and as far from Christianity as you can get! Again, in Mormonism salvation is about works, not about what Jesus accomplished at the cross. If requiring personal blood sacrifice doesn't fit the definition given of a cult—I don't know what does!

Symbols

The cross is a symbol of Christianity—a reminder of the price Jesus paid for man's redemption.

Mormons have likewise rejected the cross of Jesus as unnecessary for the redemption of mankind and therefore do not display the cross of Jesus, but instead adorn their temples with various symbols, many actually occult in nature.

Instead of the cross, the fictional angel Moroni raising a trumpet is seen atop Mormon temples.

Let's look at the definition of a cult once more: a particular system of religious worship, especially with reference to its rites and ceremonies. A religion or sect considered false, unorthodox, or extremist, with members often living outside of conventional society under the direction of a charismatic leader.[71]

Understanding the false teachings and all that is required of the members of the Mormon religion qualifies it as a cult, not just another church, and most assuredly not a Christian denomination.

With that being said, Mr. Hannity, the above evidence gives great cause for concern for the truth presented herewith. Just because a religion uses the name of "Jesus Christ," its members are not necessarily Christians. It's like me standing in my garage does not make me a Cadillac. A study of the Bible plainly shows that Mitt Romney's "faith" is unequivocally *not* Christian. Furthermore, the Mormon religion is utterly blasphemous to the living God and His word, purposely misleading to the citizens of the United States of America and the world and to those who are caught up in and believe in it, including presidential candidate Mitt Romney.

Chapter 7

If Mitt Lives in Deception, Should We Not Question His Judgment to Discern the Truth in All Dominion of The Office Of The Presidency of the United States of America?

Mitt Romney has boldly proclaimed that he will not separate himself from his faith—even though, as proven in this book and many others, his faith/religion is steeped in dishonesty. Though his religion is cloaked under the guise of God loving poster family perfection with wholesome values, it is filled with *deception.*

Keep in mind as with any religion in which one spends his life practicing, he has lived through years of instruction and has had plenty of time to discover the error in the prophecies and doctrine he is involved in. Mitt Romney has had ample time to discover the fraudulence in Mormonism, yet he still upholds allegiance to it in which case, one of two scenarios are involved:

1. Mitt Romney is aware of the deception, yet chooses to not only live in it, but also to propagate it; or
2. Mitt Romney is unable to discern for himself deception from truth.

Either scenario makes him a dangerous consideration for president of the United States.

If one blindly follows those over himself, the Bible says that they both shall fall. Read the following counsel of the Bible found in Luke 6:39;

"And he spake a parable unto them, Can the *blind* lead *the blind?* Shall they not both fall into the ditch?" (KJV). [Emphasis added]

There are many prophecies based directly on the writings of Joseph Smith that have failed the litmus test of time. For a more exhaustive look at these prophecies, visit Ed Decker's site http://blogs.myspace.com/index.cfm?fuseaction=blog.view&friendId=241586834&blogId=390826932. Mr. Decker catalogues over forty verifiably false prophecies made by the founder of the Mormon Church, Joseph Smith.

The Bible is clear on the process of determining false prophet**s** and what to do with them once you find them.

Deuteronomy 18: 21–22 says, "And if thou say in thine heart, How shall we know the word which the LORD hath not spoken? [22] When a prophet speaketh in the name of the LORD, if the thing follow not, nor come to pass, that is the thing which the LORD hath not spoken, but the prophet hath spoken it presumptuously: thou shalt not be afraid of him" (KJV).

Thus, it is an easy test to determine if a person is a false prophet or true prophet. Simply allow the prophecy to testify as a witness to whether or not the individual is a true prophet. Using the Bible's prescribed method of testing, Joseph Smith horribly fails the test on numerous occasions.

Herewith, I will highlight just seven of the prophecies that *have not,* and *cannot* come to pass. Keeping in mind that according to Mormon teachings, all words spoken or written by a Mormon prophet are equally weighted as Scripture and prophecy, the following testify against Joseph Smith. This is not an attempt to be an exhaustive study of all of the false prophesies that the church has manufactured its deception on, but merely a sampling.

False Prophecy #1

This prophecy was spoken concerning David W. Patten as revelation given through Joseph Smith the prophet, at Far West, Missouri, April 17, 1838, found in *The Doctrine and Covenants* Section 114:

> Verily thus saith the Lord: It is wisdom in my servant David W. Patten, that he settle up all his business as soon as he possibly can, and make a disposition of his merchandise, that he may perform a mission unto me next spring, in company with others, even twelve including himself, to testify of my name and bear glad tidings unto all the world.

> For verily thus saith the Lord, that inasmuch as there are those among you who deny my name, others shall be planted in their stead and receive their bishopric. Amen.[72]

Notice that the prophecy was given *April 17, 1838;* the problem with this prophecy was that David Patten died in *October 1838,* before having an opportunity to fulfill this prophecy. This is the first of many failures from the so-called prophet who claimed to write the most perfectly written book in the history of the world.

False Prophecy #2

Joseph Smith said, "I prophesy in the name of the Lord God of Israel, unless the United States redresses the wrongs committed upon the Saints in the state of Missouri and punish the crimes committed by her officers that in a few years the *government will be utterly overthrown and wasted,* and there will not be so much as a potsherd left ..." [73]

Was he a true or false prophet? A total of 175 years later the United States government is still moving forward into the future. This is another false prophecy by the false prophet leader who has led so many a stray, *including* Governor Romney.

Joseph Smith prophesied on February 14, 1835, "Go forth to prune the vineyard for the last time, or the *coming of the lord,* which was nigh even fifty-six years, should wind up the scene." [74]

This prophecy is reaffirmed by Mormon clerk Oliver Boardman Huntington and is found in Volume 2 of the *Journal of Discourses*

"On the 14th of Feb. 1835, Joseph Smith [said] that God had revealed to him that the coming of Christ would be within 56 years, which added to 1835 shows that before 1891 and the 14th of February the Savior of the world would make his appearance again upon the earth and the winding up scene take place."[75]

According to the test of time (fifty-six years) this prophecy has also failed. Jesus has not yet returned. In fact, Jesus, when speaking of his own return said this in Matthew 24:36: "But of that day and hour knoweth no man, no, not the angels of heaven, but my Father only."

Yet this blatant deception is still something that Romney does not want to distance himself from.

False Prophecy #3

Joseph Smith prophesied again on May 18, 1843, on the destruction of the United States.

"I prophesy in the name of the Lord god of Israel, unless the United States redress the wrongs committed … in a few years the government will be utterly overthrown and wasted, and there will not be so much as a potsherd left."[76]

The United States government did not redress any of the alleged wrongs against the Mormons in Missouri and in fact drove them out of the region, yet the government is still intact.

One-hundred-fifty-seven years after the prophecy, the United States government is still in existence, and now Governor Romney wants to be at the helm of it.

How can an educated man, such as Mitt Romney, possessing several degrees from some of the best educators of our time, align himself with an organization in which its foundation is completely marred with evidentiary fallacies while claiming to represent the ultimate truth?

Mormon doctrine teaches that all religions, Christian or otherwise, are false and tainted; yet Mormons do not examine their own blatantly false doctrine with any kind of factual scrutiny. We must seek the truth, no matter how many opportunistic deceivers seek to hide it. We must be able to discern the basic differences between fact and fiction in order to function correctly as a society, and most importantly, in the highest office in the land.

False Prophecy #4

"While discussing the petition to Congress, I prophesied, by virtue of the holy Priesthood vested in me, and in the name of the Lord Jesus Christ, that, <u>if Congress will not hear our petition and grant us protection, they shall be broken up as a government, and God shall damn them, and there shall be nothing left of them—not even a grease spot"</u>. See also History of the Church

(HC), vol. 6, p. 116, though when this prediction was incorporated into the official history, Mormon Church leaders decided to leave out the "grease spot" element.) [77]

Here is yet another attempt by Joseph Smith to accomplish his means by way of a threat under the guise of a prophetic utterance upon a government that has outlasted the so-called prophet. Strong and threatening language is common throughout the history of the Mormon Church, yet Mormons are made up to be peace-loving people who fear God and serve him humbly.

The petition was not heard, nor was protection granted nor was Congress ever broken up, but continues to function to this day. It is interesting that the compilers of *History of the Church* added an editorial note on page 116 in an attempt to soften or explain this prophecy. They state, "*This prediction doubtless has reference to the party in power; to the 'government' considered as the administration.*" [78] According to the note in *History of the Church*, this means the Democratic Party, which was in control at the time. The prophecy was that "*Congress* shall be broken up as a government" and Congress is made up of both parties. The LDS church was making an appeal to the entire United States government and not just the Democratic Party. This is an attempt to whitewash the story into existence by the Mormon Church, which knows full well that the prophecy is in error.

False Prophecy #5

According to the *History of the Church 2*: 465–466 , this revelation was given through Joseph Smith, the prophet, at Salem, Massachusetts, on August 6, 1836.

To set the background, "*At this time the leaders of the Church were heavily in debt due to their labors in the ministry. Hearing that a large amount of money would be available to them in Salem, the Prophet, Sidney Rigdon, Hyrum Smith, and Oliver Cowdery traveled there from Kirtland, Ohio, to investigate this claim, along with preaching the gospel. The brethren transacted several items of church business and did some preaching. When it became apparent that no money was to be forthcoming, they returned to Kirtland. Several of the factors prominent in the background are reflected in the wording of this revelation.*"[79]

Prophecy Found in Section 111 in *The Doctrine and Covenants*

I, the Lord your God, am not displeased with your coming this journey, notwithstanding your follies.

I have much treasure in this city for you, for the benefit of Zion, and many people in this city, whom I will gather out in due time for the benefit of Zion, through your instrumentality.

Therefore, it is expedient that you should form acquaintance with men in this city, as you shall be led, and as it shall be given you.

And it shall come to pass in due time that I will give this city into your hands, that you shall have power over it, insomuch that they shall not discover your secret parts; and its wealth pertaining to gold and silver shall be yours.

Concern not yourselves about your debts, for I will give you power to pay them.

Concern not yourselves about Zion, for I will deal mercifully with her.

Tarry in this place, and in the regions round about;

And the place where it is my will that you should tarry, for the main, shall be signalized unto you by the peace and power of my Spirit, that shall flow unto you.

This place you may obtain by hire. And inquire diligently concerning the more ancient inhabitants and founders of this city;

For there are more treasures than one for you in this city.

Therefore, be ye as wise as serpents and yet without sin; and I will order all things for your good, as fast as ye are able to receive them. Amen.[80]

The problem is that there was never any treasure found at Salem, not only making this a false prophecy, but it also demonstrates disregard for just and honest debts. This does not teach good stewardship or credit management. You cannot let these situations go and maintain fiscal responsibility in your personal or public accounts.

False Prophecy #6

Regarding pestilence, hail, famine, & earthquake to destroy the wicked:

> *And now I am prepared to say by the authority of Jesus Christ, that not many years shall pass away before the United States shall present such a scene of bloodshed as has not a parallel in the history of our nation; pestilence, hail, famine, and earthquake will sweep the wicked of this generation from off the face of the land, to open and prepare the way for the return of the lost tribes of Israel from the north country. The people of the Lord, those who have complied with the requirements of the new covenant, have already commenced gathering together to Zion, which is in the state of Missouri; therefore I declare unto you the warning which the Lord has commanded to declare unto this generation, remembering that the eyes of my Maker are upon me, and that to him I am accountable for every word I say, wishing nothing worse to my fellow-men than their eternal salvation; therefore, "Fear God, and give glory to Him, for the hour of His judgment is come." Repent ye, repent ye, and embrace the everlasting covenant and flee to Zion, before the overflowing scourge overtake you, for there are those now living upon the earth whose eyes shall not be closed in death until they see all these things, which I have spoken, fulfilled.* [81] [Emphasis added]

This simply has not happened and no one who was alive during the prophecy is living today. It would seem that threats were the main source of Smith's prophecies. Smith's threats were unfulfilled and suggest that he had no supernatural awareness of the future. He went from one tirade to another without any results and yet men like Governor Romney still attest that Joseph Smith was a "true" prophet of the church, and continue to follow his false teachings.

False Prophecy #7—

This prophecy regarding the temple being built in Zion Missouri comes directly from *The Doctrine and Covenants*, section 84, the introduction of which states:

> *A revelation of Jesus Christ unto his servant Joseph Smith, Jun., and six elders, as they united their hearts and lifted their voices on high.*

Yea, the word of the Lord concerning his church, established in the last days for the restoration of his people, as he has spoken by the mouth of his prophets, and for the gathering of his saints to stand upon Mount Zion, which shall be the city of New Jerusalem.

Which city shall be built, beginning at the temple lot, which is appointed by the finger of the Lord, in the western boundaries of the State of Missouri, and dedicated by the hand of Joseph Smith, Jun., and others with whom the Lord was well pleased.

Verily, this is the word of the Lord, that the city New Jerusalem shall be built by the gathering of the saints, beginning at this place, even the place of the temple, which temple shall be reared in this generation.

For verily this generation shall not all pass away until an house shall be built unto the Lord, and a cloud shall rest upon it, which cloud shall be even the glory of the Lord, which shall fill the house. [82]

Mormons fled Missouri due to mounting pressure and persecution. The temple was never constructed on the "Temple Lot" in the lifetime of Joseph Smith or anyone living at the time. These are only seven of the numerous false prophecies Joseph Smith imparted during his lifetime.

I would like to direct your attention to what the Bible says about false prophecies. First, there is no such thing as a batting average when it comes to prophecy; you are either a true prophet or a false prophet. The next several passages are from the Holy Bible.

Matthew 7:15 says, "*Beware of false prophets, which come to you in sheep's clothing, but inwardly they are ravenous wolves.*"

2 Corinthians 11:4 warns of preaching "another" Jesus or "another" gospel. The Book of Mormon claims to be just that— "another" gospel of Jesus Christ. "*For if he that cometh preacheth* another Jesus, *whom we have not preached, or if ye receive another spirit, which ye have not received, or another gospel, which ye have not accepted, ye might well bear with him*" *(KJV).*

2 Corinthian 4:13–15 also warns about false apostles and deceitful workers, who transform themselves into apostles of Christ, warning that Satan comes as an angel of light, as do "his" ministers. *"For such are false apostles, deceitful workers, transforming themselves into apostles of Christ.*

And no wonder! For Satan himself transforms himself into an angel of light. Therefore it is no great thing if his (Satan's) *ministers also transform themselves into ministers of righteousness, whose end will be according to their works* (NKJV)." [Emphasis added]

Furthermore, Galatians 1:6 –9 continues to expound on the dangers of following after "another gospel" or false teachers or prophets: "I marvel that ye are so soon removed from him that called you into the grace of Christ unto another gospel: *Which is not another; but there be some that trouble you, and would pervert the gospel of Christ. But though we, or an angel from heaven, preach any other gospel unto you than that which we have preached unto you, let him be accursed. As we said before, so say I now again, if any man preach any other gospel unto you than that ye have received, let him be accursed."*

In fact, the above Scripture plainly states that if any man or even an angel from heaven preach any other gospel, let him be cursed.

"Now the Spirit expressly says that in latter times some will depart from the faith, giving heed to deceiving spirits and doctrines of demons" (1 Timothy 4:1 NKJV).

And according to 2 Peter 2–3, these false prophets and teachers will bring in destructive heresies, leading many away from the truth.

> *But there were also false prophets among the people, even as there will be false teachers among you, who will secretly bring in destructive heresies, even denying the Lord who bought them, and bring on themselves swift destruction. And many will follow their destructive ways, because of whom the way of truth will be blasphemed. By covetousness they will exploit you with deceptive words; for a long time their judgment has not been idle, and their destruction does not slumber.* [Emphasis added]

1 John 4:1 warns to not believe every teaching or every spirit: "*Beloved, do not believe every spirit, but test the spirits, whether they are of God; because many false prophets have gone out into the world."*

I believe that the Bible, the one and only word of God, gives an accurate example of the Mormon Church and its leaders as false prophets. I believe the Bible is the standard by which "truth" is and should be measured. I believe that if anything is preached from the pulpit that does not line up with the word of God, it is patently false and misleading. The Bible strongly warns against *believing* or *following* false doctrine.

The deception of the Mormon religion is blatantly plain to see and hard to evaluate without concluding that the Mormon Church is utterly rooted in heresy and fallacies. Knowing what you have learned herewith, would it not be difficult to cast a vote for a man who, although polished and educated, does not seem to possess the cognitive skills to discern simple truth, based on the historic and completely false writings and records of his church? Or maybe even worse, Mitt knows the truth but purposely glosses it over in order to accomplish the mission.

We have already experienced one candidate that *said* whatever was convincing to the American people in order to achieve the elected position of president. Very little, if any, of what Obama *said* to get elected bears out in the reality of what he has *done* and continues to *do*. In fact, Barack Obama has *done,* in most cases, just the opposite of what he *said* that he would do.

Can America afford to elect another candidate based on his "words" and smooth demeanor, versus doing the diligence to bear out the facts of who this candidate is, what he believes and even more crucial, what his true agenda points are?

More Deception and Danger—Polygamy

Known today as "*The Principle,*" polygamy has been a practice and a part of the teaching of the Mormon Church throughout its history. The doctrine of plural marriage in the LDS church dates back to 1843 when Joseph Smith Jr. recorded what became foundations for polygamy, believing that the practice was required to reach the highest level of the Mormon third heaven, the Celestial Kingdom, in order to become "gods." This teaching is written in *The Doctrine and Covenants*:

> *And again, as pertaining to the law of the priesthood—if any man espouse a virgin, and desire to espouse another, and the first give her consent, and if he espouse the second, and they are virgins, and have vowed to no other man, then is he justified; he cannot commit adultery for they are given unto him; for he cannot commit adultery with that that belongeth unto him and to no one else.*

> *And if he have ten virgins given unto him by this law, he cannot commit adultery, for they belong to him, and they are given unto him; therefore is he justified.*[83]

While the Mormon Church denies that it supports such a teaching and points to the fundamentalist Mormons as to being the ones to practice it, this teaching has not been removed from its doctrines.

Further investigation lends to the fact that polygamy ceased to be practiced by non-fundamentalists only for a time (due to pressure from the government) but that it would ultimately return again to be performed as an open and accepted part of the religion.

In 1890 at an October conference, Mormon President Wilford Woodruff presented a "Manifesto" which declared that the church no longer taught or practiced plural marriages. However, it remains in their *Doctrine and Covenants* today.

Polygamy was prominent throughout Mitt Romney's family tree. Mormon Church genealogical records, among the most detailed and complete of any religion, show that two of his great-grandfathers had five wives and at least one of his great-great grandfathers had twelve.

In 1897, more than thirty years after federal law prohibited the practice and six years after Mormon leaders banned it, Romney's great-grandfather, Miles Park Romney, married his fifth wife.

As previously mentioned, Romney's great-great grandfather, Mormon apostle Parley Pratt, had at least twelve wives. In an 1852 sermon, Pratt's brother Orson became the first church official to not only defend polygamy but to publicly proclaim it as a direct revelation from God.

Mitt Romney's father, former Michigan Governor George Romney, was born in Chihuahua, Mexico, where Mormons had fled in the 1800s to escape religious persecution and US laws forbidding polygamy. He did not return to the United States with his family until 1912, more than twenty years after the church issued "The Manifesto" which banned polygamy.

Upon realizing the important part polygamy played in the history of the Romney family, it causes one to wonder if Mitt supported gay marriage in his state with an ulterior motive in mind. If gay marriage is legalized, the next step could easily be the legalization of polygamy.

Church Finances

The Mormon Church is one of the wealthiest organizations on the planet. With its resources in real estate and business interests layered in both for-profit and non-profit corporations, it is hard to document the worth of the church today.

One of the most uncompromising principals of the Mormon Church is the faithful "mandatory" 10 percent of the "gross" of the church members' income to the church, with no exceptions. One of the most important tasks for the Mormon bishop to accomplish is to police the finances of the church members, even to the extent that, if necessary, the church members' financial and tax records can be presented to the bishop in order for verification that the members have not skimped on their 10 percent owed to the church. Remember that the ticket into the sought-after utopia, Mormon Temple, is the faithful tithe payment.

The book *The Mormon Corporate Empire* by John Heinerman and Anson Shupe gives in-depth details about the wealth of the church. It should be noted that the church does not handle its finances like other mainstream denominations. The handling of collected funds and disbursements are kept to a select few members in the upper echelon of the church, whereas most churches give financial reports to the local congregations on a regularly scheduled basis. This obligatory disclosure from the Mormon tithe payer does not work both ways. It's a one-way street and the Mormon emperors have a sweet deal going for themselves.

With deep pockets, the Mormon Church is more than capable of buying a seat in the political arena, including that of the office of the president of the United States of America, which would very likely give the Mormon Church control over the direction of our country and a voice at the table with the top leaders of the world. Moreover, this would also allow the political agenda of the church to be achieved through the means of financial resources of the Mormon Church.

The Agenda

Behind the scenes of the Mormon Church is a secret political agenda that the leaders don't want you, the public, to know about. It's the reason that although the Mormon religion is the fastest-growing religion in the world, there is a continued push for more converts and the motive behind the expense put toward its missionary program.

Birthed within the Church, yet distinct from the church, is a secret organization formed by Joseph Smith during early Mormon history. This organization is the political machinery of the "priesthood" of the Mormon Church, named "the Kingdom of God" and "the Government of God."

The goal of the Mormon Church through "the Kingdom of God," according to J. Stewart in *Joseph Smith the Mormon Prophet,* is to "**bring the United States Government under the rule of the priesthood.**" [84]

Mormons believe the prophecy from the book of Daniel, chapter 2, verse 44 that says *they* (the Mormon Church and its corporate empire assets and resources) will be the chief element in a millennial overthrow of the United States government.

> *And in the days of these kings shall the God of heaven set up a kingdom, which shall never be destroyed; and the kingdom shall not be left to other people, but it shall break in pieces and consume all these kingdoms, and it shall stand forever* (KJV).

Brigham Young stated in *The Journal of Discourses, "No more or less than the complete overthrow of the nation, and not only of this nation, but the nations of Europe."* [85]

Mormon President John Taylor explains in *The Journal of Discourses,* "*The priesthood will be the only legitimate ruling power under the whole heavens; for every other power and influence will be subject to it. When the millennium is introduced all potentates, powers, and authorities—every man, woman, and child—will be in subjection to The Kingdom of God; they will be under the power and dominion of the priesthood of God.*" [86] (Emphasis added)

Mormons believe that they are the only true church and their main objective is to be ready when the time comes for the millennial reign by having their leaders ready to rule or already in key places of authority and power.

This agenda is confirmed in *Mormon Doctrine* by Bruce R. McConkie: "*During the millennium the church will have the rule and government of the world given to it.*"[87]

Their ultimate goal is to better serve their agenda by being able to rule and govern *before* the millennium actually takes place!

How might they accomplish this secret agenda?

One way, according to authors Heinerman and Shupe, will be "directly related to general *public ignorance* about their methods and ends." [88]

Additional ways could be by:

- Acquiring worldwide Mormon Church membership. According to 2008 year-end statistics there were over 13 million members so as of the printing of this book the number will be more like 14 million.
- Implementing all-out media campaigns and public relations campaigns. Think of all the propaganda, television commercials, and door-to-door visits by nice, wholesome young missionaries.
- Accumulating corporate wealth. Along with federal church tax exemptions, the Mormon Church is a very wealthy and powerful organization of which its money is hidden beneath many corporations, acquisitions, and venues with no accountability to the members who give to the church.
- Establishing Mormons in key political positions, such as president of the United States, senators, and congressmen.

In a nutshell, the political agenda of the church is to place a Mormon man in the presidential office in order that the church may take over and control our country and further the world for the "Kingdom of God." Just as is mentioned in the White Horse Prophecy below, Joseph Smith has been at war with the US government since the 1830s. Mitt Romney is the latest champion of the Mormon Church *through* whom they may accomplish their means. The goal is first states, then the country, and ultimately the planet. Make no mistake: Mitt Romney and the Mormon Church have more in mind than just the Oval Office.

In closing the spiritual part of this book, I will leave you with what is often called "The White Horse Prophecy" given by former prophets of The Church of Jesus Christ of Latter-day Saints:

You will see the constitution of the United States almost destroyed. It will hang like a thread ... A terrible revolution will take place in the land of America ... [T]he land will be left without a Supreme Government ... [Mormonism] will have gathered strength, sending out Elders to gather the honest in heart ... to stand by the constitution of the United States ... In these days ... God will set up a Kingdom, never to be thrown down ... [T]he whole of America will be made the Zion of God.[89]

Will the constitution be destroyed? No: it will be held inviolate by this people; and, as Joseph Smith said, "The time will come when the destiny of the nation will hang upon a single thread. At that critical juncture, this people will step forth and save it from the threatened destruction." It will be so.[90]

End of Part I

Part II

Political Portion

Chapter 8

The Mormon Church and Its Image Machine: A Clean-Cut Corporation

Since 1959 the Mormon Church has maintained a tight shroud of secrecy regarding its finances. Three sources offer a glimpse into the vast financial empire of the LDS church: the 1985 book *The Mormon Corporate Empire* by John Heinerman and Anson Shupe, a 1991 *Arizona Republic* article, and a 1997 article in *Time* magazine.

The largest source of income for the Mormon Church comes from its members. As stated earlier, Mormons must tithe 10 percent of their gross income. As church membership grows, so do the financial resources deemed necessary to usher in their kingdom on earth.

In 1983, the church's wealth was estimated at around $2 billion, with three-quarters of its income coming from tithes.[1] In 1991, it was estimated that the church received $4.3 billion a year from its members.[2] In 1996 approximately $5.2 billion were sent to the church by its 9.7 million members worldwide.[3] With a current estimated 14 million members, worldwide, you can almost estimate that church member tithing gross receipts would be close to double of the 1996 estimate, mostly tax free.

The LDS church also has income flowing in from its investments. In 1997, LDS assets were estimated at a minimum of $30 billion with an annual church gross income of $5.9 billion, which would have placed "LDS Inc." above Nike and Gap in the Fortune 500. In 1997 *Time* estimated $6 billion of the church's wealth was "invested directly in church-owned, for-profit concerns, the largest of which are in agribusiness, media, insurance, travel and real estate."[4]

According to Latayne Colvett Scott, author of *The Mormon Mirage*, "the Mormon Church does now or has recently owned hotels, department stores, newspapers, bookstores, publishing companies, a funeral home, farms, canneries, mills, factories, salvage stores, food-producing industries, cattle grazing land, banks, mines and much of the land and buildings in downtown Salt Lake City. It finances supermarket chains and food processors and controls the copper and sugar-beet industries. Mormons own automobile factories and control paper mills and newspaper chains."[5]

In fact, the largest beef ranch in the United States is the Deseret Cattle and Citrus Ranch, which is located near Orlando, Florida, and is owned by the Mormon Church. The mere real estate value of the 312,000-acre ranch was estimated at $858 million in 1997. LDS's Deseret Management Corporation, which controls almost all of the church's commercial assets, was "one of the largest owners of farm and ranchland in the country, including 49 for profit parcels in addition to the Deseret Ranch" in 1997.[6]

In 2000, it was estimated that the church's assets were over $50 billion.[7] However, it was rumored on various web sites that the assets are more in the $80 to $100 billion range.[8] As Charles Wood, author of *The Mormon Conspiracy*, writes, the church's income seems to benefit only a few of its members.

> "The General Authorities are funneling over $1 billion in tithing income into investments. The Mormon church members who are struggling to meet the church's demands for 10 percent of their incomes would wonder why this income is not spent for church (religion) related activities. The church leaders seem unconcerned about the financial needs of the large concentration of Mormons living in mobile home communities throughout the state of Utah populated by people who are barely able to make ends meet. Faithful as they are, these poor souls are encouraged by the church to raise large families and they are barely scraping together enough to feed, clothe and house their children. Given the opportunity, they would surely question the siphoning of their tithing dollars for lucrative business deals made by the church hierarchy. They would surely wonder if some of the church's money could be used to improve their lot."[9]

With close to fourteen million members, the finances of the church are controlled by only fifteen people: The First Presidency (the prophet and two counselors) and the Twelve Apostles.[10] A significant amount of this money is spent on a massive media campaign to craft and control the image of the church, concealing its doctrines, rites, and rituals, and instead portraying Mormonism as a normal Christian religion. In 1983 the estimated value of all LDS communications holdings was $547,640,000.[11] Wood estimates that in 2004 these would be worth $4 billion.[12]

In 1985, *before* the explosion of the Internet, Heinerman and Shupe wrote, "Mormon influence in communications touches virtually every person in the United States, and increasingly, millions of people beyond North America."[13]

One of the church's largest communications holdings is Bonneville International Corporation, the fourteenth largest radio chain in the United States. Today, Bonneville owns stations in Los Angeles, Chicago, Washington, D.C., Seattle, Phoenix, St. Louis, Cincinnati, and Salt Lake City.[14]

Janis Hutchinson, author of both *The Mormon Missionaries* and *Out of Cults and into the Church*, writes on her blog janishutchinson.com that leaders of the Mormon Church "are determined to see that their message reaches every home … And what's that message? Not that individuals can become gods, or that temple rituals are required for full salvation, or that heaven can only be gained through the certification of Joseph Smith—these doctrines and others are concealed. Rather they bombard the public with Christian values. More specifically, that happiness and family solidarity can be gained by following the teachings of Jesus Christ as contained in the Book of Mormon, the latter offered free through an 800 number."[15]

More recent advertisements now offer a free Bible instead. What the callers do not realize is that their names and addresses are forwarded to local LDS mission offices near the callers' residences. The free book they order comes attached with two Mormon missionaries.[16]

The "Homefront" ads which focused on wholesome pro-family issues, rather than Mormonism, hit the airwaves in the 1970s. By 1994 these ads had been "shown on over 5,000 radio and 800 television stations on NBC, CBS, ABC and several cable channels in the U.S. and Canada."[17]

University of Maine at Presque Isle Communication Professor Kenneth Petress and student Anne E. Chapman in their paper "The Mormon Church and Image Advertising: Appeals for Family Unity and Community Responsibility," found that "the basic commercial appeal is to show the church is keenly aware of family and interpersonal needs and desires that most people feel sympathetic toward and that the Mormons are much like mainstream America in basic desired visions; and that if they want to join others who practice traditional and adjusted family activities and interpersonal behaviors, they need only join the Church of Jesus Christ of Latter Day Saints."[18]

The Mormons want the world to know that they are just like you, while at the same time masking history, doctrine, and rituals that would appall most Christians. Noah Feldman notes in his January 2008 *New York Times* article *What Is It about Mormonism?* that "(s)peaking esoterically about faith has a firm basis in LDS tradition." Feldman writes, "The church's most inviting public symbols—pairs of clean-cut missionaries in well-pressed white shirts—evoke the wholesome success of an all-American denomination with an idealistic commitment to clean living. Yet, at the same time, secret, sacred temple rites and garments call to mind the church's murky past, including its embrace of polygamy, which has not been the doctrine or practice of the mainstream church of Jesus Christ of Latter Day Saints for a century." [19]

Speaking esoterically was a mastery of the late President Hinckley who enjoyed a lengthy public relations career in the church and is often credited for more recent LDS image campaigns. When interviewed for the 1997 *Time* article, the author noted, "On whether his church still holds that God the Father was once a man, he (Hinckley) sounded uncertain (saying) 'I don't know that we teach it. I don't know that we emphasize it ... I understand the philosophical background behind it, but I don't know a lot about it, and I don't think others know a lot about it.'"[20] This was a bold-faced lie.

While concealing the true church, the LDS also focuses intently on the clean-cut, industrious, and successful Mormon. Feldman wrote "In the elite East Coast where Romney made his career, Mormonism signifies personal rectitude, professional competence, and an idiosyncratic-but-impressive rejection of alcohol and caffeine. If anything, the systematic overrepresentation of Mormons among top business people and lawyers affords LDS affiliation a certain cachet—rather like being Jewish but taller." [21]

LDS purposely and consistently highlights its successful members, almost careful to point out their faith as a key to their success. You will hear hints of this from convert Glenn Beck, insinuating through various ways of communication that his "faith" is what makes him what he is today.

The highly touted Mormon Tabernacle Choir, for example, has produced over one-hundred albums and boasts five gold and two platinum records. Over 500 stations around the world air "Music of the Spoken Word," a weekly radio/television program which features the choir. [22]

Athletes are particularly heralded, especially in the Olympics which will be discussed in a later chapter. Recently John Moody, an executive at News Corporation, authored the book *Kiss it Good-bye: The Mystery, the Mormon, and the Moral of the 1960 Pittsburgh Pirates.* The book, published by Shadow Mountain, an imprint of Deseret Books, heralds the career of Pittsburgh Pirate Vernon Law. Moody writes "to understand how Law's faith shaped his character and wrote the code by which he lived as a player and spent the rest of his life. It helps to know what his religion teaches, and why its doctrines and beliefs are a sore point for many Christians who view the Mormon church with disdain."[23] Moody sanitizes the history of the Mormon Church, including the "martyrdom" of Joseph Smith. [24]

Shadow Mountain also published *Surround Yourself with Greatness*, a book about Mormon NFL player Chad Lewis. "Three time Pro-Bowl tight end Chad Lewis says that every good thing in his life is a direct result of his family and faith," the publisher's website says in describing the book.[25]

Mormons are also quick to point out many successful Mormons in the entertainment industry, beyond Donnie and Marie Osmond. A 2009 article in *LDS Living Magazine* chronicles Mormons in the film industry, such as Dean Jagger: "Little-known theatre actor Dean Jagger, who depicted the title character in *Brigham Young*, had something special about him. In fact, according to George D. Pyper, a consultant on the film who had actually known the prophet Brigham, said he looked like him, sounded like him, and even had some of the same mannerisms. His portrayal of the 'frontiersman' proved to be his breakthrough into film.

Jagger went on to star in *White Christmas* and *Twelve O'Clock High*, which earned him an Academy Award for best supporting actor. He also won two Emmys for his television show, *Mr. Novak*. Then, in his late 60s, he came back to his breakthrough role, but in a way he may not have expected: after marrying his third wife, the LDS Etta Mae Norton, Jagger was baptized a member of the church. At the time, one headline read, "Brigham Young Becomes a Mormon." Subsequently, he donated his awards, theatrical files, and several scrapbooks to the BYU Library, where they still reside. He died in 1991 at age 87. [26]

The article lauds Mormon achievement in cinema. "The scope of Mormon film is grander than one might guess at first, stretching back to the beginning of film in the 1890s. Some 3,000 films have been made by and about Latter-day Saints, representing an enormous contribution to Mormon culture and to the history of film in general."[27]

Nowhere have Mormons sought legitimization more than through politics. Today, there is a significant overrepresentation of Mormons on several levels of the government including the CIA and FBI. *Presidents and Prophets*, published by the LDS Covenant Communications Inc., chronicles the Mormon influence on US presidents. "From Washington to Bush, each president and his relationship with the Mormons is explored, and we see the church rising from obscurity to political clout as America's fastest growing religion," the book's inside jacket claims.[28]

Nothing could elevate the clout of the Mormon Church more today than a highly successful, clean-cut Mormon with a beautiful family and high political aspirations. In Romney, the LDS found someone to further its public relations campaign. And in the LDS church, Romney found the perfect strategy to further his.

Throughout his life, Romney has followed the same playbook as the LDS church: amass vast financial wealth and use it to finance a massive public relations campaign, playing on emotion rather than substance so others will join him in his own campaign for power.

Like the LDS church, Romney likes to highlight his successful business career, particularly at Bain Capital. In 1984, while working at Bain & Company, Romney was asked to found the private equity firm. Under Romney, Bain Capital became "one of the world's largest and most successful private equity firms with billions in assets." From his success, Romney's wealth was estimated at between $190–250 million in 2007. [29]

Some of Romney's (and Bain's) success resulted in losses for others, however. While many of the companies Romney and his team managed did wind up healthier and more profitable, "in some cases Romney's team closed US factories, causing hundreds of layoffs or pocketed huge fees shortly before companies collapsed," according to the *Los Angeles Times.*[30]

In 2007, former Bain managing Director Marc B. Wolpow told the *Los Angeles Times,* "They're whitewashing his career now … We had a scheme where the rich got richer. I did it, and I feel good about it. But I am not planning to run for office."[31]

Described as vain and bottom-line oriented by some of his colleagues, Romney with his team developed a plan to go beyond managing and controlling start-up companies, and set their sights on established ones as well. They would use bank loans or debt to leverage their investments.[32]

"To help pay off the debt, Romney's group immediately pulled money out of target companies, typically by stripping assets and paying itself high monthly management fees, preferred dividends and numerous other payments. Then they sold their stake, or took the company public, as early as possible."[33] This strategy became quite a fast-turning moneymaker for Romney and his team.

For example, in 1986 Bain Capital put up $1 million and borrowed $10 million to purchase equity in Calumet Coach, a manufacturer of mobile medical systems. When Bain sold its stake in the company two years later, Romney and his team pocketed thirty-four times their initial investment.[34]

Not all ventures helped the companies and their employees, however. Romney's team purchased a stake in DDi Corporation in 1997. In 2000 Bain Capital took the company public, reaping a cool $36 million in profit. Romney sold his shares for $4.1 million. Soon after, however, DDi saw its stock plummet and eventually filed for bankruptcy in 2003, when 2,100 workers lost their jobs.[35]

Bain and DDi eventually settled a class-action lawsuit that awarded $4.4 million to shareholders. (Romney was not named in the suit.)

According to the *Los Angeles Times*, the suit "argued that DDi was poorly managed and 'hemorrhaging cash' before the stock offering, court records show."[36]

In 1990 Romney and his team purchased a stake in Damon Corp, a medical testing company, where Romney subsequently served on its board. Three years later, when the company was bought by Corning, Inc., Bain took in three times its investment. Romney reported $100,000 in capital gains when he sold his stock.[37]

In 1996, however, Damon pled guilty to overbilling Medicare and paid $119 million in criminal and civil fines. When asked about this during his gubernatorial race in Massachusetts, Romney claimed he was a whistleblower in the scandal. US Attorney Donald K. Stern, however, had no recollection of such actions by Romney.[38] In fact, "Court records suggest that the Damon executives' schemes continued throughout Bain's ownership and prosecutors credited Corning, not Romney with cleaning up the situation. Bain meanwhile tripled its investment. Romney personally reaped $473,000," according to the *Boston Globe*.[39]

Romney aides would later claim that reporters "misunderstood" his whistle-blowing claims—something his aides would continue to do on a number of Romney's misrepresentations of the truth.[40]

One of the most memorable debacles of Romney's career at Bain was Ampad. During his senate race against Ted Kennedy in 1994, Romney claimed that he created more than 10,000 jobs at the companies he helped manage under Bain. Senator Kennedy shot back, revealing that the paper products company in which Bain invested $5 million in 1992 wound up filing for bankruptcy, laying off workers, and cutting salaries and benefits.[41]

"Bain Capital didn't escape Ampad's eventual bankruptcy unscathed. It held about one-third of Ampad's shares, which became worthless. But while as many as 185 workers near Buffalo lost jobs in a 1999 plant closing, Bain Capital and its investors ultimately made more than $100 million on the deal," according to the *Boston Globe*.[42]

All in all, Romney's stint at Bain made him a wealthy man, enabling him to use his fortune to promote his image and career, while at the same time making him the quintessential successful Mormon poster boy.

Following in the LDS tradition in which he grew up, Romney used his wealth to craft and control a public relations campaign that he hoped would hand him the presidency. The following chapters in the book will include detailed accounts of how Romney used his wealth to:

- Hand him the governorship of Massachusetts;
- Manipulate straw polls in presidential primaries;
- Set up a political action committee operating in key states that circumvented federal election laws;
- Buy influence in conservative organizations such as National Review and the Heritage Foundation;
- Tap colleagues at Bain Capital for large donations—while at the same time Bain Capital purchased media giant Clear Channel, which airs Rush Limbaugh, Sean Hannity, Glenn Beck, and Fox News Radio, among many others.
- Coordinate with the LDS church for donations and boots on the ground for his campaign.

Most importantly, the later chapters will unmask Romney's massive public relations campaign, exposing a hollow shell of a man who is merely another highly marketed brand. Romney's wavering positions on almost every social and public policy issue are based solely on cash flow and political expediency. *He is just as dangerous to America as the highly branded politician who currently occupies the White House.*

As a casting director, image consultant, and political strategist, I have been called to comment on many national TV cable news shows on the imaging, posturing, and positioning that creates the public persona of presidential candidates, as portrayed to US voters. Some of the candidates I was called on to critique were Al Gore, Bill Clinton, and George W. Bush.

The spin masters of the church are proficient and seasoned at marketing and displaying the proper Mormon image in which to exhibit to the public. Romney, his wife, and children's apple pie, attractive, clean, and wholesome image make the poster of what a Mormon family is taught to present. From his perfectly placed hairstyle, to his chiseled looks, to his humble mannerisms, Romney is properly displaying the "image" that he has been brought up in the church so well to portray.

Barack Obama is also a great image projector, a completely smooth operator with the ability to come across as a messiah who would literally save the world. Obama counted on being able to fool the American people into electing him, not based on experience or qualifications but on his personality alone. He's the smoothest operator that I would venture to say has ever achieved the office of the presidency. Obama won through the same smoke and mirrors strategy in which our media generation grew up: fairytales and entertainment magic dust.

Romney is not quite as skillful of a teleprompter orator as Obama, but from his quaffed hair, to his completely contrived facial expressions, to his perfect image of "family" and all things good, he *presents* himself as the perfect candidate. *Presents* is the key word. Romney has been trained to *present* this perfect image growing up in the Mormon Church, as the Mormon Church's agenda is to *present* the perfect image in order to sell its religious product. The church is a walking commercial, as Romney and his family are. Again, smoke and mirrors, fairytales, and entertainment magic dust used as a means to an end.

Obama and Romney have a lot in common. Obama fooled the American people into voting for him so that he could enact his radical socialist agenda. Romney is basing his candidacy on the same strategy of deceiving the American public into voting for him so that he can bring legitimacy to his religion, another dangerous agenda for the American people. Same strategy, similar motives. It is up to the American people to decide whether or not they are fooled again.

Chapter 9

Mormons In Politics

As Noah Feldman wrote in the *New York Times*, "Another part of the Mormon assimilationist strategy was to participate actively in politics at the state and national levels."[43] In order to appear as a normal religion, while at the same time establishing the framework for its kingdom on earth, the LDS church has increasingly expanded its web into the political arena. Ten Mormons from Joseph Smith to Ezra Taft Benson to George Romney have all unsuccessfully sought the highest office in the land.

The LDS' involvement in political issues has not been the result of principle or the desire to serve the American people, but rather political expediency. Back in the 1880s when Utah was seeking statehood, LDS officials were concerned about which side its members would support, Democrats or Republicans. According to Brigham Young University law professor Lynn Wardle, in an effort to appear politically neutral the LDS instructed its members to split along party lines. According to Wardle, "The church realized it was in a no-win situation. It sent apostles to various communities and said we want you to divide."[44]

Wardle cites an old friend and Utah judge who recalled others discussing the day the apostles arrived: "The apostle came to town and said everyone who lives on this side of the street becomes Republicans, and people on that side of the street should register as Democrats."[45]

The admittance of African-Americans into the LDS church is another example. The policy hurt George Romney when seeking the Republican nomination for president in 1968 and Morris K. Udall in 1976 when seeking the Democrat nomination against Jimmy Carter. The LDS president had a "revelation" in 1978 overturning the policy. According to Newell Bringhurst, a scholar and author of two books about African-Americans and the Mormon Church, the most significant reason for the reversal "came from the Mormon Church wanting to expand outside the United States … Potential growth was being impeded in places like Brazil and Africa."[46] LDS influence in politics has always been about expanding the Mormon agenda, regardless of party and principle.

This was in addition to the political pressure on the Mormon hierarchy to change its stance on the church's blatant racism toward blacks as discussed in part 1 of this book.

Mormon Influence in Utah

There is no doubt that the Mormon Church is highly influential in Utah. Approximately 70 percent of Utahans are members of the LDS church.[47] According to the *Deseret News,* "Before each general session, GOP and Democratic leaders in the House and Senate sit down separately with The Church of Jesus Christ of Latter-day Saints special affairs committee, a group made up of church general authorities, church public relations officials and their lobbyists, to discuss any items on the minds of both legislators and church leaders."[48] While typically branded as Republicans, LDS members also have influence in the Democrat party. In 2003 over 90 percent of Democrat candidates in Utah were Mormons.[49]

Romney's presidential bid highlighted the Utah/LDS influence. When George W. Bush ran for re-election in 2004, political contributions ranked Utah fortieth in the United States. In 2007, when Romney was running for the GOP presidential nomination, Utah ranked thirteenth in the nation. Ninety-one percent of all Utah political contributions in the first quarter of 2007 were sent to the Romney campaign. Salt Lake City in 2007 "emerged as one of the most generous cities of the '08 cycle, along with traditional toppers Los Angeles and New York." Salt Lake City also moved up its primary to "Super Duper Tuesday" in February 2008 to join twenty-six other states and was a leading contender to host the 2012 RNC Convention.[50]

Mormons in Political History

B.H. Roberts:

A prominent member in the LDS church, Roberts was elected to the US House of Representatives to represent Utah in 1898. The problem, however, was that Roberts was living with his three wives that he had married prior to the church's reversal on polygamy. With the country outraged, seven million signatures arrived on Capitol Hill demanding Roberts be refused his seat. Roberts was eventually replaced by another Mormon with only one wife.[51]

Reed Smoot:

In 1903 Smoot, an LDS apostle, was elected to the US Senate. Concerns over the practices of Mormonism led to several hearings before Smoot was eventually seated. Smoot served five terms until Democrat Mormon Elbert D. Thomas defeated him for a sixth term.[52]

The Marriotts:

In the 1920s J. Willard and Alice Marriott set up their A&W Root Beer stand in Washington, D.C. and the first LDS branch was established in the capital city. The Marriotts would go on to become one of the most successful hotel chains in the United States (and a Romney campaign donor).[53]

Ezra Taft Benson:

Perhaps one of the turning points of Mormons in politics came in 1952 when President Eisenhower named Ezra Taft Benson as secretary of agriculture. According to Feldman, "In just a century, the leaders of the Latter-day Saints had gone from being murdered outcasts to being appointed to the cabinet."[54]

According to Michael K. Winder, author of the gushing book about Mormon influence on presidents, *Presidents and Prophets,* "It was one thing to have an Apostle as a United States Senator and confidant to presidents as Reed Smoot did in the early twentieth century, but it was quite another for a president to have an LDS Apostle and future church president in his cabinet for eight years."[55]

Because of the appointment of Benson as well as Mormon Ivy Baker Priest as US treasurer, Eisenhower earned "immense popularity" among LDS members according to Winder.[56] It is important to note that the quote on the very first page of Mitt Romney's book *No Apologies* is by none other than Dwight D. Eisenhower.

Other Mormons would also serve as cabinet members: Stuart Udall as secretary of the interior under JFK and LBJ, David M. Kennedy as secretary of the treasury, and George Romney as secretary of HUD under Nixon.[57]

With more Mormons in Washington, D.C., the first LDS temple east of Utah was built in 1974 in Kensington, Maryland.[58] Since then the Washington, DC. temple has become a landmark in the area and a means to boost the Mormon image, especially with its well-publicized Christmas tree lighting. In 2005 the *Salt Lake Tribune* reported that Ann Santini (wife of former Congressman James Santini) hosted fifty to sixty ambassadors each year at the ceremony or fall party at the Marriott ranch in Virginia. Bill Marriott told the *Tribune*, "It's slow but worth the effort … I just got off the phone with an Arab ambassador who was at the Christmas lighting. He now has a better, more favorable image of the church."[59]

Today, there are more Mormons per capita in the Washington, D.C. area than any city east of Denver.[60] According to the *Salt Lake Tribune,* "Though their numbers are relatively small, legions of Latter-day Saints are tucked into every corner of the nation's capital." Mormons can be found from the Peace Corps to the Treasury to the Bureau of Land Management, and advising Congress on issues from social security to education to war. The LDS church even has a public affairs office located down the street from 1600 Pennsylvania Avenue. According to the *Tribune*, the LDS also has "a high-powered advisory committee to vet national and international issues that affect the church's vital interests."[61]

While the Mormons constitute only 1.7 percent of the population, they represent 3.2 percent of Congress.[62] In 2008, the Latter-day Saint Congressional Staff Organization was formed and now has ninety registered members.[63]

Each of the wards in the DC area has "employment specialists" to provide lists, phone numbers, and job openings for LDS members to network.[64] Networking inside the D.C. wards has its political advantages.

According to Mormon lobbyist Bill Nixon, "You have a desire to give your time, talent and energy to building the kingdom … it doesn't end at the chapel door or the office door. It's part of your life." According to the *Tribune*, when then Senator Bob Bennett was approached by a lobbyist attempting to connect with a federal official regarding a terrorism insurance bill during the Bush Administration, Bennett replied, "I'll just talk to him at church."[65]

When LDS officials met with Mormon senators Bennett, Hatch, Reed, Smith, and Crapo to express their interest in leasing some federal land, all of them said they would support the measure. The lease was granted by Congress.[66] In a 2001 *Slate* article titled "The Mormon Stem-Cell Choir," Drew Smith noted that the group of five Mormon senators were a powerful force in the support of embryonic stem-cell research. According to Smith, "The LDS church, not the Vatican, is playing the pivotal role in the struggle over stem cells."[67]

Another area where Mormons have a significant influence is the Central Intelligence Agency (CIA). Mormons are disproportionately represented in the CIA as well as the FBI. In a 1981 Associated Press article, Denver CIA recruiter Jack Hansen said, "Utah is one of our good sources … A lot of people here have language or foreign culture experience … That's what we look for." The three qualities the CIA, and often other government agencies, look for are foreign language, foreign culture experience, and having lived abroad.[68]

The CIA reportedly accepts almost all applicants from BYU (Brigham Young University), precisely because both of BYU's and the LDS church's grooming of their members fit their agendas. According to Charles Wood, BYU educates its students "to provide leadership for the domination of the governments throughout the world." Unlike other universities, BYU offers thirty-seven languages and twenty-one different cultural studies programs.[69] Moreover, the LDS required two-year missionary experience provides foreign experience abroad.

It is important to point out that LDS missionary service not only served and continues to serve the Mormon Church in expanding its empire, it also has disproportionately allowed draft deferments during the Vietnam War for its members, including Mitt Romney. According to the *Boston Globe*, a "minister of religion" could be eligible for deferment. "The exemption for Mormon missionaries created controversy at the time," reported to the *Globe*. "Non-Mormons in Utah filed a lawsuit against the federal government in 1968. The suit was still in court two years later, at a time when 'the church and the Selective Service System worked hand-in-hand in deferring missionaries,' according to an article from the period published by the *New York Times*."[70]

Mitt Romney himself would benefit from this. According to the *Globe*, "Romney's home state was Michigan, making his 4-D exemption as a missionary all but automatic because of the relatively small number of Mormon missionaries from that state." Romney obtained almost three years of deferments while in France as a missionary and as a student. When he was finally eligible, Romney drew a high number.[71]

According to Richard Leedy who filed the Utah lawsuit, "The substantial number of deferments to missionaries made the likelihood for us non-Mormons going to Vietnam a lot more likely."[72] Romney would later claim his five sons' work on his campaign were also equivalent to service in the military.[73]

This ploy could not be further from reality. In the military, soldiers fight with their lives to protect our country. When young men go on Mormon missions, they are simply recruiters for the cult, nothing more. The more members, the more tithe payers. Many Mormon youths have avoided fighting in wars by going on Mormon missions. For Mitt Romney to portray that there is any comparison between serving our country in the military and recruiting vulnerable "seekers" in to this well masked cult, it is an astounding smoke screen to the truth about this ruse to avoid serving our country.

The LDS Ingratiation into the Christian Right

According to Adam Reilly of the *Boston Phoenix*, "If there's a moment that marks the beginning of the LDS ascendancy, it came in 1979 when right-wing Christian fundamentalist Jerry Falwell announced the formation of the Moral Majority."[74] The Mormon Church, eager to appear mainstream, joined the organization and began its quest to assimilate itself into additional Christian organizations with the hopes of gaining acceptance as just another religion with the same cultural goals. The LDS church also set out to prove that its wealth and obedient members would make the Mormons a valuable force to achieve their common societal goals, particularly with regards to gay marriage.

In 2008, Quin Monson, a BYU political science professor, told the *Los Angeles Times* "Being against gay marriage puts the church right in the mainstream of American religious behavior."[75] The Mormon Church would also have the boots on the ground and the money in the bank to further their cause. Mormon and Notre Dame political science professor David Campbell told the *Salt Lake Tribune* in 2008 that Mormons are "uniquely situated to be mobilized into politics ... But they only get mobilized when a match is lit, and that doesn't happen very often ... they have a lot of money and are willing to work for a socially conservative cause."[76] The match was lit and the Mormons set out to prove themselves.

(It is important to note that the Mormon Church refuses to declare homosexuality as a choice and is weary of programs designed to cure homosexuality.)

After then Prophet Hinckley publicly denounced gay marriage in 1994, Mormon churches across the country received fliers offering recommendations on how to form pro-family political action committees. During the 1990s LDS officials encouraged members to campaign against gay marriage initiatives in other states. The LDS church also donated hundreds of thousands to campaigns against gay marriage throughout the United States.[77] In a 1997 memo general authority Loren C. Dunn confirmed Hinckley's approval of members participating in a campaign against same-sex marriage in Hawaii. Hinckley wanted the LDS church to appear as part of other normal Christian religions and not on the fringe, as Dunn stated in the memo. "The church should be in a coalition and not out front by itself."[78]

Perhaps the one initiative that ingratiated the LDS with the Christian right more than any other was Proposition 8 in California in 2008. Proposition 8 called for a constitutional amendment to define marriage as only between a man and a woman. While other Christian groups had already joined the fight early on, the LDS church was late to the game. After the Roman Catholic archbishop of San Francisco asked the Mormon Church to join the campaign, the LDS, seizing an opportunity to be part of a Christian coalition of mainstream religions, went in full force.[79]

At first, both sides of Prop 8 had generally raised the same amount of money. Once the Mormon machine joined the cause, things changed. Steve Smith of No on 8, Equality for All told the *Wall Street Journal* in 2008, "All of a sudden in the last few weeks they are out-raising us, and it appears to be Mormon money."[80]

Prophet Monson sent a letter to all Mormon congregations in Utah urging members to "do all you can to support the proposed constitutional amendment by donating your means and time." Broadcasts such as "30 People in Each Ward" and "More than Four Hours Per Week" were heard in LDS churches nationwide.[81]

Conference calls were also arranged by members of the Quorum of the Seventy suggesting $25,000 donations from prominent members of the church. LDS leaders told members that donating to the campaign was "a matter of personal conscience."[82] The church also warned that they could lose their coveted tax-exempt status if they refused to officiate same-sex marriages.[83]

LDS member and wife of a stake president Gayle Teuscher told *Time* magazine, "If I believe that the Prophet is a true prophet of God and disregard his counsel, what does that say about my belief in God?"[84]

Proposition 8 was passed by in large with the influence of the Mormon Church. Half of the $40 million used in the campaign was raised by Mormons. Eighty to 90 percent of the initial door-to-door volunteers were also Mormons.[85] The LDS church had succeeded in wiggling its way into a mainstream Christian coalition as a formidable force in cultural issues. After the passage of Prop 8, more than 4,000 online signatures were collected thanking the Mormon Church for its help. Signatures included James Dobson of Focus on the Family, Tony Perkins of the Family Research Council, and Richard Land of the Southern Baptist Convention.[86] Perkins also penned an editorial in the *Deseret News* defending the LDS church from the rising criticism of the LDS church and its tax-exempt status.[87]

Following the criticism from the left for what appeared to be a large Mormon involvement in Prop 8, as well as the LDS detaining two gay men kissing at Mormon plaza in Salt Lake City, once again public relations trumped principle in LDS leadership.

After two months of secret meetings between mid-level LDS leaders and a handful of the Utah's most influential gay activists, the LDS church supported two Salt Lake City ordinances that protected gay and transgender citizens from housing or employment discrimination in 2009.[88]

Jim Dabakis, a founder of Equality Utah and the Utah Pride Center who was contacted by LDS leadership, told the *Salt Lake Tribune,* "They are really trying to put some of the Prop 8 stuff behind them. The discussions we have had over the last several months have shown what a caring, loving, concerned institution [the LDS church] is."[89] Aww. Public relations at its best.

Mormons Ingratiating Themselves on a Global Level

Today there are more Mormons outside the United States than inside. The LDS church is now in 176 countries and territories, with temples in over forty countries. There are 8,400 Mormon meeting houses abroad with a "new one built nearly every day." Six thousand churches are consistently in sync with Salt Lake City thanks to the extensive LDS satellite system.[90]

"For those who work in the international realm, though, Mormon activism is nothing new," according to Michelle Goldberg, the *New York Times* bestselling author of *Kingdom Coming: The Rise of Christian Nationalism.* According to Goldberg, while women's rights, particularly abortion rights, have gained status as a human rights issue on the international stage, the LDS church has led an effort to join with other conservative Christian organizations to counter pro-abortion measures.[91]

According to Goldberg, "This in turn has led to a conservative counter-movement, with Mormons playing a leading role in a world-spanning alliance of right-wing Christians and Muslims who have banded together to defeat threats to patriarchal tradition."[92]

One of the first Mormons to seize upon this international opportunity to ingratiate the LDS church with legitimate Christian religions around the world was BYU law professor Richard Wilkins. According to Jennifer Butler, author of *Born Again: The Christian Right Globalized*, Wilkins founded the World Family Policy Center (WFPC) at BYU in 1997 after a successful speech at the UN Conference on Habitats in Istanbul.[93]

According to Wilkins, "At the conclusion of my short remarks, I emphasized the essential message of the First Presidency's Proclamation on the Family … [The] fundamental connection between a decent society and the reinforcement of strong stable families." Wilkins urged the conference "to consider seriously the need to protect traditional values in drafting and implementing the Habitat agenda."[94]

Wilkins stated that the response to his speech was "remarkable," noting that the Arab delegation at the conference declared it would not sign the agenda unless changes were made regarding marriage and family.[95]

After the establishment of the WFPC, Wilkins found a partner to build the WFPC influence: The Howard Center. Named after Dr. John Howard (who has an honorary degree from BYU among others) and headed by Director Allan C. Carlson, "the Howard Center for Family, Religion and Society strives to be the leading source of fresh ideas and new strategy for affirmation and defense of the natural family, both nationally and globally."[96]

According to Butler, "The WFPC and the Howard Center began efforts to organize into an interfaith lobby of pro-family NGOs and governments by convening a conference call the World Congress of Families I (WCF) in Prague in March of 1997. The coalition was solidified at a meeting the World Congress of Families II, convened in Geneva during the fall of 1999."[97]

According to Allan Carlson director of the Howard Center and part of the WCF, "Financial support for this meeting came from many sources; the largest single donor was the World Family Policy Center, part of the law school at Brigham Young University." Carlson also noted that the WFPC "was emerging as a key organization in countering the aggressive secularism of the UN."[98]

According to Butler, the Family Research Council "was a co-convening organization of both conferences." Butler also states that "Press accounts suggest that at least half of the representatives were from the United States and a large percentage was Mormon."[99] No surprise, since Mormon missionaries span the globe.

The Roman Catholic Church funded most of the WCF meeting in 2004. Wilkins himself was asked by the royal family of Qatar to set up the subsequent Doha Conference which was funded by the royal family.[100] Top LDS officials have spoken at the WCF including Quorum of the Seventy Elder Bruce Hafen and Quorum of the Twelve Elder Russell M. Nelson.[101]

Current partners of WCF which LDS leaders can integrate and rub shoulders with are as follows:

American Family Association

Alliance Defense Fund

Alliance for the Family

Americans United for Life

Associazione per la Difesa Dei Valori

Cristiani - Luci sull'Est, Italy

Catholic Family and Human Rights Institute

Concerned Women for America

Ethics and Public Policy Center

Euthanasia Prevention Coalition

Family First Foundation

Family Watch International

Family Research Council

Father Peter Skarga Institute (Poland)

Fellowship of St. James

Focus on The Family

Grasstops USA

HazteOir.org

His Servants

Home School Legal Defense Association

Human Life International

Media Research Center

Parents Forum Switzerland

Population Research Institute

Real Women of Canada

Red Familia (Mexico)

Tradition, Family, & Property

United Families International[102]

According to Goldberg, "Some of the lessons the right-wing Mormon activists learned globally have likely contributed to their new found success in influencing American politics."[103] That could not be more true with the rise of their white horse Mitt Romney.

Ten Mormons have run for president, from Joseph Smith all the way to Mitt Romney. None of them were successful. Through ingratiating themselves with traditional Christians and maintaining large war chests, both Romney and the LDS church were putting their bets on the 2008 presidential election, and would do almost anything to get a Mormon in the White House—even if it meant bribing organizations or potentially violating election laws.

Chapter 10

Politics in the Family, Like Father, Like Son: George and Mitt Romney

Mitt Romney and his father, George, have a little more in common than most fathers and sons. Each spent two years in Europe as a missionary, married his high school sweetheart after he returned, amassed a fortune in the business world, was elected governor at age fifty-five, and ran for president at age sixty.[104] "From his slicked, carefully coifed hair to his data-driven business principles to his unwavering devotion to his oft-maligned Mormon faith, Mitt Romney is the spitting image of his father physically, professionally, and morally," wrote AP reporter Steve LeBlanc in 2007.[105]

"My dad is my life hero," Romney told the reporter back then. "I probably would have never thought about politics; it would have never crossed my mind, had I not seen him do it. He's the real pioneer."[106]

Both Romney and his father would prove themselves more progressive than "pioneer" in the Republican Party, and each would first need his "white horse" moment to do so.

The Romney Roots

After converting to Mormonism and being baptized in England in 1837, Miles Romney immigrated to Nauvoo, Illinois, where he served as a prominent leader in the LDS church. His son, Miles Park Romney, a polygamist, took three wives, including Hannah Hood Hill, and had several children. One of those children was Gaskell Romney, the son of Miles Park Romney and Hannah Hood Hill.[107]

After the Edmunds-Tucker Act, Miles Park Romney and his multi-family fled to Mexico. While in Mexico with his family, Gaskell Romney married Anna Pratt, his only wife, and had six children, including George Romney (Mitt's father). When the Mexican Revolution broke out, Gaskell and his family left almost everything behind and fled back to the United States.[108]

In his book, *No Apology*, Mitt Romney describes his father's often displaced and struggling family. "Once back in the United States, they struggled. They moved time and again, and work was always hard to find. My grandfather established a construction business, but he went bankrupt more than once. Dad used to regale us kids with claims that one year in Idaho his family lived on nothing but potatoes—for breakfast, lunch, and dinner."[109]

After serving as a missionary in Great Britain, George Romney went to Washington, D.C. In 1929, he dropped out of college to be closer to his high school sweetheart, Lenore La Fount. La Fount's father was serving in Calvin Coolidge's administration at the time. "Inspired by their friend J. Willard Marriott, whose root beer stand would grow into a hotel empire, Romney opened a dairy bar across the Potomac that quickly folded." Romney then went to work as a legislative aide to Democratic Senator David Walsh of Massachusetts.[110]

"It also opened a familiar revolving door. A year later, George Romney left to become a lobbyist and spokesman, first for Alcoa and then the Automobile Manufacturer's Association."[111]

George and Lenore married, eventually had four children (Mitt being the youngest), and moved to Michigan where George later became an executive of Nash-Kelvinator Corporation. While there, he oversaw the merger of Nash-Kelvinator and Hudson Motor Car Corporation.[112]

"It was late in his career in 1950, when the company that later became American Motors hired him and put him in charge of promoting its novel compact car. Four years later, he became chief executive and bet the company on the small vehicle, called the Rambler."[113]

The gamble paid off. "Romney's business skills not only saved American Motors but also made him a multimillionaire … [He] attracted national media attention, highlighted in a *Time* magazine cover story that appeared on April 6, 1959."[114] This gave George Romney his "white horse" moment, which he would laud in launching his political career.

In *No Apology*, Romney writes, "What Dad accomplished at American Motors prepared him for the challenges that would follow."[115] As David D. Kirkpatrick of the *New York Times* notes, "Even at American Motors, though, George Romney was never far from politics. He made headlines testifying on Capitol Hill about the twin evils of 'big labor' and 'big business' and calling for a federal breakup of the big three carmakers. He led a push for a tax increase to improve the Detroit schools, then a new state Constitution to make raising revenue easier."[116] It wasn't until 1961 when running for delegate however that George Romney publicly referred to himself as a Republican.[117]

Capitalizing on his turnaround artist image, George Romney entered politics in Michigan as a Republican. Romney won the nomination unopposed and the gubernatorial race by a slim margin, garnering only 50.9 percent of the votes.[118]

As a "moderately progressive" Republican, Romney instituted several liberal policies to tackle the state's deficit. Romney introduced Michigan's first minimum wage, a 2.5 percent income tax, and a 5.6 percent tax on business profits.[119]

"In general, Romney's record as governor paid political dividends. He was reelected in 1964 and again in 1966, each time by increasingly large margins." In fact, his record "as a progressive governor allowed him to emerge as a front-runner for the 1968 Republican presidential nomination."[120]

Like his son would later do, George Romney published two books to bolster his image: *Romney's Way: A Man and an Idea*, a biography written by T. George Harris, and *The Concerns of a Citizen*, written by Romney himself.[121]

"What few remember is that Romney was to win the presidency," wrote Alex Beam of the *Boston Globe* in 2004. "In early 1967, both the Harris and Gallup polls showed him with a significant lead over Johnson. The problem was, the more people saw of Romney, the less sure they liked him. Even before he was quoted in an unfair context, many believe as saying Johnson administration officials had 'brainwashed' him about progress in Vietnam, his mouth was getting him into trouble."[122]

His ties to the LDS church also caused some concern among voters. "It is certainly true that Romney's religious faith was a core element of his personal identity. A somewhat unfriendly article published in the *National Review* in late 1967 concluded that if Romney won the nomination, he would be the 'most avowedly religious candidate since the fundamentalist Bryan last ran in 1908.'"[123]

This was especially true regarding his relationship with Prophet David O. McKay. "Romney, in fact, enjoyed a close relationship with McKay, one going back to the 1950s and Romney's service as president of the Detroit LDS stake. McKay had been a houseguest at the Romney's Bloomfield Hills home in 1959 when the Mormon leader had traveled to Michigan for the dedication of a new LDS Detroit stake center. Romney also visited with the Mormon leader on two different occasions in 1966–67. Romney's initial audience was during the summer of 1966, when he and his wife, Lenore, traveled to Utah. Romney's second meeting with McKay, also in Utah, took place the following winter, in February 1967. Again Romney was accompanied by his wife, along with other family members. Also included in the party was Ann Davies, whose fiancé, Mitt, was then serving as an LDS missionary in France. The second meeting between Romney and McKay received extensive media coverage from 'a bevy of national and local television, radio, and newspaper reporters.'"[124]

George Romney was compelled more than once to discuss his religion in public. In a February 1967 speech, Romney called the separation of church and state in America a "vital necessity." "Addressing this group of non-Mormon clergymen, he sought to allay their anxieties concerning his Latter-day Saint faith."[125]

The Mormon Church's stance on blacks particularly haunted Romney, who refused to criticize his church's policy.[126] In his February 1967 speech Romney stated, "Actions speak louder than words and I feel my actions of the past twenty-five years have made it crystal clear that I believe in equal rights and full equality of citizens regardless of race, creed or color." He went on to state "If my church prevented me as a public official from doing those things for social justice that I thought right, I would quit the church."[127]

Speaking esoterically on other subjects also haunted Romney, particularly when it came to the war in Vietnam. Originally a strong supporter of President Johnson's conducting of the war, Romney's conflicting and vague statements left many confused and critical. "In the wake of such criticism, Romney moved toward an increasingly anti-war position. In an August 31, 1967, speech the candidate described in greater detail circumstances of his earlier November 1965 fact-finding trip to Vietnam. He asserted that he had been misled by American military and political officials. In Romney's own words, 'I had the greatest brainwashing that anyone can get … Not only by the generals, but also by the diplomatic corps over there, and they did a very thorough job.'"[128]

The comment drew such national criticism that *Time* magazine's September 1967 article *Republicans: The Brainwashed Candidate* led with the following paragraph:

> "Many Americans of late have altered their views about the complex and bewildering war in Viet Nam without feeling obliged to offer elaborate justifications. Politicians, too, change their minds, and the good ones do so with such grace that people hardly notice, or such logic that everyone understands. Last week Michigan's Governor George Romney offered so inept an explanation of his shifting views on Viet Nam that it could end his presidential ambitions."[129]

The article went on to point out that the *Detroit News*, which had initially supported George Romney, would no longer back his campaign and hinted that perhaps Nelson Rockefeller would make a better candidate because Rockefeller was a person "who knows what he believes."[130]

These comments, as well as his views on social and economic issues, which "placed him to the left of the core of the Republican party," contributed to his decline in Republican support.[131] This could have been seen in his failure to endorse Republican Presidential Candidate Barry Goldwater in 1964. In fact, during his gubernatorial campaign, when Romney and Goldwater were both at a Republican senatorial committee fundraiser, Goldwater congratulated Romney when he "decided to join the Republican Party."[132]

As Kirkpatrick wrote in 2007, "Some of George Romney's former advisors said they were not sure he would even be a member of today's more conservative Republican Party."[133] Mitt Romney, who disputes this, however, and told Kirkpatrick that he (Mitt) "is not so much a conservative Republican or a liberal Republican, he said, as he is a George Romney Republican— 'a very intensely practical person' less committed to any ideology than to bridging divides and 'helping people.'"[134]

Romney also had an image problem. His "piety" disconnected him from the average voter. "Romney's politics and his piety were inseparable, and the damage was more than his presidential aspirations could withstand."[135]

When Nelson Rockefeller entered the race, Romney knew his candidacy was doomed and pulled out of the race. He would later lament that when Rockefeller entered the race "there was no way I could get the nomination fighting both Rockefeller and Richard Nixon."[136]

Romney would later go on to serve in Nixon's cabinet as secretary of housing and urban development, and help campaign for his wife in her unsuccessful US Senate bid.[137]

"George Romney, who died in 1995, has in many ways become the ghost in Mitt Romney's political machine. It has been the son's peculiar challenge to try to repeat the best moments of the father's life while avoiding the worst. And maybe earn a little redemption along the way for a father whom history remembers more for a singular failure than for his many successes," wrote Scott Martelle in the *Los Angeles Times.*[138]

"'I always felt that his father's [presidential campaign], and the fact that it turned out badly, made a very distinct impression' on Mitt Romney, said Ben Snyder, a retired teacher at the elite Cranbrook Schools who supervised a foreign-exchange student at the Romney's while Mitt was in high school. 'He is now in a position to, perhaps subconsciously, succeed in representing his dad.'"[139]

To Romney, it was a quest. In 2007 he told Kirkpatrick, "Like a baton has passed, like a relay team where the baton passed from generation to generation … I am a shadow of the real deal."[140]

Mitt Romney's Political Beginnings

It is interesting to note that Mitt Romney seems to have aligned himself with whichever party seemed to have momentum at the time. In 1988, following the era of Reagan, he donated $2,000 to the GOP and another $1,000 in 1989. From July 1989 until October 1993 (after Clinton's election) Mitt Romney "exclusively financed" three Democrats.[141]

The year 1992 was good for Democrats following the "no new taxes" flip-flop by President George H.W. Bush and the slick presidential candidate Bill Clinton. In 1992 Romney donated $250 to US Representative Dick Swett's (D-NH) campaign for reelection. That year, Swett, as *Human Events* writer Deroy Murdock notes, "had a 32 (out of 100) rating from the American Conservative Union and an 85 from the liberal Americans for Democratic Action."[142]

That same year, Romney also donated $1,000 to Democrat Douglas Delano Anderson's unsuccessful bid for a seat in the US Senate representing Utah and gave $250 to Representative John J. LaFalce (D-NY). Murdock points out, "That year, LaFalce scored a 12 ACU rating and a Swett-like 85 from the ADA."[143]

More pointedly, Mitt Romney was registered as an independent until he ran as a Republican for the US Senate seat in 1994 and voted for Democrat presidential candidate Paul Tsongas in the 1992 primary in Massachusetts.[144]

After the failure of HillaryCare and a momentum was building for a historical Republican sweep of Congress, Romney registered as a Republican just four months before announcing his intention of unseating Massachusetts Senator Ted Kennedy.[145] To be elected in liberal Massachusetts, he cloaked himself in liberal stances on issues.

"It was the year Newt Gingrich was pushing his Contract with America, but Romney distanced himself from Gingrich and rejected help from that national right-wing apparatus," wrote Neil Swidey and Stephanie Ebbert in the *Boston Globe* in 2007. Romney at the time stated, "I don't want their money. I don't want their help … this is my race."[146] During a debate with Ted Kennedy in 1994 Romney would not endorse the Contract with America.[147]

Romney also apparently did not want the help of the coattails of Ronald Reagan either. During a debate with Sen. Kennedy, he stated, "I was an independent during the time of Reagan-Bush. I am not trying to return to Reagan-Bush."[148] That year, he told the *Washington Post,* "My hope is that, after this election, it will be the moderates of both parties who will control the Senate, not the Jesse Helmses."[149]

And a moderate, or one could say liberal, candidate he was, particularly on the issues of abortion, gay rights, and gun control.

Abortion

During a debate in 1994, Romney stated, "I believe that abortion should be safe and legal in this country."[150] He went on to state "I have since the time that my mom took that position when she ran in 1970 as a US Senate candidate. I believe that since Roe v. Wade has been the law for 20 years we should sustain and support it."[151]

According to the *Boston Globe* "Romney sought to reassure Massachusetts voters of his pro-choice bona fides by citing his mother's example. Lenore had run for the Senate on an abortion rights platform, a stance forged by the death of her son-in-law's teenage sister from an illegal abortion." The Globe quotes Romney at that time: "My mother and my family have been committed to the belief that we can believe as we want, but we will not force our beliefs on others on that matter. And you will not see me wavering on that."[152]

In 1994 the *Boston Globe* also reported Romney's stance on the RU–486 abortion pill, quoting Romney as saying, "I don't really understand how it works or when it works but my understanding is it's an effective morning after pill and I think it would be a positive thing to have women have the choice of taking morning-after pills … I would favor having it available."[153]

In 2007, ABC News reported on a photograph taken of Romney and his wife attending a fundraising reception for Planned Parenthood in 1994 and a check written out to the pro-abortion organization from the couple's joint bank account. "When asked by reporters earlier this year whether the former governor had ever donated money to Planned Parenthood, the Romney campaign said no. Aides subsequently conceded that Romney's wife, Ann, wrote a $150 check to the group in 1994."[154]

Neither Romney, nor his wife could recollect the event. Nicki Nichols Gamble, who was president and CEO of the Planned Parenthood League of Massachusetts at the time and in the photo with the Romneys at the event, was surprised at their lack of memory. "I can understand that he might not remember the check—it's surprising to me that he would not remember the event. His main motivation for being there was a political motivation."[155]

On his own 1994 campaign flyer, Romney lists "Retain a woman's right to choose" as one of his prominent issues.[156] When asked what were the differences between Romney's and Kennedy's stances on abortion, Romney's political consultant at the time, Charles Manning stated, "It's tiny nuances."[157]

Conveniently, right before he was gearing up for a presidential run and needed national Republican support, Romney would have a conversion moment and suddenly become pro-life after examining the stem cell research issue. Writing in the *National Review*, Byron York wondered how this sudden conversion would sit with voters.

"Romney's description of his conversion strikes some activists on both sides of the abortion issue as unusual … Oran Smith, pro-life, questions Romney's explanation in a more subtle way. In talks with conservative Christians, Smith points out, Romney has often addressed the issue of his Mormon faith by saying something to the effect of, 'Our faiths are different, but they bring us to the same positions on the issues.' But by all accounts, Romney was a faithful Mormon when he was solidly pro-choice, and he is a faithful Mormon today. How, precisely, did his faith bring him to different positions, then and now? 'Christians generally like for someone to have a conversion experience and a mea culpa moment,' says Smith. 'But he doesn't have that to turn to. He can't say 'My faith changed and therefore my views changed.' That's the normal thing with Republicans who move to the right on some issues—they claim to have had some spiritual transformation.'"[158]

Gay Rights

In 1994 candidate Romney told *Bay Windows*, New England's largest GLBT newspaper, "When Ted Kennedy speaks on gay rights, he's seen as an extremist. When Mitt Romney speaks on gay rights, he's seen as a centrist and a moderate."[159]

In fact, Romney, seeking the endorsement of the Log Cabin Republicans, wrote in a letter to the group, "As we seek to establish full equality for America's gay and lesbian citizens, I will provide more effective leadership than my opponent."[160] Romney received the endorsement from the Log Cabin Republicans. According to *Bay Windows,* he received the endorsement "primarily based on his support for the federal Employment Non-Discrimination Act (EDNA), a pro-gay piece of legislation that at the time had little Republican support."[161]

Many Log Cabin Republicans helped in Romney's campaign. Mark Goshko, former president of the LCR told *Bay Windows* that gay Republicans had "multi-level involvement" in the Romney campaign. "Our people were very involved officially and outside of [the campaign]."[162]

In 1994 *Bay Windows* asked Romney if he would have supported federal legislation that would refuse federal funding to public schools that are "encouraging or supporting homosexuality as a positive lifestyle alternative." Romney stated he would oppose the measure because it "grossly misunderstands the gay community by insinuating that there's an attempt to proselytize a gay lifestyle on the part of the gay community."[163]

During the campaign Romney also expressed open support of gays in the military and as Boy Scout leaders. In his letter to LCR, Romney wrote regarding Clinton's "Don't ask, Don't tell" policy: "I believe that the Clinton compromise was a step in the right direction. I am also convinced that it is the first in a number of steps that will ultimately lead to gays and lesbians being able to serve openly and honestly in our nation's military."[164]

When asked about gays serving as Boy Scouts leaders, Romney is quoted as saying "I feel that all people should be allowed to participate in the Boy Scouts regardless of their sexual orientation."[165]

Conveniently, when gearing up for a presidential run, Romney had another conversion moment and became a staunch defender of marriage between man and woman, supported nothing further than "Don't ask, Don't tell," and angered the Log Cabin Republicans.

Gun Rights

During his campaign, Romney supported two pieces of gun legislation that the National Rifle Association staunchly stood against: the Brady Bill and an assault weapons ban. Interviewed by the *Boston Herald*, Romney stated, "That's not going to make me the hero of the NRA."[166] When asked about the Brady Bill, which instituted a five-day waiting period before purchasing a handgun, Romney told the *Boston Herald,* "I don't think [the waiting period] will have a massive effect on crime, but I think it will have a positive effect."[167] At a campaign stop in 1994, Romney told reporters, "I don't line up with the NRA."[168]

Conveniently, one year before his presidential run, Romney joined the NRA and became a strong supporter of the second amendment.

Health Care

In 1994 when HillaryCare was unpopular, Romney's own campaign flyer stated the differences between Senator Kennedy and himself. The flyer proudly boasted that, while Kennedy supported a government takeover of the health care system, employer mandates, and increased taxes to pay for government-run health care, Romney was adamantly opposed to these.[169]

Conveniently, with no signature issue as governor when gearing up for his presidential run, Romney worked with Senator Kennedy to pass RomneyCare in Massachusetts. In 2007, Romney told Kirkpatrick "If you listen to what my opponents have to say, 'Romney is just trying to move to the right to appeal to the right wing of the Republican Party.' Well, why is it that in the last months of my governorship that I helped push through a plan to help give health insurance to everybody in the state?"[170] After the passage of ObamaCare and the disaster of the Massachusetts health care debacle, Romney would scramble to continually defend his possible Waterloo.

Campaign Finance Reform

Back when Romney was up against Ted Kennedy and the Kennedy fortune for the US Senate seat, Romney advocated limited spending on house and senate elections. He suggested the Massachusetts' senate campaign be capped at $6 million. At a 1994 press conference, Romney said, "These kinds of associations between money and politics in my view are wrong. And for that reason, I would like to have campaign spending limits … I also would abolish PACs … I don't like that kind of influence."[171]

Romney also supported restrictions far beyond McCain-Feingold. According to the *Concord Monitor*, "Back then [since his days as a senate and gubernatorial candidate in Massachusetts], Romney advocated more stringent measures than McCain-Feingold ultimately included, such as a spending limit for federal elections and a tax on political contributions."[172]

In 1996 he would finance advertisements against then-presidential candidate Steve Forbes' plan to eliminate the capital gains tax, calling it a "tax cut for fat cats."[173]

Conveniently, when gearing up for his presidential run, Romney established his own PACs, spent millions of his own money, and called McCain-Feingold a violation of free speech.

Romney ultimately lost his senate bid to Ted Kennedy and returned to Bain Capital where he would search for his "white horse" national moment like his father's. He would ultimately find it in Salt Lake City.

Chapter 11

The White Horse: Salt Lake City and the Olympics

The relationship between Mitt Romney and the LDS church is symbiotic. The LDS church needs Romney to aid in ushering in the kingdom on earth while portraying the Mormon faith as a wholesome, mainstream religion. Romney needs the LDS church and its vast network to finance, support, and promote his political aspirations. Nowhere was this more apparent than the Salt Lake City Olympics—the Greatest Show on Earth for the Mormon Church and Mitt Romney—all funded in part by you, the US taxpayer.

In his 2007 article in *Olympika,* an *International Journal of Sports Studies,* David J. Lunt writes, "During the 1980s and 1990s, the LDS church created an Olympic identity which capitalized on its Olympic associations both to emphasize its unique culture, teachings and doctrines, as well as claim status as a mainstream American religion. During this time, Mormons constructed an Olympic identity by highlighting the achievements of contemporaneous Mormon athletes and by revisiting the accomplishments of past Mormon Olympians. The LDS relationship with the Olympic Games culminated in the 1990s with the church's strong support for Salt Lake City's bid for the 1998 and 2002 Olympic Winter Games."[174]

Lunt notes how the LDS church uses the success of Mormon athletes to link Olympic athletes' accomplishments specifically to the Mormon faith. "In a movement directed mainly at the church's adolescent members, LDS leaders consistently cited the achievements of Mormon Olympians as evidence of God's blessings to faithful church members."[175]

The first Utah Olympic athlete was Alma Richards, who in 1912 in Stockholm won the high jump and set an Olympic record. Very little attention was given to Richards' feat back then, but during the 1980s and 1990s his name suddenly reemerged.[176]

After the 1980s, especially after the 1984 Games in Los Angeles, when the Olympics were gaining popularity and media coverage, the LDS church began to see the benefits of tying the LDS church to the Olympics:

According to Lunt: "In conjunction with the Olympic Games' increased appeal and prestige, LDS faithful emphasized Richards' Olympic experience much more strongly than the 1920s' LDS leaders, who were more impressed by Richards' achievements as a track star."[177]

Richards' career was touted in *Deseret News* reporters Lee Benson and Doug Robinson's 1992 book, *Trials and Tribulations: Mormons in Olympic Games.* The book describes Richards as he prepared for his high jump by taking off his hat and "in full view of the 22,000 spectators, knelt down, bowed his head and prayed." Lunt points out that in later writings, Richards himself never accounts to kneeling publicly and that he simply prayed to himself while walking out to the event.[178]

Nevertheless, in the 1990s, billboards were popping up in Salt Lake City with Richards' image promoting the Salt Lake Olympics. In fact, during the 2002 Olympics in Salt Lake City, the torch run included a run through Parowan, Richards' hometown, in his honor.[179]

Another athlete lauded by the LDS and featured in Benson and Robinson's book was Peter Vidmar, a Mormon gymnast who captured the first US gold medal in the team event. In 1984, Richard Romney, associate editor of *New Era* (an LDS youth magazine) wrote an article on Vidmar, describing Vidmar as a "normal fellow" who participated in church meetings, completed his homework, and read Scripture. Richard Romney emphasized that Vidmar's most memorable moment at the Olympics was not winning the gold, but rather when he was able to discuss his Mormonism with another athlete and facilitate her conversion to Mormonism.[180]

According to Lunt, "[Richard] Romney's article is illuminating in several aspects. It demonstrates how LDS leaders used accomplished LDS athletes to promote devout LDS behavior. By associating Vidmar's athletic achievements with his devotion to the LDS faith, Romney implied that the two were inherently related."[181]

Another LDS athlete, Henry Marsh was also heralded by LDS leaders—that is until his career hit a few stumbling blocks. Marsh was the number one steeplechaser in the world in 1981, 1982, and 1985, and set four US records. Unfortunately a series of setbacks, such as a virus, boycott, cracked ribs, etc., ultimately hurt his Olympic performances. He never earned a medal in the 1976, 1980, 1984, and 1988 Olympics.[182]

"In contrast to this characterization of Marsh's career," Lunt writes, "a July 1984 article in the LDS publication *New Era* downplayed Marsh's mishaps and emphasized the runner's religious goals over his temporal ones. Published four months before the 1984 Olympics, *New Era* highlighted Marsh's religious devotion and explicitly connected his running success with his religious faith. The article stated that Marsh 'unashamedly acknowledges the hand of the Lord in his success' and believed that his running accomplishments were part of God's plan for him"[183]

Unfortunately, after Marsh's fourth place in the 1984 Games and sixth in the 1988 Olympics, Mormon publications no longer connected his career with his faith.[184]

"LDS faithful viewed the Olympic Games as a possibility to exude a positive image to the world, both to cultivate possible converts as well as to foster the world's good favor," Lunt notes.[185] According to the *Boston Globe*, Prophet Hinckley "made no secret that he viewed the Games as a vehicle to fulfill pioneer Brigham Young's prophecy that Salt Lake City would 'become the great highway of the nations … kings and emperors and the noble and the wise of the earth will visit us here,' Hinckley said, quoting Young."[186]

From 1985 to 1995 LDS-owned businesses contributed $210,938 to Salt Lake City bid committees. In 1998, the Mormon Church established its own Church Olympic Coordinating Committee to mobilize Mormon volunteers for the Olympics. According to Lunt, "Clearly from the beginning of the bid process, the LDS church and the Salt Lake City organizers enjoyed a cozy relationship and the Bid Committee did little to separate Salt Lake City from its dominant church in official presentations to the IOC."[187]

The Olympics, notorious for the greasing of members of the IOC (International Olympic Committee) in order to secure games in a specific city, met the mother of all scandals. After an ABC News affiliate received a tip regarding Salt Lake City's landing of the 2002 Winter Games, all hell broke loose. It was revealed that in bribing IOC delegates to secure Salt Lake as the 2002 host, members of the organizing committee spent more than $1 million in "cash, college tuition, medical-care payments, jobs, lodging, beds and bedding, bathroom fixtures, Indian rugs, draperies, doorknobs, dogs, leather boots and belts, perfume, Nintendo games, Lego toys, shotguns, a violin, and trips to spa resorts, Las Vegas and a Super Bowl in Miami." According to the *Boston Globe*, "Almost no request from an IOC member went unmet." Ultimately, ten members of the IOC resigned or were removed from their positions.[188]

With the fate of the Olympics on US soil, and a predominately Mormon city in the balance, the organizing committee searched for its white horse to salvage not only the Olympics, but Salt Lake City.

"They fast settled on Romney, whose ties to the state ran deeper than his ancestral roots. Romney had visited Utah as a child, married his wife, Ann, at the great Mormon temple in Salt Lake City, attended Brigham Young University, where two of his boys were enrolled at the time. Ann, struggling with her recently diagnosed multiple sclerosis, was finding some relief in the mountain air of Park City, Utah, where she and Mitt had just built a magnificent vacation home, now assessed at $5.2 million," according to the *Boston Globe*.[189]

More importantly, Mitt Romney was a Mormon. According to Robert Garff, Salt Lake Organizing Committee chairman, member of the LDS Quorums of Seventy, and someone who has known Romney since they were kids, "He [Romney] had high credentials in and out of the church ... It would have been a disaster if we just picked a stranger and they didn't understand the mores of the community."[190]

The relationship would benefit Romney as well. "Romney offered a more personal reason for taking on the Olympic challenge. Having been defeated in his Senate race against Senator Edward M. Kennedy in 1994, Romney knew his political fortune hung on the fate of the Games," the *Boston Globe* reported in 2007.[191]

According to the Globe, when Romney met with the president of John Hancock Mutual Life Insurance, David D'Allessandro, in his office while soliciting Olympic support, Romney told him, "If this doesn't work, I can go back to private life, but I won't be anything more in public life."[192]

Garff himself told the Globe in 2007, "He had done what he wanted to do in business and was looking to leapfrog into the world of public service. This was the thing he could do to propel himself into the national spotlight, which I believe was all part of his overarching plan of his life."[193]

Ken Bullock, a member on the organizing committee told the *Globe*, "He tried very hard to build an image as a savior, the great white hope ... He was very good at characterizing and castigating people and putting himself on a pedestal. Bullock (not to be confused with Romney friend Fraser Bullock) has been described as a Romney foe, particularly with regards to their standoff, when Bullock refused to endorse Romney's idea of deferring payments owed to the state of Utah. Romney is allegedly quoted as telling Bullock, "You don't want me as an enemy."[194]

Another perceived enemy was Tom Welch. Welch and David R. Johnson were accused of defrauding the organizing committee. "Mitt didn't save the games. It was a publicity ploy from the beginning to build his platform in politics," he told the *Deseret News*. "Mitt's objection was to look as good as he could."[195] Romney urged Welch to accept a plea bargain, which he refused. All fifteen felony charges against Welch were thrown out by Judge David Sam who said, "I can only imagine the heartache, the disappointment, the sorrow that you and your loved ones suffered through this terrible ordeal. My hope is that you will now be appropriately recognized and honored for your efforts."[196] Romney refused to acknowledge his efforts or accept Welch's innocence, calling the prosecutors "inept."[197]

His image as the white horse and turnaround artist like his father however does not sit well with all of those involved in the SLC Olympics. According to the *Boston Globe*, "His determination to present himself as a white knight came at a cost. Some colleagues now say he magnified the extent of the Olympics committee's fiscal distress, risked some possible conflicts of interest among board members, and shunted aside other people whose work had been instrumental in promoting the Games."[198]

Garff told the *Congressional Quarterly* in 2007, "I know that's a sensitive issue out here [in Utah]. Did he do it all by himself? No. Does he deserve all the credit? No. Was it bankrupt? No." Garff does contend that Romney's securing the sponsorship of John Hancock did help.[199]

Sydney Fonnesbeck, who was on the Salt Lake City Council and a friend of Welch's, said, "He just came in and gathered the money that was already (pledged) … He didn't want to give anyone else any credit. We became nobodies. A lot of us were hurt and angry. It didn't surprise any of us when he ran home and ran for governor."[200]

"A *Globe* review of archived records showed the organizing committee already had secured commitments of nearly $1 billion in revenues, including the $445 million as its share of the NBC contract and nearly $450 million in contracts for sponsorships, before Romney arrived." [201]

Perhaps the biggest scandal is the amount of federal tax dollars used to highlight Salt Lake City and at the same time bolster Romney's national stature—for which Romney—outrageously—showed little concern.

In January of 2002, the Associated Press reported, "The Olympics have grown into an expensive extravaganza, where sporting events cost less than the pomp, pageantry, and the elaborate technology, according to a budget released to the Associated Press by organizers of the 2002 Winter Games."[202]

In their December 2001 *Sports Illustrated* article *"Snow Job,"* Donald L. Barlett and James B. Steele wrote, "For the past few years, while attention was focused on the Great Olympic Bribery Scandal … private and public interests have siphoned an estimated $1.5 billion out of the US Treasury, all in the name of the Olympics."[203] Barlett and Steele cited four "Olympic records" set by the Salt Lake City Olympics:

1. **Federal Handouts**: The amount of federal taxpayer money spent in Utah was more than "the amount spent by lawmakers to support all seven Olympic Games held in the US since 1904—combined. In inflation-adjusted numbers."[204]

2. **Private Interests:** "For the first time, private enterprises—primarily ski resorts and real estate developments—stand to derive significant long-term benefits from Games-driven congressional giveaways."[205]

3. **Milking of Government Agencies:** "Utah's five-member congressional delegation has used the Olympics to drain money from an unprecedented number of federal departments, agencies

and offices—some three dozen in all, from the Office of National Drug Control Policy to the Agriculture Department."[206]

4. **Most Amount of Taxpayer Money per Athlete:** "Federal spending for the Salt Lake City games will average $625,000 for each of the 2,400 athletes who will compete. (Not a penny of it will go to the athletes.) That's a 996 percent increase from the $57,000 average for the 1996 Atlanta Olympics. It's a staggering 5,582 percent jump from the $11,000 average for the 1984 Summer Games in Los Angeles. Again, these are inflation-adjusted numbers."[207]

One could argue that following the September 11 attacks, more money would be needed for increased security, but as Tom Schatz from Citizens Against Government Waste noted in January 2002, "just over 50 percent (of federal money earmarked for the Games) is for security and the rest is for infrastructure and other activities that in many ways don't have national significance." At the Los Angeles Games in 1984, "95 percent of the federal share was for security." [208]

In fact, in a 2002 article in *The New American*, William Norman Grigg noted "of the estimated $1.3 billion in federal money spent on the Salt Lake Winter Games, $342 million was spent in direct outlays for the events themselves; the rest was spent on construction and other projects that were funded as Olympic 'necessities.'"[209]

Some of these "necessities included the following:

- $500 million in new or improved infrastructure including electronic highway-information systems;
- $326 million for a light rail transit system;
- $30 million for parking lots;
- $2 million for new sewers and media housing;
- $16 million for Salt Lake City airports;
- $1 million for a weather forecasting system that went to the University of Utah's meteorology department.[210]

According to Barlett and Steele, "To be sure, at least a few of these federal dollars would have found their way to Utah even if there were no

Olympics. Such is the case with some of the money spent on highway improvements. However, because work on them was put on a fast track, similar projects were shelved in other cities and states. Thus taxpayers not only subsidized the Salt Lake City Games, but also lost out because highway work in their own areas was deferred."[211]

In 2000 Senator John McCain railed against the "pork barrel spending" and "fiscal abuse" of taxpayer money used for the Salt Lake Games. "The American taxpayer is being shaken down to the tune of nearly a billion and a half dollars," he said. "He (McCain) repeatedly denounced 'pork barrel subsidies' for the 2002 Games, identifying earmarks for construction projects, road improvements, new post offices and other infrastructure in and around Salt Lake City."[212]

On her blog, Debbie Schlussel wrote in February 2002, "US taxpayers will pick up nearly $1 out of every $5 spent on the Salt Lake City event … That doesn't include the $1.1 billion in federal transportation funding of projects like Interstate 15 reconstruction and building light rail in Salt Lake … Romney won't scale down Olympic spending, including the $28 million opening ceremony and an exorbitant, commissioned Alvin Ailey choreographed dance tribute to the late Florence Griffith Joyner? There isn't even a bidding process to scale down costs. More money was blown on his choice of sand 'legacy bricks' that disintegrated in cold weather and twice building the Utah Olympic Oval after screw-ups. It is this waste of our money that led to the brisk sale of 2,500 'Mitt Happens' pins in Salt Lake."[213]

While the federal government subsidized other Olympic games, according to Barlett and Steele, "no federal tax dollars were spent to significantly increase the long term value of private business interests in Los Angeles, Atlanta or Lake Placid."[214] Not so for the Salt Lake Games.

California contractor Clinton Charles Meyer was able to swap his 386-acre tract of land used for Olympic Park in Utah in return for an access road across another piece of land in which he held a majority stake. The road cost taxpayers $2 million.[215] "With the access road in place, 750 acres were opened up for condominiums and luxury homes. The land value of Meyer's Summit Ranch development, where the new homes were built, skyrocketed from $3 million in 1990 to $48 million in 2000—a windfall, underwritten, in part, by US taxpayers."[216] Another $3 million road also benefitted Meyers as well as the LDS church.[217] According to Barlett and Steele "The church's real estate arm, Property Reserve, Inc. (PRI), owns 450 prime acres through which the road runs, a tract long coveted by developers for its gorgeous mountain backdrop (which now includes the ski jumps) and proximity to Park City (10 minutes) and other nearby resorts."[218]

Robert Earl Holding, the owner of Snowbasin Ski Resort in Utah, also benefitted from federal tax dollars. Holding had wanted to expand his resort, but the federal government owned the land required for expansion. Once Salt Lake City was announced as the host for the Olympic Games, Senator Orrin Hatch (R-UT) and Representative Jim Hansen introduced legislation to allow a "land swap" for Holding. Holding would receive the 1,320 acres of federal land in exchange for "land of approximately equal value" to the government.[219]

"Holding (who comes in at number 236 on the Forbes 400 list of wealthiest Americans) also received taxpayer funds to build a $15 million road through his newly acquired lands to his ski resort." [220]

Romney friend Kem Gardner was able to build the Olympic Legacy Park in his brand new shopping mall which increased visitors to his mall. "In addition, Gardner became eligible for millions of dollars in tax reimbursements by creating a plaza on the site and making other improvements," according to the *Boston Globe.* The *Globe* also reported that, although Romney claimed Gardner offered to build the $5 million plaza, "Because Romney's Olympic Organizing Committee brokered the deal with Gardner's private company, city officials had no say in the matter and no knowledge of how the deal transpired." The *Globe* cited a city council woman, Nancy Saxton, who believed the plaza should have been built on public land. The *Globe* also reported that "there was no competitive bid process for the project."[221]

In 2007, the *Boston Globe* also reported, "But despite overall insistence on high ethical standards, Romney himself risked the appearance of conflicts by soliciting companies, such as Staples and Marriott International that listed him on their boards of directors. As a director he was responsible for protecting the companies' interests, as CEO of the organizing committee, he had promised to get the best deal for the Olympics."[222]

The Mormon Church, however was probably one of the biggest beneficiaries. With help in part from federal tax dollars, Salt Lake City and Mormonism were showcased to the world.

Despite Hinckley's declaration that there would be no proselytizing on the streets during the Games, the Mormon church "had no intention of standing idly by," according to Lunt.[223] In fact, according to the *Boston Globe*, documents showed "church officials recommended employees to the organizers, commented on committee policies, and sought direct public relations benefits from the Games."[224] Mormon Elder Robert Hales himself traveled to New York City to meet with NBC executives volunteering his input on televising the Games. Romney also solicited donations and loans from the LDS church.[225]

"Wary of appearing to dominate the games, [LDS] leaders asked Romney to scale back his requests for aid, which he did," the *Globe* acknowledged.[226] While the Mormons attempted to appear to back off, they did not stand by idly. The LDS church donated a plaza which was used for the medal ceremonies and offered free concerts by the Mormon Tabernacle Choir.[227] The Mormons also set up a Family History Center and hosted a free program entitled "Light of the World" each night which stressed the Mormon values and heritage.[228] An LDS company also published the book *Why I Believe* for the games, which highlighted fifty Mormons, including Romney, discussing their faith.[229]

Romney also asked the president of Brigham Young University, Merrill Bateman, to close the school during the Games in order that BYU students could volunteer at the Games. Mormon publication *Ensign* magazine also published a story, "Being A Good Host to Visitors During the Games," to promote volunteerism in the Games among LDS members.[230]

According to Lunt, "The church clearly sought to use the Olympic Games to impress upon the world the value of its doctrines, traditions and morality. So concerned with its public image was the Mormon Church, that three months after the Olympics, in May 2002 *Ensign* published excerpts from newspapers around the globe which made positive comments about the LDS church in conjunction with Olympic coverage."[231]

Richard Ostling, author of *Mormon America: The Power and the Promise*, told *Time* in 2008, "It was a great civic success for Salt Lake City … a come from behind success for Mitt Romney that made his presidential campaign feasible, and it brought Mormonism very much to the fore, as the successful hosts of a kind of national festival."[232]

In essence, the Salt Lake City Olympics was a boom for the Mormon Church as well as for Mitt Romney's political aspirations. All courtesy of you, the US taxpayer.

According to the *Boston Globe*, "The day Mitt Romney took over the scandal-tainted Salt Lake City Olympics in 1999, he pledged not to exploit the role for political gain and announced that he would not accept any severance pay when he finished the job. Public records show otherwise." [233]

In addition to his $922,980 total salary, Romney received a $476,000 severance. When asked about the severance pay and his pledge, Romney spokesman Eric Fehrnstrom said that Romney donated both his salary and severance to charity. When pressed, Fehrnstrom replied that Romney does not discuss his charitable contributions.[234]

Romney also significantly increased the severance pay of the twenty-five senior managers on the board, many of whom donated to his gubernatorial campaign shortly after the Winter Games ended. After the Atlanta Games, senior managers received an average of two months' salary as a severance. Severance pay after the Salt Lake Games was initially supposed to be one year's salary. Romney proposed changing it to eighteen months' salary plus $10,000 put into their retirement plans. While some members on the committee were reluctant about the change, they approved Romney's recommendation.[235]

Athlete and board member Joan Guetschow told the *Globe*, "A few of us were surprised by how big [the severance packages] were, but I didn't have the experience to know what would be acceptable for that level of management, so I didn't object."[236]

Seventeen of these twenty-five members donated to Romney's campaign or the Massachusetts GOP. Fourteen of the fifty-three members on the board of trustees of the organizing committee also donated to Romney's campaign or PACs. Romney's committees also received money from Olympic sponsor Nu Skin's executives or families in the amount of $118,500. Fraser Bullock (not to be confused with Romney foe Ken Bullock), member of the Quorum of the Seventy in the LDS church, who worked with Romney at Bain and was appointed by Romney as his top assistant in Salt Lake, donated $53,000 to Romney's campaign committees and the Massachusetts GOP.[237]

David Simmons, who pled guilty to tax fraud in the Salt Lake City Olympic scandal, donated to Romney's Massachusetts and New Hampshire PACs. When asked about Simmons' donation, Fehrnstrom replied, "What Simmons did was wrong, but he expressed regret for it and accepted responsibility for his actions. It's time to put the past behind us."[238] Too bad Romney did not feel the same way about Welch and Johnson, whose charges against them were thrown out of court.

According to the *Globe*, "All told, Romney reaped more than $1.5 million in campaign funds during his governorship from individuals and families with ties to the Olympics." Moreover, in 2007 "Many of his Olympic-related donors have since joined a massive fundraising movement for Romney's presidential campaign."[239]

Romney's quest for his white horse moment to ultimately reach the prize of the presidency for his father and his church has not been surprising. Like his father, he would first need a governorship under his belt. According to the *Globe*, "Mitt Romney began spending on a campaign for governor early in March, laying the groundwork for his possible run even while completing the Winter Olympics in Salt Lake City, new campaign finances show."[240]

Speculation after the games was whether it would be Utah or Massachusetts that Romney would run as governor. Conveniently he had residences in both states. It would ultimately depend not on which constituents Romney felt he could best serve, rather on which governorship would best launch his presidential campaign.

Chapter 12

Romney as Governor

Even before the Olympic flame was extinguished, the buzz regarding Romney's next political move was in full force. "Mitt will be a golden boy after the Olympics," political consultant Rob Gray told the *New York Times* in February of 2002.[241]

"What will Mitt do next has become an Olympic event of its own here [in Salt Lake City], and even the average pin-trading volunteer seems to have an opinion. Romney himself does little to dispel the speculation—he will only say that he is looking for a race he can win and that he will not return to his business" (New York Times, February 12, 2002).[242]

"In the months leading to the Olympics, Mr. Romney made no secret of his desire to run for public office again" *(New York Times,* February 25, 2002).[243]

"Romney has not only played the part of white knight, he looks it. With his 'Meet the Press' hair and perfect teeth, he seems almost impossibly handsome and happy."[244]

There was no question Romney would run. The real questions were where and which party?

According to the *Boston Globe*, "Future public service was likely, he declared, either Massachusetts or Utah, where some pundits theorized *he might fit in as a Democrat*" [Emphasis mine].[245] Utah, with its large concentration of LDS members, would certainly benefit Romney. Some hypothesized that Romney would run in conservative Utah after he responded to a *Salt Lake Tribune* article that described him as pro-choice. Romney wrote in a letter to the editor at the time, "I do not wish to be labeled pro-choice."[246]

(Running for governor in liberal Massachusetts, however, Romney would later adamantly describe himself as "pro-choice.")

Romney would make his decision not based on the state he could best serve, rather the state that would best serve his presidential aspirations. A 2001 *Deseret News* article cited "sources close to Romney who believed 'he wants a position with enough national exposure to launch a presidential campaign.'"[247]

Romney ultimately decided on Massachusetts, after Jane Swift, the Republican governor at the time, who was facing ethical charges, pulled out of the race. Romney, who won the Republican nomination unopposed, was in a good position to win. After all, like his father, Romney successfully crafted a national image as a turnaround artist with the 2002 Olympics and even was named as one of *People* magazine's "50 most beautiful people."[248]

Romney's initial indecision on where he would run, however, led to questions regarding his residency pounced on by Democrats.

"Initially, Romney's campaign insisted that he had filed his federal income taxes as a resident of Massachusetts. But soon after, he acknowledged he had filed as a Utah resident for two years and had amended those tax returns after announcing his candidacy to show Massachusetts as his home," according to the *Boston Globe.* [249]

The State Ballot Law Committee listened to testimony regarding Romney and his Utah home which had been classified as his "primary residence," and provided him $18,000 in property tax breaks for three years.[250]

"Romney attributed the mistakes to his accountant and the local tax assessor, who under oath acknowledged the error and after the commission proceedings, sent him a new bill to recoup $54,587," the *Globe* reported. The board ultimately came to a unanimous decision that Romney had always maintained his ties to Massachusetts.[251]

The Campaign in Full Force

Romney, in order to win his springboard position to the national stage, first had to win a governorship in which a majority of the electorate was more to the left than right. "In a state where Democrats outnumbered

Republicans by almost a three to one ratio, Romney rarely identified himself as a Republican," according to the *Boston Globe.*[252]

As in 1994, Romney tried to rely on his clean-cut, wholesome image again, which this time fell flat. In a television ad titled "Ann," the Romneys spoke about their fairytale courtship and Ann described her husband as "very romantic," while Mitt gushed, "Ann's just good to the core." The end of the ad showed a bathing suit-clad Mitt goofing around with his sons in a lake.[253]

After the ad, Romney's poll numbers tanked. "Internally, some advisors thought the cloying tone of the ad encased the candidate in plastic," according to the *Boston Globe.* A series of missteps, however, by his opponent helped him recoup his poll numbers later on.[254]

Romney on the Issues 2002

Romney's positions on the issues in 2002 were somewhat similar to those in 1994 and seemed to be part of his larger plan for the presidency. Romney would first have to portray himself as a progressive Republican to win the votes of the Massachusetts people. Once becoming governor, Romney would then have to portray himself as a more conservative Republican to win the votes of the American people. Attempting to serve these two mini-masters would ultimately expose Romney's only consistent position: he wanted the presidency and would do and say whatever it took to get him there.

Abortion

Answering a Planned Parenthood questionnaire in 2002, Romney made his position on abortion well known:

> Question: Do you support the substance of the Supreme Court decision in Roe v. Wade?
>
> Romney's answer: Yes.[255]
>
> Question: Do you support efforts to increase access to emergency contraception?
>
> Romney's answer: Yes.[256]

When asked how Romney's prochoice stance compared to his Democratic opponent Shannon O'Brien, his running mate Kerry Healy stated "There isn't a dime of difference between Mitt Romney's position on choice and Shannon O'Brien's."[257]

In fact, Romney's 2002 campaign website stated, "As Governor, Mitt Romney would protect the current pro-choice status quo in Massachusetts. No law would change. The choice to have an abortion is a deeply personal one. Women should feel free to choose based on their own beliefs, not the government's."[258]

Most striking is the claim by MassResistance.org, a website that highly documents the Romney record. According to MassResistance, "Notes taken by key leaders of the nation's most radical pro-abortion group, the National Abortion Rights Action League (NARAL), reveal that at a 2002 meeting, Romney assured them he would work to soften the GOP stance on abortion and said that the GOP's pro-life position was 'killing them.'"[259]

Gay Rights

Romney's 2002 campaign website stated, "All citizens deserve equal rights, regardless of their sexual orientation." While he does not support gay marriage, Mitt Romney believes domestic partnership status should be recognized in a way that includes the potential for health benefits and rights of survivorship."[260]

During the campaign a pink flyer was released for the gay pride event in Boston with Romney and his running mate Kerry Healy. The flyer read, "Mitt and Kerry wish you a Great Pride weekend! All citizens deserve equal rights, regardless of their sexual preference."[261]

Jonathan Spampinato, a gay Republican activist who served as deputy political director for Romney's gubernatorial campaign, told the *New York Times* that Romney "explained his position to Log Cabin club members early on by saying, 'Regardless of what you call it, if you look at the benefits I support and the benefits Shannon [his Democrat opponent] supports, there's probably a hair of a difference."[262]

Most revealing was a 2007 *New York Times* article describing Romney's meeting with Log Cabin Republicans at a gay bar in Boston as he sought their endorsement. According to the *Times*, "When the discussion turned to a court case on same-sex marriage that was then wending its way through the state's judicial system, he said he believed that marriage should be limited to the union of a man and a woman. But, according to several people present, he promised to obey the courts' ultimate ruling and not champion a fight on either side of the issue."[263] This is one of the few issues on which Romney would keep his promise as governor.

Romney Wins Governorship, Immediately Runs for President

After spending $6 million of his own money, Romney was elected governor of Massachusetts, defeating O'Brien by 106,000 votes.[264]

Romney didn't waste any time once he was governor in setting up the scaffolding for his presidential run. According to the *New York Times*, "He almost immediately began parlaying his own wealth, a network of his fellow Mormons and financiers ..."[265]

The *New York Times* went on "Soon after he was elected governor of Massachusetts, Mr. Romney turned into a fund-raising machine, setting up a series of federal and state political action committees that together let individual donors give far more than the federal spending limits." The *Times* also noted, "To fill them, Mr. Romney turned in part to connections in the tight-knit world of wealthy fellow members of the Church of Jesus Christ of Latter-day Saints."[266]

According to the *Boston Globe*, "In the summer of 2003, barely six months into Romney's governorship, Robert White, a confidant, had huddled in Washington with political strategists Michael Murphy and Trent Wisecup and a top GOP lawyer, Benjamin Ginsberg, to ponder Romney's next move. At Ginsberg's law office near Georgetown, and later over a steak in a private room at Morton's the seeds for Romney's presidential campaign were planted."[267]

Romney once again used his wealth to facilitate his quest for the White House and essentially attempted to buy future endorsements. According to the *Globe*, "They [Romney advisors] conceived the Commonwealth PAC, a political action committee that enabled Romney to travel the country with a checkbook, currying favor with Republican leaders by contributing to their campaigns and causes."[268]

The Commonwealth PAC was designed to maximize Romney's influence in crucial primary states and raise as much money as possible for his presidential campaign. "Romney's advisors organized the PAC in an innovative way, setting up affiliates in six key states—including some states with no limits on contributions, which allowed Romney's wealthy associates to give five- and six-figure sums. In all, the PAC raised $8.8 million and doled out $1.3 million, much of it in key presidential-primary states," according to the *Globe*.[269]

Romney's full court press for the presidency did not stop with his PAC. He also ingratiated himself into the Republican Party for increased exposure. According to the *Boston Globe,* "Romney also positioned himself to lead the Republican Governors Association, advancing from chairman of the group's annual dinner in 2004 and vice chairman in 2005 and putting himself in line to be chairman in 2006. The job would give Romney visibility, contact with Republican donors, and the chance to visit other states."[270]

Romney's Economic Record

Romney consistently likes to paint himself as a turnaround artist in Massachusetts, claiming he "closed a nearly $3 billion budget deficit without raising taxes" while governor. The facts do not back this up.

According to Reuters, "The $3 billion deficit projected by Romney and state legislators in January 2003 at the start of his Administration never rose that high because a surge in capital gains taxes more than halved the shortfall to $1.3 billion."[271]

President of the Massachusetts Taxpayer Foundation, Michael Widmer told Reuters in 2008, "There's never been under his [Romney's] watch an economic turnaround to speak of ... We added a few jobs over the last three years of his tenure, but very few. He also raised corporate taxes and the (deficit) gap turned out to be less than $3 billion."[272]

According to the *Boston Globe,* "Romney's success in steering the state through the fiscal maelstrom was one of his key achievements, but in the retelling he and his aides often overstate the accomplishments and understate the side-effects: big fee increases and pressure on local property taxes."[273]

Romney proposed or raised so many fees, he earned the nickname "Fee-Fee." Almost no Massachusetts citizen was immune from the fees he imposed. "Romney and Democratic lawmakers ended up approving hundreds of millions in higher fees and fines, making it more expensive to use an ice skating rink, register a boat, take the bar exam, get a duplicate driver's license, file a court case, install underground storage tanks, sell cigarettes or alcohol, comply with air quality rules and transport hazardous waste," according to the Associated Press.[274]

Carla Howell, co-founder and president of the Center for Small Government, and sponsor of a 2002 ballot initiative to end the Massachusetts state income tax, explained on the blog LewRockwell.com in 2007, "Each of the four years Romney served as Governor, he raised taxes—while pretending he didn't. He claims he only raised mandatory government 'fees.' But government mandatory fees are nothing but taxes, and taxes are nothing but mandatory government fees."[275]

When questioned in 2008 by the late Tim Russert on *Meet the Press*, Romney tried to explain himself.

> Russert: The AP says it this way: "When Romney wanted to balance the Massachusetts budget, the blind, mentally retarded and gun owners were asked to help pay. In all, then-Governor Romney proposed creating thirty-three new fees," "increasing fifty-seven others." The head of the Bay State Council of the Blind said that your name was "Fee-Fee," that you just raised fee after fee after fee. That's a tax … A fee's not a tax?
>
> Romney: A fee—well, a fee—if it were a tax, it'd be called—it'd be called a tax. But …
>
> Russert: Governor, that's, that's gimmick.
>
> Romney: No, it's, it's reality. It is. But—and I have no—I'm not trying to hide from the fact that we raised fees. We raised fees \$240 million.[276]

According to the *Boston Globe,* "One major fee hike was clearly excessive—a 2-cent-per-gallon increase in a special gasoline fee, implemented during the fiscal crisis without fanfare, even though it affects every motorist in the state." The fee was raised from .5 cents to 2.5 cents per gallon under Romney in 2003, in addition to an already twenty-one cent per gallon state tax.[277]

According to Howell, "He [Romney] also increased several taxes by 'closing loopholes' to enable collection of a new Internet sales tax and by passing legislation that enables local governments to raise business property taxes. This, he claims, is not raising taxes."[278]

Writing on the Official Blog of the National Taxpayers Union in 2008, Sam Batkins pointed out "Romney raised taxes or fees seven times in Mass, but only cut taxes three times … Overall, during Romney's four years in office, taxes increased $175 million. This total is nothing compared to some tax-hikers like Jon Corzine (D-NJ), but Romney doesn't have a great record as a tax cutter."[279]

Romney also refused to endorse the Bush tax cuts, with his spokesman claiming "It's just not a state matter" at the time. When Romney met with an all- Democrat group of House and Senate members in Washington, D.C. in 2003, he reportedly said he would not be a "cheerleader" but that "I have to keep a solid relationship with the White House."[280]

Liberal Democrat Congressman Barney Frank commented at the time, "I was very pleased … Here you have a freshman governor refusing to endorse a tax cut presented by a Republican president at the height of his wartime popularity."[281]

Romney's claims of cutting the state budget by $2 billion also do not ring true, according to Howell. "These 'cuts' were merely budget games," wrote Howell in 2007. "Spending cuts in one area were simply moved into another area of the budget."[282] According to the National Taxpayers Union, under Romney, spending in the Bay State rose 20.7 percent (from $22,848 billion to $27,588 billion).[283]

While Romney may blame the primarily liberal state legislature, "When it comes to tax and spend policies, he's not only in lockstep with the Democrats, he leads the way," according to Howell. "Each of the four years Romney served as Governor, he started budget negotiations by proposing an increase of about $1 billion. Before the legislation even named a budget figure."[284]

In a typical smoke and mirrors fashion, Romney would accept a few line-item budget increases from the legislature. However, when Romney would veto a few other line item increases, "The media helped him out again by making fanfare of his vetoes and portraying him as tough on spending—*after he had already given away the store!*"[285]

How did the people of Massachusetts fare under Romney? According to Northeastern University economist Andrew Sum, in number of jobs created, economic growth, and wage increases, not well. Sum told Reuters in 2008, "As a strict labor market economist looking at the record, Massachusetts did very poorly during the Romney years ... On every measure you've got, the state was a substantial underperformer."[286]

During Romney's term Massachusetts was in the bottom three of the nation for job creation, only above Michigan and post-Katrina Louisiana, according to Sum.[287] Moody's Economy.com was a little more generous ranking Massachusetts as the fourth weakest state during the period. Only 24,400 new jobs were netted during Romney's term, an anemic 0.8 percent increase.[288]

Wages did not fare much better either during Romney's term. The weekly wage, adjusted for inflation, from 2001 to 2006 increased a mere $1.00 and "real output of goods and services—a broad measure of economic performance—grew 9 percent, below the 13 percent rate for the United States," under Romney.[289] Massachusetts did rank in the top three in another category, however; the third highest for population loss in a state from 2002 to 2006. [290]

The Romney camp responds to such criticism that if it weren't for Romney, Massachusetts would have fared much worse. According to Romney spokesman in 2008 Kevin Madden, Romney brought Massachusetts "back from the brink of financial disaster."[291] That sounds eerily familiar to our current president's rhetoric.

Massachusetts Gay Marriage

After the Massachusetts Supreme Judicial Court ruling (called the *Goodridge* decision) regarding same-sex marriage, Joan Vennochi wrote in her 2004 article "Romney's Real Goal in Gay Campaign" in the *Boston Globe,* "Washington is on Romney's mind, not Boston ... He sees more

TV cameras in his future, not real chaos from same-sex marriage in this state."[292]

Romney, who had been eying a presidential run for years, was in a pickle. He had to appease the liberal left in Massachusetts as well as the Log Cabin Republicans on whom he relied for support to win the governorship, but also had to appear as a conservative to voters nationwide in order to win the Republican nomination for the presidency.

According to a May 2004 Associated Press article, "For three days after the legislation of gay marriage on Monday, Romney remained in seclusion, quietly avoiding the international media that descended on the state … When he finally emerged on Thursday, Romney appeared to try to distance himself from the issue, even as he took the fight to a new legal level."[293]

Romney did appeal to the attorney general to stop clerks from issuing licenses to out of state couples. Romney himself, however, expressed joy for the newly married gay couples under his watch stating, "I'm pleased for them and for their ability to establish a further relationship with the people they love."[294]

Larry Sabato, political science professor at the University of Virginia, told the Associated Press, "He's clearly taken a side and it's clear that he's not happy about the gay marriage situation in Massachusetts. There's no way a pro-gay marriage Republican governor would ever be nominated president or vice president. He had to do something to indicate his displeasure."[295]

In a May 2004 *National Review* article titled "The Missing Governor," Hadley Arkes wrote, "The deeper failure must go to the man who stood as governor, holding the levers of the executive. And if it is countdown for marriage in Massachusetts, it is countdown also for Mitt Romney, whose political demise may be measured along the scale of moves he could have taken and the record of his receding, step by step, until he finally talked himself into doing nothing, or nothing much."[296]

Romney not only did nothing or nothing much to stop gay marriage in Massachusetts, he illegally instituted gay marriage in Massachusetts, mainly by accepting a court's opinion as law, changing the state's marriage licenses, and ordering judges to perform same-sex marriages or face repercussions.

According to MassResistance, "Some time in early 2004 (no record can be found of the order), Romney directed his Department of Public Health to change the state marriage license to read 'Party A' and 'Party B', replacing 'Husband' and 'Wife.' None of this was required by any law or passed by the legislature or even ordered by the court."[297]

Romney's chief legal counsel, Daniel B. Winslow, told justices of the peace on April 25, 2004, "Your task is straightforward and can be summed up in three words: follow the law." Justices uncomfortable with performing same-sex marriages were pressured to resign.[298]

In no way was Romney required by law to do these things. As MassResistance points out: "The court ruling simply advised the legislature to pass legislation codifying its opinion on changing the marriage statutes. Romney was *not* bound to enforce same-sex marriages prior to legislative action."[299]

According to MassResistance, the *Goodridge* decision, *which issued an opinion, not a law* stated four things:

1. Existing law does not allow same-sex marriage.

   Ruling: "The only reasonable explanation is that the Legislature did not intend that same-sex couples be licensed to marry. We conclude, as did the judge, that G.L. c.207 may not be construed to permit same-sex couples to marry."

2. No existing marriage laws were being struck down.

   Ruling: "Here, no one argues that striking down the marriage laws is an appropriate form of relief."

3. Denying same-sex marriages violated the Massachusetts Constitution.

   Ruling: "We declare that barring an individual from the protections, benefits, and obligations of civil marriage solely because that person would marry a person of the same sex violates the Massachusetts Constitution."

4. The Legislature had 180 days to "take such action as it may deem appropriate."

> Ruling: "We vacate the summary judgment for the department. We remand this case to the Superior Court for entry of judgment consistent with this opinion. Entry of judgment shall be stayed for 180 days to permit the Legislature to take such action as it may deem appropriate in light of this opinion."[300]

In December 20, 2006 a hand-delivered letter to Romney signed by almost fifty pro-family activists laid out exactly what Romney should have done regarding same-sex marriage in Massachusetts. (Romney never acknowledged the letter.)

The letter disagreed with Romney's decision to "execute the law" after the *Goodridge* decision. After all, the court issued an *opinion* not a law.

Romney had two choices in the beginning. He could have deemed the ruling unconstitutional and therefore void as Jefferson did in *Marbury v. Madison*. Or he could have deemed the ruling not enforceable to Massachusetts citizens because the case only applied to specific plaintiffs in the case and not the general population as Lincoln did in the Dred Scott decision.[301]

"Instead," the letter stated, "you [Romney] asserted that the court's opinion was 'law' and thus binding. Though the Legislature never revoked the actual law, you issued—with no legal authority—the first 'homosexual marriage' licenses in American history."[302]

The letter went on citing sections of the Massachusetts Constitution which specifically prohibit the judicial branch from making laws, especially with respect to marriage.

"All causes of marriage … shall be heard and determined by the governor and council, until the legislature shall, by law, make other provision."

"The people of this commonwealth are not controllable by any other laws than those to which their constitutional representative body have given their consent."

"The judicial shall never exercise the legislative and executive powers, or either of them: to the end it may be a government of laws and not of men."[303]

The letter also pointed out that the Massachusetts Constitution was so protective against judicial activism that even laws passed before the constitution itself was written could not be changed by the judiciary. They again cited a provision in the Massachusetts Constitution which reads:

"All the laws which have heretofore been adopted, used and approved ... shall still remain and be in force until altered or repealed by the legislature."[304]

Again, the letter pointed out that the current marriage law banning same-sex marriage was never struck down by the court in the *Goodridge* decision.

The letter stated, "We note that even the Goodridge majority said they were *not* suspending the marriage statute."

They cited the judges' opinion: "Here, no one argues that striking down the marriage laws is an appropriate form of relief."

The letter went on: "In fact, they [the judges] admitted that under the statute, Chapter 207 of the Massachusetts General Laws, homosexual marriage is illegal."

The letter again cited the court's opinion: "We conclude, as did the judge, that M.G.L. c. 207 may not be construed to permit same-sex couples to marry."[305]

Romney still refused to act as the chief executive of the state. He chose to play it both ways: try to appear as a defender of traditional marriage on the national stage by criticizing the opinion of the court, while at the same time doing nothing, in fact, facilitating gay marriage in Massachusetts to pander to the left that elected him governor. It wasn't just gay marriage that Romney let slip in Massachusetts, however, it was a complete gay agenda aimed at Massachusetts children.

Governor Romney's Administration and the Homosexual Agenda in Massachusetts Schools

The Governor's Commission on Gay and Lesbian Youth was already in place before Romney became governor. Romney had the power to dissolve the commission, or at least command its leadership and funding. Instead,

Romney let the commission run rampant with a pro-homosexual agenda toward Massachusetts children.[306]

This commission wasn't simply a support apparatus to protect gay students from bullying. According to MassResistance, "The Governor's Commission was perhaps the largest government-sanctioned promoter of the homosexual agenda to children in the United States. This entity spent millions of state tax dollars promoting the gay-lesbian-bisexual-transgender (GLBT) radicalism in Massachusetts schools by inundating them with GLBT speakers, presentations, films, books, parades, dances, posters, handouts and help establishing GLBT clubs on campus."[307]

One example of the commission's organized activities was the Youth Pride Parade. Gay activists marched in the parade along with gay youth, some dressed in drag. Governor Romney issued a celebratory proclamation of the day in 2004. The day would end with a GLBT "Prom" promoted by the commission and sponsored by the Boston Alliance of Gays, Lesbians, Bisexuals and Transgender Youth (BAGLY), "a group that has promoted adult-child sex and has received funding from the Governor's Commission." The event was attended by children as young as middle school *and* homosexual adults.[308]

Romney proposed doubling the 2006 funding for the commission as governor. To achieve political cover, he then vetoed the funding once the legislature approved of it, knowing that his veto would be overridden. "This enabled Romney to appear 'pro-family' while the homosexuals still got their funding."[309]

MassResistance showed Romney photographs of some of the outrageous activities and events that were sponsored or organized by the commission in 2006. "A few days later, Romney announced his intention to dissolve the commission. But within hours of that announcement, under pressure from the homosexual community, the governor changed his mind."[310]

The homosexual agenda was also pushed by several of the Romney Administration departments. Surfing Romney's Department of Education's website, one could find helpful information such as how to start a Gay Straight Alliance, how to come out of the closet to family and friends, and others under tabs such as "Safe Schools" or "Anti-Bullying." Romney's Department of Public Health was a contributor to *The Little Black Book: Queer in the 21st Century* which provided middle and high school students graphic information on homosexual practices, such as fisting. Romney would later call this "grossly inappropriate" but there were no repercussions to any staff at the department and Romney never demanded any oversight on DPH spending on programs. Romney also awarded a Massachusetts district court judgeship to Stephen Albany, part of the Massachusetts Lesbian and Gay Bar Association and a proponent of the repealing of sodomy laws in the Bay State.[311]

Romney's Republican Party Legacy

Romney not only left his mark on the Republican Party in Massachusetts—he decimated it. In 2004, Romney helped the Massachusetts GOP raise $3 million and campaigned for over forty Republican candidates in the state. Romney himself made close to seventy stops around Massachusetts.[312] Romney, however, may have had the magic touch that Obama seems to be having with Democrat candidates.

According to the *Boston Globe*, "For Romney and the anemic GOP, it was a train wreck. The party suffered a net loss of two seats in the House and one in the Senate."[313] Worse, during Romney's term the number of Massachusetts residents that registered as Republican fell 31,000, while those registering as Democrats rose 30,000.[314] The *Washington Post* reported in 2006, "Romney is leaving office with the state GOP weaker than he arrived."[315]

According to the *Boston Globe*, "After his failure to elect more Republican legislators in the 2004 campaign, Mitt Romney met with the *Globe's* editorial board and made a surprising declaration: No longer could he put so much time in promoting his party."[316] No, Romney was more interested in promoting himself for the presidency. He told the *Boston Globe* editorial board at that same meeting, "From now on it's me—me—me."[317]

Gay marriage was not his finest moment on the national stage. Romney needed something to bolster his stature. According to the *Globe*, "What the governor lacked, however, was a defining achievement after two years in office. He seized on health care reform."

Shortly after his meeting with the *Globe's* board, Romney wrote an op-ed for the newspaper titled "My Plan for Massachusetts Health

Insurance Reform." Two days after the opinion piece ran, Romney received an encouraging response from none other than his buddy Senator Ted Kennedy.[318]

RomneyCare

Senator Kennedy said at the time, "We're basically stalemated [in Washington] so the states are going to have to try to come up with a response."[319]

Romney aides and Romney himself would work together with Ted Kennedy and his staff to completely overhaul the Massachusetts health care system.

In 2006, "After months of hard bargaining by Romney aides, legislators, advocates, business leaders, insurers and health care providers, a compromise bill emerged from the Legislature in early April with a goal of providing coverage for virtually all of the state's more than 400,000 uninsured."[320]

Romney vetoed eight items in the bill such as a $295 per person fee for employers with eleven or more employees that did not offer health plans. Romney knew the vetoes would be overridden. According to the *Boston Globe*, "Politically, Romney was able to have it both ways. With the stroke of a pen, the would-be presidential candidate signed a landmark law and used his line-item veto to wash his hands resembling a tax increase to help pay for it. The vetoed parts of the bill were certain to be overridden in both the House and the Senate anyway."[321]

Ted Kennedy joined Romney as he signed the bill into law. After the signing, reporters asked Governor Romney what the difference between his plan and HillaryCare was, to which Romney replied, "Mine got passed and hers didn't."[322]

Michael Tanner from the Cato Institute cited in his briefing paper in 2006 several problems with RomneyCare and why it would fail:

> "The individual mandate opens the door to widespread regulation of the health care industry and political interference in personal health care decisions."
>
> "The act's subsidies are poorly targeted and overly generous."

"The Massachusetts Health Care Connector, which restructures the individual and small business insurance markets, is a form of managed competition that has the potential to severely limit consumer choice."

"The act imposes new burdens on business and creates a host of new government bureaucracies to manage the health care system."[323]

How has Massachusetts fared under RomneyCare?

According to the *Wall Street Journal*, "The liberal Commonwealth Fund reports that Massachusetts insurance costs have climbed anywhere from 21 percent to 46 percent faster than the US average since 2005. Employer-sponsored premiums are now the highest in the nation."[324] The average premium for family coverage was higher than $15,000 a year in 2009.[325]

It has also been a budget buster. *Forbes* noted in 2009, "In the last two years alone, spending on free and subsidized plans for low-income citizens of the Bay State has doubled from $630 million in 2007 to an estimated $1.3 billion this year."[326]

Romney has been forced to defend his plan since the ObamaCare bill passed. Romney told *Newsweek* in April 2010, "What we did was insist on personal responsibility … in my view, and others may disagree, expecting people who can afford to buy insurance to do so is consistent with personal responsibility, and that's a cornerstone of conservatism."[327]

What about personal responsibility? Grace-Marie Turner, president of the Galen Institute, wrote in the *Wall Street Journal* in March 2010, "While Massachusetts' uninsured rate has dropped to around 3%, 68% of the newly insured since 2006 receive coverage that is heavily or completely subsidized by taxpayers. While Mr. Romney insisted that everyone should pay something for coverage, that is not the way his plan has turned out. More than half of the 408,000 newly insured residents pay nothing, according to a February 2010 report by the Massachusetts Health Connector, the state's insurance exchange."[328]

As predicted, subsidies under RomneyCare are indeed overly generous. Citizens of the Bay State with incomes up to 300 percent of the federal poverty level can qualify for subsidies. A single individual with an income of $30,480 would qualify for a subsidy as well as a married couple with two children with an income under $63,000.[329]

Others are gaming the system. Harvard-Pilgrim, one of the state's health benefits companies, reported an increase in short-term customers. "These new customers purchase coverage for several months, run up big medical bills and then drop their insurance policies once their treatment has ended." From April 2008 to March 2009, 40 percent of Harvard-Pilgrim customers were on the plan less than five months, with an average medical bill of $2,400 per month.[330]

In 2009 the *Wall Street Journal* cited Charlie Baker, CEO of Harvard-Pilgrim, who wrote on his blog, "It is raising prices paid by individuals and small businesses who are doing the right thing by purchasing twelve months of health insurance, and it's turning the whole notion of shared responsibility on its ear."[331]

As predicted, increased government regulation has also contributed to rising costs. According to the *Wall Street Journal*, "As in Washington, the political class and providers blame insurers, but a better culprit is the state's insurance regulation."[332] As Turner wrote, "A 2008 study by the Massachusetts Division of Health Care Finance and Policy found that the state's most expensive insurance mandates cost patients more than $1 billion between July 2004 and July 2005. The Massachusetts health reform law [Romney's plan] left all of them in place."[333]

All of this has led to higher penalties on businesses, increased fines on those who do not purchase insurance under the individual mandate, higher taxes on hospitals and insurers, rising premiums, and the inevitable rationing of care in the Bay State.[334] The average wait time to see a primary care physician for new patients is forty-four days and less than half of Massachusetts internal medicine doctors are accepting new patients.[335] While the average wait time to see a specialist has declined nationally to twenty-one days, it increased to fifty days in Boston.[336]

"As a result, many patients are insured in name only: they have health coverage, but can't find a doctor." Visits to the emergency room increased 7 percent from 2005 to 2007, with half of these visits able to be treated in a doctor's office rather than in the ER.[337]

Perhaps the most tragic part of RomneyCare has been the cost to the unborn. Having an abortion under Romney's plan costs a mere $50 co-pay. According to the *Politico*, "Even worse, the plan does not include any exceptions, which means Massachusetts taxpayers are forced to fund abortion-on-demand." RomneyCare also requires by law that Planned Parenthood plays an instrumental part in naming members to the policy board.[338]

RomneyCare has been a disaster for Massachusetts and a preview for our nation under ObamaCare. Romney was so eager to pass his signature achievement, he didn't care about the long term effects; he would be out of office by then and on the presidential campaign trail.

Romney's Greek Columns Moment

Romney's last day in office was arguably his first official day on the presidential campaign trail. Called "a masterpiece of political stagecraft" by the *Boston Globe*, Romney and his wife Ann sauntered down the steps of the State House, stopping several times to draw attention to his record as governor before leaving office.[339] Televised, minus the Obama Greek columns, Romney milked the moment for every bit of political capital he could.

The *Globe* reported, "He greeted the family of Melanie Power, a 13-year-old killed by a repeat drunk driver and memorialized by Melanie's Law, the tough drunken driving bill signed by Romney. He met students attending state colleges under the John and Abigail Adams merit scholarships he created. And he hailed two families who should be able to afford medical insurance under the state's new healthcare law."[340]

Even before the Romneys took their last step out of the State House as governor and first lady, the years of sowing the seeds for higher office had already started to take root and begin to sprout. According to the *Globe*, "An hour before Romney departed the State House, the Federal Election Commission docketed a four-page form establishing the Romney for President Exploratory Committee."[341]

Chapter 13

The 2008 Presidential Campaign: The Mormons, Mitt, and DeMoss

In November 2006, *Time* magazine reported, "A Mormon church official and a public relations executive shuttled recently from the Fox News Washington bureau to the *Washington Post* to the online political digest the *Hotline.* The two were engaging in a little pre-emptive rearguard action, gearing up for the impending Republican presidential campaign of Massachusetts Governor (Willard) Mitt Romney, 59, whose family has long been part of the church's elite."[342]

Clearly the LDS church was licking its chops at the prospect of a Mormon president to usher in its kingdom on earth, and was no doubt in full public relations mode to portray Mormonism as just another traditional religion.

Time reported that Michael Otterson, the director of media relations for the LDS, had traveled to Washington, D.C. to meet with several political reporters. Otterson told *Time,* "The message in a nutshell is, remember that we're politically neutral as an institution. The church is about preaching the gospel of Jesus Christ. Anything else is a distraction."[343]

In other words, pay no attention to the real history and bizarre rites, rituals, and doctrines of the Mormon Church. Just look at this clean-cut, successful Mormon candidate Romney who, like us, is just like you. The LDS church went on the public relations offensive, in an attempt to dispel the facts about Mormonism before most of America could actually find out the truth. In other words, focus on *how we are just like you.*

A Mormon president would be a boon to the LDS church's public relations campaign to portray itself as a normal religion. When *Meridian* magazine asked LDS film director Mitch Davis in 2006 how a President Romney would help put a human face on Mormonism, Davis replied, "How could it not? It's one of the most visible jobs in the world! Having a Mormon in that office would be like having the Olympics in Salt Lake City everyday for four years in a row—eight years if he runs for reelection!" If Romney amassed a large war chest and an army of supporters, according to Davis, "He will go from dark horse to white knight."[344]

Davis directed the documentary *Could a Mormon be President?* and headed the political organization runmittrun.org. To Davis, a Mormon, a President Romney would "take our Church places it might not otherwise ever go in terms of world perception."[345] In essence, a Mormon in the White House would finally give the credence to a faux religion that it does not deserve. As to whether or not Evangelicals would support a Mormon candidate, Davis replied, "They are voting for someone whose values mirror their own, *never mind doctrinal quibbles.*" [Emphasis mine][346]

The LDS church certainly was gearing up for a closer look into its false religion with a Romney campaign on the horizon. While they claimed they remain "politically neutral," documents show otherwise.

In 2006 the *Boston Globe* broke a story regarding direct contact between the LDS church and the Romney campaign. According to the *Globe*, Romney's "political team has quietly consulted with leaders of the Mormon church to map out plans for a nationwide network of Mormon supporters to help Romney capture the presidency in 2008, according to interviews and written materials reflecting plans for the initiative."[347]

It is important to note that there are approximately 5.5 million Mormons in the United States. As it is fair to assume that approximately 80 percent of LDS members would vote for a Mormon as president, Romney would enjoy his own voting bloc of Mormons, as Obama did with African-Americans. The nationwide network put into place by the LDS church and the Romney campaign would help mobilize this bloc.

The "initiative" the *Globe* is referring to is the Mutual Values and Priorities (MVP), a program that would use Brigham Young University's forty business school alumni chapters throughout the United States to garner money and support for the Romney campaign. According to the *Globe*, members of both BYU and Romney's PAC sought help from "prominent Mormons to build the program."[348]

The *Globe* outlined the details of the meetings between the campaign and the church. On September 19, 2006 Romney's son, Josh Romney, and Romney's Commonwealth PAC paid consultant Don Stirling met in Jeffrey R. Holland's office. Holland, one of the Twelve Apostles and former BYU president, headed the MVP initiative for the LDS. Kem Gardner, one of Romney's largest donors, was also in attendance. According to the *Globe*, Holland "suggested using the alumni organization of the university's business school, the BYU Management Society, to build a network for Romney, according to the documents."[349]

Because the LDS church and BYU are considered non-profit and tax exempt, it is *against federal law* for either institution to advocate for a candidate or political party. Since the BYU Management Society is an official part of the BYU business school, it is also subject to the same federal election laws.[350]

On September 27, 2006 Spencer Zwick, a top Romney aide, and Romney's brother Scott Romney hosted a dinner at private club in Salt Lake City "for other prominent Mormons, where they discussed the initiative further," according to the *Globe*. Steve Albrecht, the associate dean of the BYU business school (The Marriott School of Management) attended the dinner.[351]

A little over a week later an email from Albrecht and Ned Hill, the dean of the business school, was sent to fifty members of the BYU Management Society and one hundred to BYU's National Advisory Council. Albrecht and Hill wrote in part:

> *Dear Marriott School Friend:*
>
> *We are writing to you as a friend to see if you have any interest in helping Governor Romney by volunteering to serve as a Community or Neighborhood Chair …*
>
> *Governor Romney's chances for success are significantly enhanced and energized by people, such as you, who are willing to help him at the grass-roots level throughout the United States.*[352]

Recipients of the email were told to contact Albrecht (at his school email) if they were interested. The email, sent from a BYU email address, was signed by Albrecht and Hill with their official BYU titles.[353]

Once again, it is important to note that because the LDS church and BYU are considered non-profit and tax exempt, it is *against federal law* for either institution to advocate for a candidate or political party. Since the BYU Management Society is an official part of the BYU business school, it is also subject to the same federal election laws.[354]

Initially when asked about LDS leaders coordinating efforts to support Romney, LDS media relations director Otterson said the claim was "nonsense" citing the so-called political neutrality of the LDS church. Otterson claimed the September 19 meeting was just "a handshake and a chat, literally a courtesy call." Otterson also claimed the meeting was at the request of Kem Garner (the large Romney donor) and that it was "simply a response to an appointment requested by an old friend."[355]

The *Globe* pointed out however, that in an earlier interview regarding the meeting Otterson stated Holland hosted the September 19 meeting to "make sure that they were doing this properly and to inform them of the church's political neutrality."[356]

Don Stirling, Romney's Commonwealth PAC paid consultant and attendee at the September 19 meeting, also had trouble with his recollection of the meeting. Initially he told the *Globe* that the LDS church had "absolutely no connection whatsoever" with the MVP initiative." When pressed about the September 19 meeting, Stirling "acknowledged the discussions but downplayed their significance," according to the *Globe*.[357]

According to the *Globe*, "Like Otterson, Stirling said that discussion with church leaders have focused on making sure the MVP effort did not run afoul of rules against political activism. He acknowledged however, that the *email from the BYU deans was part of the MVP initiative*." [Emphasis mine][358]

Once again, it is important to note that because the LDS church and BYU are considered non-profit and tax exempt, it is *against federal law* for either institution to advocate for a candidate or political party. Since the BYU Management Society is an official part of the BYU business school, it is also subject to the same federal election laws.[359] How can such intelligent, savvy business leaders not know?

BYU associate dean Albrecht said Kem Garner asked him to connect with his friends to support Romney and that he regretted sending out the email in BYU's capacity.[360]

In an effort to portray the MVP initiative as not exclusively LDS oriented, Stirling told the *Globe* that their efforts went beyond the LDS church and to members of other faiths. Stirling, however, could not recall any meetings with leaders of other religions regarding the program.[361]

"In fact, Romney's operatives, in their campaign to identify people in each state to serve as MVP leaders, appear to be focusing solely on members of the church," the *Globe* reported. "Documents show that at least two Latter-day Saints have already been tapped to help lead efforts in Utah and in California."[362]

Romney's PAC at the time was also focusing on prominent Mormons. The fundraising arm of the PAC led by Spencer Zwick also involved the efforts of his father, W. Craig Zwick, a member of the Mormon Church Quorum of the Seventy. Top Mormon business leaders tapped for cash included Sheri L. Dew, chief executive of Deseret Book Co., Mac Christensen, president of the Mormon Tabernacle Choir, and Richard Eyre, a prominent LDS writer.[363]

While the MVP program did not pan out as they had expected, the LDS church continued its PR campaign, especially after Romney's faith became more troubling to the American people.

One year later the LDS church established a twenty-four-hour hotline for political commentators and writers to contact regarding any questions they had about Mormonism. In addition to this pre-emptive damage control, high church officials met face to face with political reporters in Washington, D.C. and across the country to let them know "if you get to that point where you're going to write, please just include us."[364]

LDS members also attempted to shape public opinion by helping finance a 2007 PBS series titled *The Mormons*. Mormon donors to the series were able to put in their 20 percent in the funding. According to *Roll Call*, "The series, which generally portrays the Mormon church in a favorable light, aired at a time when polls and pundits indicate Romney's presidential campaign may not be able to overcome voters' lack of familiarity with the Mormon faith. The series included segments on polygamy and some other controversial aspects of the church's history."[365]

Mormons who helped fund the series included Romney donors such as Blake Roney, Steven Lund, Sterling Colton, and the J. Willard and Alice S. Marriott Foundation. 366

Members of the LDS voting bloc also contributed heavily to Romney's campaign. Utah, the state with the largest concentration of Mormons, was dubbed "the second most generous state" to Romney's campaign in April 2007, according to the Associated Press. The state which is seen as a "seldom go to state for politicians seeking money" seemed to have a large effect on presidential campaign money.[367]

With a handful of delegates and a population of only 2.6 million, Utah donated almost 92 percent of its contributions to the Romney campaign in the first quarter of the 2008 election. In the 2004 presidential election, Utah was fortieth in political contributions, the year of Romney they ranked thirteenth. In the first quarter of the 2008 election cycle alone, Utah's contributions to Romney were almost half the amount the state donated to all candidates in the entire 2004 election.[368]

According to Lindsey Renick Mayer of the Center for Responsive Politics, Salt Lake City "emerged as one of the most generous cities of the '08 election cycle, along with traditional toppers Los Angeles and New York."[369] Some Utah zip codes donated almost ten times the amount donated to Bush in both elections.[370] A zip code in Provo, Utah, in three months donated $209,105 to Romney while from 1999–2000 donated only $27,000 to Bush.[371]

In Idaho, the state with the second largest concentration of LDS members, Romney dwarfed other candidates, with $214,756 compared to only $11,700 to Hillary Clinton and $10,950 to Giuliani. Wyoming, coming in at third for LDS members, gave $32,250 to Romney and only $14,900 to Obama, $2,050 to Clinton, and $5,600 to Giuliani.[372]

While Romney had LDS members tucked tightly in his corner, he still would have to use his wealth to buy off support from otherwise "conservative Christians."

Romney's Commonwealth PAC Slush Fund

As stated in an earlier chapter, Romney's presidential campaign was on the ground running only months after he was sworn in as governor of Massachusetts in 2003. In 2004 Romney established his Commonwealth PAC. A PAC for presidential candidates is typical and legal, but Romney went a step further and established PAC affiliates in several key electoral states, such as Michigan, Iowa, New Hampshire, Alabama, and South Carolina.[373]

According to the *Politico*, The Commonwealth PACs complied with state rules rather than federal law, allowing some wealthy Romney backers to donate as much as $250,000 to his operation—well above the $2,300 federal cap for individual contributions."[374] Romney's state PAC affiliates bypassed federal law and served as merely a slush fund for Romney to buy endorsements and influence.

"The stated purpose of the Commonwealth PAC is to elect GOP candidates, but its indirect role of raising Romney's profile and amassing chits, or at the very least good will, is apparent from an analysis of PAC spending this year," wrote Brian C. Mooney of the *Boston Globe* in December 2006.[375]

In 2006 Mooney noted that Romney's PAC donated to 400 candidates in thirty-six states and 300 GOP state, county, and local committees. He donated $49,500 to the Michigan GOP, $20,000 to the New Hampshire GOP, and even $5,000 to South Carolina Senator Jim DeMint's campaign committee even though he was not up for reelection until 2010.[376]

The largest amount of Commonwealth PAC money went to candidates and party committees in the following key states: Iowa and Michigan ($276,165), New Hampshire ($164,150), South Carolina—the first southern state with a primary ($144,500) and Alabama—which moved up its primary to February ($143,500).[377]

Romney, surely realizing his pro-abortion and anti-family record in Massachusetts, his "Fee Fee" pro-tax reputation, as well as his membership in an anti-Christian church, also sought to buy his influence among Christian and conservative organizations.

In Massachusetts, Romney's foundation donated $15,000 to Massachusetts Citizens for Life, $10,000 to Massachusetts Citizens for Limited Taxation, and $10,000 to the Massachusetts Family Institute (which is affiliated with the Family Research Council and Focus on the Family) in December 2006.[378]

In March 2005, after Romney's convenient conversion to pro-life, the *Boston Globe* reported that "Marie Sturgis, legislative director of

Massachusetts Citizens for Life said she hasn't detected any change in Romney's stance. The group considers Romney to be an abortion rights supporter, as do national anti-abortion groups such as the Family Research Council."[379]

Yet in March 2007, the *New York Times* quoted Sturgis: "Granted, when he began his role as governor, he certainly was not with us … but toward the end, if you look at the record, especially in the stem cell debate, he certainly took the pro-life position consistently."[380]

In addition to Massachusetts groups, Romney's foundation also donated $25,000 to the conservative Heritage Foundation, which coordinated with him on his disastrous RomneyCare, $35,000 to the Federalist Society, a network of conservatives focused on judicial nominations, and $5,000 (along with another $5,000 from Evangelicals for Mitt) to help sponsor a dinner for the National Review's website. According to the *New York Times*, "*All the groups said he had never contributed before, and his foundation's public tax filings show no previous gifts to similar groups.*" [Emphasis mine][381]

Romney enjoyed a cover and positive comments from the *National Review*, and eventually received its endorsement in 2007. The Review itself had a hard time justifying Romney's record, instead blaming the liberal state of Massachusetts: "He [Romney] may not have thought deeply about the political dimensions of social issues until, as Governor, he was confronted with the cutting edge of social liberalism."[382]

In South Carolina, a key primary state, Romney's PAC donated $9,500 to the Palmetto state's GOP, $500 to South Carolina Citizens for Life, $1,000 to South Carolina's Club for Growth, $1,000 to South Carolinians for Responsible Government , $2,000 to South Carolina Victory, and $2,000 to Charleston school board candidates.[383]

Romney's money would also be used to buy support in other areas, particularly the conservative media.

Romney's Bain Capital Purchases Clear Channel—What Could Go Wrong?

Ask yourself if you have heard Rush Limbaugh, Sean Hannity, Glenn Beck, or anyone on Fox News Radio criticize Romney's abysmal pro-abortion and pro-gay marriage record, discuss his numerous flip-flops, or his lackluster economic record in Massachusetts. Why not? All of these hosts have something in common—their shows are all aired on Premiere Radio Networks, Inc., the number one radio network in the nation.[384]

Premiere is a subsidiary of media giant Clear Channel Communications, Inc. In 2006 Clear Channel announced that Thomas H. Lee Partners, L.P. and Bain Capital Partners, LLC had agreed to acquire Clear Channel. The deal was finalized in July 2008 for $17.9 billon.[385]

CNNMoney.com reported in 2007 that "Almost 43 percent of the Romney portfolio is tied up in private equity investments through Bain Capital Management."[386]

There is no doubt that Rush Limbaugh's show is the most popular talk radio program. Why then would Clear Channel bump Rush off one of its stations for a local host in the profitable time slot Rush occupied for fifteen years? In March 2010, Clear Channel announced that Massachusetts' station WRKO-AM would be replacing Rush with a local host; a guy by the name of Charley Manning, who just happened to have served as Romney's campaign advisor. Old trusty Rush was moved to a new station, WXKS-AM.[387]

Romney's Pro-life "Conversion"

Answering a Planned Parenthood questionnaire in 2002, Romney made his position on abortion well known:

> Question: Do you support the substance of the Supreme Court decision in Roe v. Wade?
>
> Romney's answer: Yes.[388]

When asked during the 1994 Senate campaign how Romney's pro-choice stance compared to his Democratic opponent Shannon O'Brien, his running mate, Kerry Healy stated, "There isn't a dime of difference between Mitt Romney's position on choice and Shannon O'Brien's."[389]

Romney's 2002 campaign website stated, "As Governor, Mitt Romney would protect the current pro-choice status quo in Massachusetts. No law would change. The choice to have an abortion is a deeply personal one. Women should feel free to choose based on their own beliefs, not the government's."[390]

Under Romney's Massachusetts health care plan an abortion costs a mere $50 co-pay, leaving taxpayers, even anti-abortion evangelical Christian taxpayers, on the hook for abortion on demand. RomneyCare also requires by law that Planned Parenthood plays an instrumental part in naming members to the policy board.[391]

Now Romney claims he is prolife. On February 21, 2007, Ruth Marcus wrote in the *Washington Post*, "Precisely two years ago [2005], the then governor of Massachusetts but already eyeing a 2008 presidential bid, sat in the coffee shop of a Washington hotel, *doing his best not to explain his views on abortion.*" [Emphasis mine][392]

Marcus went on to describe the 2005 meeting with Romney and a few of her colleagues from the *Post*. "It was also hard to see how a man with deeply held convictions on abortion rights—either for or against—could take a position so calibrated and inconclusive." Romney had told the group, *"I can tell you what my position is, and it's in a very narrowly defined sphere, as candidate for governor and as governor of Massachusetts, what I said to people was that I personally did not favor abortion, that I am personally pro-life.* However, as governor I would not change the laws of the commonwealth relating to abortion. Now I don't try and put a bow around that and say what does that mean you are—does that mean you're pro-life or pro-choice, because that whole package—meaning I am personally pro-life but I won't change the laws, you could describe that as—well, I don't think you can describe it in one hyphenated word." [Emphasis mine][393]

What? As an image consultant and strategist, I can tell you that this was a desperate attempt to throw the interviewer off by talking out of both sides of his mouth on the issue. No wonder the meeting left Marcus and her colleagues perplexed.

"It was hard to know what Romney actually thought about abortion rights other than that this was a political minefield it was best to avoid stepping into for as long as possible," Marcus recalled of the 2005 meeting. "Listening to Romney that day was like watching a chameleon in the fleeting moment that its color changes to suit its environment. Indeed, several months later, after vetoing a bill to expand access to emergency contraception, Romney wrote in the *Boston Globe* about how his views on the subject had 'evolved and deepened.'"[394]

Romney claims his "conversion" to pro-life came after a change of heart he had when meeting with a scientist at the Harvard Stem Cell Institute in November 2004. According to a 2006 interview Romney gave, the scientist, Dr. Douglas Melton, supposedly told Romney, "Look, you don't have to think about this stem cell research as a moral issue, because we kill the embryos after 14 days."[395]

In 2007 at a campaign stop in South Carolina, Romney recalled the meeting. "It struck me very powerfully at that point, that the Roe v. Wade approach so cheapened the value of human life that someone could think that it's not a moral issue to destroy embryos that have been created solely for the purpose of research," he said. "I said to my chief of staff and that's been two and a half years ago, I said to her, 'I want to make it very clear that I'm pro-life.'"[396]

There are several problems with this "conversion." First, if Romney was "personally pro-life" when he ran for governor and as governor of Massachusetts, why did he need a "conversion" in the first place?

Second, as Jennifer Rubin noted in the *Weekly Standard* in 2007, Dr. Melton denied Romney's account. According to Rubin, a spokesperson with the institute stated, "The words 'kill' and 'killing' are not in Dr. Melton's professional vocabulary, a vocabulary used to discuss finding cures for diseases in order to save lives."[397]

Third, just two months after Romney's "conversion," Governor Romney appointed a well-known pro-abortion Democrat to a judgeship. Matthew J. Nestor, a Democrat who ran as a "pro-choice" candidate for Massachusetts state representative, was given a lifetime appointment to the Somerville District Court in the Bay State. Republican strategist Keith Appell told ABC's Rick Klein and Jake Tapper in 2007, "This would appear to be evidence that he bowed to political pressures instead of following his supposed judicial philosophy, and that's what the conservative base is very leery of. If you espouse a certain judicial philosophy, your appointments should reflect it."[398] How about, if you have had such a profound conversion regarding the sanctity of human life, your actions should protect it?

Finally, if Romney's conversion was so profound because of what he witnessed with stem cell research that showed him how human life was "cheapened"—the hallmark of his conversion—why would he support the destruction of human life after his "conversion?"

In February of 2005, just three months after his so-called "conversion," the *New York Times* reported, "Mr. Romney said in an interview this week and again on Thursday that he supported allowing scientists embryos left over from in-vitro fertilization at fertility clinics, a position that goes beyond what President Bush supports. Fertility clinic embryos are likely 'going to be destroyed or discarded' anyway, the governor said, so using them for research 'does make sense.'"[399]

Human life, according to so-called "pro-life" Romney, is apparently not "cheapened" if it is going to be "destroyed or discarded anyway."

The *New York Times* was referring to a bill in Massachusetts introduced by state senate president Robert E. Travaglini that would further embryonic stem cell research in the state. Gubernatorial candidate Romney supported embryonic stem cell research, but Governor-wanting-to-be-President-Romney announced he would veto the bill, *not because it "cheapened" human life, but because the bill included cloning.* Romney told the *Times*, "For Ann and me, that's a line [cloning] we concurred we could not cross."[400] Perhaps Travaglini summed it up best when he said at the time, "There's evidence that he is clearly concerned with a national agenda."[401]

Romney also supported a bill in the US House of Representatives in 2005 that proposed lifting the ban on federal funding for embryonic stem cell research. Romney stated at the time, "The United States House of Representatives voted for a bill that was identical to what I proposed. They voted to provide for surplus embryos from the in-vitro fertilization processes to be used for research and experimentation. That's what I have said I support. That's what they have just supported." Romney, less than a year after his pro-life "conversion" because he saw how life had been "cheapened" when discussing stem cell research, supported using US taxpayer dollars to fund it. Conveniently, in 2007 Romney then claimed he opposed the bill.[402]

It appears Romney himself did not believe embryonic stem cells were not even human life at all; at least that is what he believed in May 2005, *six months after his "conversion."* When appearing in an interview with Boomer Esiason, a former NFL quarterback and supporter of embryonic stem cell research, Romney responded to the following question by Fox News' Chris Wallace:

Wallace: But if I may ask you, Governor, specifically, you don't see, as I understand it, the use of these leftover embryos in fertility clinics as destroying life?

Romney: That's right.[403]

In response to CBS' Katie Couric's question in December 2007—more than two years after his "conversion"—as to whether or not he supports the use of discarded embryos for stem cell research, Romney answered, "Yes, those embryos are commonly referred to as surplus embryos from in-vitro fertilization. Those embryos, I hope, could be available for adoption for people who would like to adopt embryos. But if a parent decides they would want to donate one of those embryos for purposes of research, in my view, that's acceptable. It should not be made against the law."[404]

Deal Hudson, director of InsideCatholic.com and The Morley Institute for Church and Culture, in December 2007 pointed out on his blog: "How can you consider a frozen embryo a moral entity capable of being adopted, while at the same time support the scientist who wants to cut the embryonic being into pieces? Even more, if Romney's conversion was about the 'cheapened value of human life,' how can he abide the thought of a parent donating 'one of those embryos' to be destroyed?"[405]

In a December 16, 2007, interview on *Meet the Press,* Romney was asked if he believed life began at conception. He replied: *"I do. I believe from a political perspective that life begins at conception."*[406]

If he believes life begins at conception, why would he support destroying it for research? Furthermore, how exactly do you define "life" from a "political perspective?" Basically what Romney is telling us in his statements is that he bases his stance on abortion and stem cell research on politics and not the sanctity of life.

It is clear that Romney's pro-life "conversion" had more to do with his presidential aspirations than the cheapening or destruction of human life. What is most striking is the "conservative, pro-life, pro-family" leaders that sold their souls out to Romney for reasons that boggle the mind.

The Wicked Web Mark DeMoss Wove

Mark DeMoss is probably the one person who was most able to pull the wool over the eyes of many evangelicals and turn them into Romney supporters. DeMoss is the son of Arthur S. DeMoss, a wealthy business man who made his fortune in the life insurance industry. After his father died, the Arthur S. DeMoss Foundation (which was first called the National Liberty Foundation) was established. This foundation gives millions of dollars in grants to religious organizations every year. For example, Franklin Graham's Samaritan's Purse received $975,495 in 2004, $5,420,744 in 2005, and $1,708,050 in 2007 from the foundation. Billy Graham's Evangelical Association received a $1 million grant in 2006 and Jay Sekulow's American Center for Law and Justice received a $1,056,275 grant in 2003. Since 2004 Chuck Colson's Prison Fellowship Ministries received over $5 million in grants from the Arthur S. DeMoss Foundation. Tony Perkin's Family Research Council also received $50,000 in 2005 and $10,000 in 2007.[407]

Mark DeMoss, a lawyer by trade, began his own public relations company, The DeMoss Group, in 1991, which boasts itself as the largest PR group that serves Christian organizations. Interestingly, all of the groups listed above, who received grants from the Arthur S. DeMoss Foundation, are or once were clients of Mark DeMoss (except for the Family Research Council). DeMoss's firm has worked with more than one hundred faith-based organizations since 1991, including Focus on the Family, Concerned Women for America, Liberty University, and Campus Crusade for Christ.[408] There is no doubt DeMoss is well-known among evangelicals, and if there were a man who held quite a bit of clout with evangelical Christians, DeMoss was the one.

In an April 2007 interview DeMoss chronicled his growing support of Romney: "I began to look into Mitt Romney and his life and his record and everything I could find out about him." DeMoss told the *National Review* in December 2006, "I had not met him, but his stand on traditional marriage as governor of Massachusetts convinced me he's a real leader."[409]

Did DeMoss even research an iota of Romney's record?

After discussing his blind admiration of Romney with a friend, a meeting was set up by the friend between DeMoss and Romney. According to DeMoss, "I said 'I'd like to help you.' Romney responded 'Well, what kinds of things can you do to help?'" DeMoss subsequently offered to amass a group of evangelical leaders to meet with Romney, sending out forty-five letters to Christian leaders throughout the country inviting them to the Romney home in October 2006 for a meeting. No one can confirm who received the letters and who attended is sketchy. DeMoss estimates that approximately fifteen leaders attended.[410]

According to reports, some of those who attended were Jerry Falwell (DeMoss' former boss), Gary Bauer, Jay Sekulow (American Center for Law and Justice), Franklin Graham, Richard Lee from First Redeemer Church near Atlanta, Richard Land from the Southern Baptist Convention, Lou Sheldon from the American Values Coalition, and Paula White from Without Walls International Church.[411]

According to DeMoss, "I had anticipated that there would be a real concentrated discussion about his faith and about what he believed theologically. Instead, only two people, there were only two questions in the three hours, about what he believed theologically, about God and Jesus, or how you go to heaven. Only two questions."[412]

When asked about his faith Romney "described it in terms similar to those he used during an interview that aired in November [2006] on *The 700 Club*, the news program hosted by Pat Robertson on the Christian Broadcasting Network," according to the *National Review*. In that *700 Club* interview, Romney stated, "I think Americans want people of faith to lead their country. Generally they don't care so much about the particular brand of faith if the people that they're looking at have the same values they have. And people of my faith have the values of other great religions that are represented here in this country."[413]

In a nutshell, presidential candidate Romney began courting Christian leaders with a page right out of the Mormon playbook: ignore the facts, the history, and the agenda, and focus on how we both share the same family values.

DeMoss threw in one more ploy: If Romney is not the nominee, Hillary Clinton will win.

After his meeting with Romney and other Christian leaders, DeMoss penned a letter to 150 influential Christian leaders urging them to support

Romney. Below is DeMoss' letter. For the sake of DeMoss' own ignorance or apathy toward Romney's beliefs and record, my comments are interspersed throughout the letter.

DeMoss' Letter[414]

To: Conservative & Evangelical Leaders
From: Mark DeMoss (Personally)
Date: October 9, 2007
Subject: The 2008 Presidential Election

In about 100 days we will likely have a Republican nominee for president. Most political observers believe it a near certainty that this nominee will face Hillary Clinton in the general election. While most people think this election cycle started too early, I'm finding that few people realize the primaries are almost upon us—and how compacted the primary calendar is.

Within about 30 days after the last college football bowl game is played, primaries (and an all-important caucus) will be held in Iowa, Nevada, New Hampshire, Michigan, South Carolina, Alabama, Arizona, Arkansas, Delaware, Florida, Illinois, Missouri, New Mexico, North Carolina, Oklahoma, Utah and West Virginia! (At least a dozen of these will fall on the same day—February 5, 2008.)

As certain as it seems that Hillary will represent the Democratic Party, it now appears the GOP representative will be either Mayor Rudy Giuliani or Governor Mitt Romney (based on polls in early states, money raised and on hand, staff and organization, etc.). And, if it is not Mitt Romney, we would, for the first time in my memory, be faced with a general election contest between two "pro-choice" candidates.

If Romney did not win the nomination, we would be forced with a general election contest between "two 'pro-choice' candidates"? Let's review Romney's pro-choice record.

- After a phony pro-life conversion based on embryonic stem cell research, he stated that such research does not destroy human life, even though he believes life begins at conception from a "political perspective" and continued to support such Nazi-like research.

- He instituted a health care program in Massachusetts that includes a $50 co-pay for abortions at taxpayers' expense after his "pro-life conversion."

- He gave Planned Parenthood an instrumental role on the policy board in his Massachusetts health care plan after his "pro-life conversion."

- He appointed a pro-choice judge to a lifetime appointment on a Massachusetts court after his "pro-life conversion."

I decided over a year ago to help Mitt Romney; and while I have not been (and will not be) paid one dollar, I have worked harder on behalf of a candidate this past year than in any election of my lifetime. Why? In large part because the next president is almost certain to appoint two to four Supreme Court justices.

Let's review Romney's judicial record. Romney.

- Altered marriage licenses and ordered judges to perform homosexual marriages in the state of Massachusetts when no law required him to do so, earning him the title of the Father of Gay Marriage in America.

- Awarded a Massachusetts district court judgeship to Stephen Albany, part of the Massachusetts Lesbian and Gay Bar Association and a proponent of the repealing of sodomy laws in the Bay State.

- Appointed a pro-choice judge to a lifetime appointment on a Massachusetts court after his "pro-life conversion."

When I began surveying the landscape of potential candidates I was looking for three things:

1. Someone who most closely shared my values;

The values in the Mormon church are by and large, good values, however it is a smokescreen to keep people in the cult under the veil of "good deeds" and "right behaviors" in order to position the Mormon church as an "angel of light" to propagate its false, blasphemous and anti-Christ religion for financial gain at the complete expense of its followers' salvation.

> *2. Someone who has proven experience and competence to lead and manage large enterprises;*

Let's review a few points of Romney's time at Bain Capital highlighted in an earlier chapter:

- While many of the companies Romney and his team managed did wind up healthier and more profitable, "in some cases Romney's team closed US factories, causing hundreds of layoffs or pocketed huge fees shortly before companies collapsed."
- In 2007, former Bain managing director Marc B. Wolpow told the *Los Angeles Times,* "They're whitewashing his career now … We had a scheme where the rich got richer. I did it, and I feel good about it. But I am not planning to run for office."

> *3. Someone who can actually win the nomination (without which it is obviously impossible to challenge or beat Hillary Clinton, or any other democrat—people who certainly don't share our values).*
>
> *So how did I settle on Mitt Romney? After spending months researching his life and his record, and hours with him (and his wife and staff) in his home, his office and on the road, I am convinced his values practically mirror my own—values about the sanctity of life, the sacredness of marriage, the importance of the family, character and integrity, free enterprise, and smaller government.*

Let's review Romney's values:

- After a phony pro-life conversion based on embryonic stem cell research, stated that such research does not destroy human life, even though he believes life begins at conception from a "political perspective," and continued to support such Nazi-like research.
- Instituted a health care program in Massachusetts that includes a $50 co-pay for abortions at taxpayers' expense after his "pro-life conversion."

- Gave Planned Parenthood an instrumental role on the policy board in his Massachusetts health care plan after his "pro-life conversion."

- Appointed a pro-choice judge to a lifetime appointment on a Massachusetts court after his "pro-life conversion."

- Altered marriage licenses and ordered judges to perform homosexual marriages in the state of Massachusetts when no law required him to do so, earning him the title of the Father of Gay Marriage in America.

- Awarded a Massachusetts district court judgeship to Stephen Albany, part of the Massachusetts Lesbian and Gay Bar Association and a proponent of the repealing of sodomy laws in the Bay State.

- Increased funding for the homosexual indoctrination of children in Massachusetts schools.

- Did not support the Bush tax cuts for which *uber* liberal Barney Frank stated he was "very pleased."

- Raised taxes and or fees *seven* times as governor of Massachusetts.

> *But more than one candidate shares my values; which leads me to my second criterion.*
>
> *The President of the United States is the CEO of the largest enterprise on planet earth, presiding over a nearly $3 trillion budget and some 2 million employees (the size of the workforces of General Motors, General Electric, Citigroup, Ford, Hewlett-Packard and AT&T combined). Mitt Romney has already been the chief executive of one of the most successful investment management firms in the world—Bain Capital, with nearly $6 billion under management;*

Let's review, as stated in an earlier chapter, how Romney's Bain Capital managed some of its companies:

In 1997 Romney and his team purchased a stake in DDi Corporation. Bain Capital earned $36 million after they took the company public in

2000. Romney sold his shares for $4.1 million. Soon after, however, DDi saw its stock collapse and eventually filed for bankruptcy in 2003, when 2,100 workers were laid off.

Bain and DDi eventually settled a class action lawsuit that awarded $4.4 million to shareholders. (Romney was not named in the suit.) According to the *Los Angeles Times*, the suit "argued that *DDi was poorly managed and 'hemorrhaging cash' before the stock offering, court records show.*" [Emphasis mine]

> *a Winter Olympic Games (Salt Lake City, 2002), where he turned a $379 million operating deficit into one of the most profitable Games ever;*

Let's review Romney's Olympic record as highlighted in an earlier chapter:

- "A *Globe* review of archived [Olympic] records showed the organizing committee already had secured commitments of nearly $1 billion in revenues, including the $445 million as its share of the NBC contract and nearly $450 million in contracts for sponsorships, before Romney arrived."
- The amount of federal taxpayer money spent in Utah was more than "the amount spent by lawmakers to support all seven Olympic Games held in the United States since 1904—combined. In inflation-adjusted numbers."
- "Federal Spending for the Salt Lake City games will average $625,000 for each of the 2,400 athletes who will compete. (Not a penny of it will go to the athletes.) That's a 996 percent increase from the $57,000 average for the 1996 Atlanta Olympics. It's a staggering 5,582 percent jump from the $11,000 average for the 1984 Summer Games in Los Angeles. Again, these are inflation-adjusted numbers."
- "Utah's five-member congressional delegation has used the Olympics to drain money from an unprecedented number of federal departments, agencies and offices—some three dozen in all, from the Office of National Drug Control Policy to the Agriculture Department."

> *and the state of Massachusetts, where he eliminated a $3 billion deficit without raising taxes or borrowing money.*

Let's review Governor Romney's record in Massachusetts:

- According to Reuters, "The $3 billion deficit projected by Romney and state legislators in January 2003 at the start of his Administration never rose that high because a surge in capital gains taxes more than halved the shortfall to $1.3 billion."
- President of the Massachusetts Taxpayer Foundation, Michael Widmer told Reuters in 2008, "There's never been under his [Romney's] watch an economic turnaround to speak of ... We added a few jobs over the last three years of his tenure, but very few. He also raised corporate taxes and the (deficit) gap turned out to be less than $3 billion."
- Romney proposed or raised so many fees, he earned the nickname "Fee-Fee." Almost no Massachusetts citizen was immune from the fees he imposed. "Romney and Democratic lawmakers ended up approving hundreds of millions in higher fees and fines, making it more expensive to use an ice skating rink, register a boat, take the bar exam, get a duplicate driver's license, file a court case, install underground storage tanks, sell cigarettes or alcohol, comply with air quality rules and transport hazardous waste," according to the Associated Press. Sound similar to the Obama administration?
- Writing on the Official Blog of the National Taxpayers Union in 2008, Sam Batkins pointed out "Romney raised taxes or fees seven times in Mass, but only cut taxes three times ... Overall, during Romney's four years in office, taxes increased $175 million. This total is nothing compared to some tax-hikers like Jon Corzine (D-NJ), but Romney doesn't have a great record as a tax cutter."
- According to the National Taxpayers Union, under Romney, "spending in the Bay State rose 20.7 percent (from $22,848 billion to $27,588 billion)."
- During Romney's term Massachusetts was in the bottom three of the nation for job creation, only above Michigan and post-Katrina Louisiana.

That kind of experience convinces me Mitt Romney could lead, manage and govern America during a critical time in world history. But can he actually win (my third criterion)? After he was the runaway winner of the important Iowa straw poll in August, Time magazine's political columnist Joe Klein wrote, "Romney now has to be considered a strong favorite to win the Republican nomination. And another prediction: if nominated, Romney will be formidable in the general election."

Let's discuss Romney's straw poll "win" in Iowa:

According to *Harpers,* "In an especially calculated move the Romney campaign has invested heavily in winning local straw polls around the country, which don't necessarily measure popular support as much as organization and financial resources. Nonetheless, victory can win a news cycle's worth of attention and hence be used to hype the candidate's supposed popularity and momentum."[415]

In fact, Romney had spent so much money in the Ames straw poll in Iowa, McCain and Giuliani backed out. The campaign purchased tickets to the event, chartered a large amount of buses, and provided a barbeque lunch to in which to draw people.[416] The campaign also paid 60 "super volunteers" an average of $500 to $1000 a month to "talk him [Romney] up."[417]

According to the *Washington Post*, "Officials with other campaigns have complained privately that some local party activists have said they would like to support their candidate but felt compelled to back Romney because of the stipends he was offering."[418] It is estimated that Romney spent a minimum of $650 per vote in the Ames straw poll.[419] Such buying of votes led to an Internet blog, *Iowa Values Not for Sale*, criticizing the tactics.[420]

Like it or not (and most of us don't), these campaigns have become obscenely expensive. It has been estimated that the two party nominees may well spend in excess of $100 million in the primaries, and several times that in the general election. One insider told me Hillary may spend half a billion dollars before it's over! This means a successful candidate must be able to come up with this kind of money. Through *the first three quarterly reporting periods, Republican candidates reported total revenues as follows:*

- *Mitt Romney: $62.4 million*
- *Rudy Giuliani: $46.1*
- *John McCain: $30.5*
- *Fred Thompson: $12.8*
- *Ron Paul: $8.0*
- *Sam Brownback: $3.3 (through 2 quarters; 3rd quarter number had not been reported yet)*
- *Mike Huckabee: $2.3*

These numbers are important for many reasons. It takes money to hire staff, recruit volunteers, send out mailings, travel the country, organize events (Mitt told me recently he had done 462 events just in Iowa so far!) and to buy TV commercial time. CNN recently reported that Romney just became the first candidate in history to buy 10,000 TV commercials at this point in the presidential campaign (by comparison, John McCain was purchasing his first commercials the same weekend).

If one is to base selecting a candidate on which campaign has the most money in its coffers at the time, consider that by the end of 2007, just a little over two months after this letter was written, Romney had spent $35.4 million of his own money.[421] According to the *Politico* in October of 2007, the same month this letter was written, "To date, 27 percent of Romney's receipts have come from his own pocket."[422]

Gov. Romney is also leading by 4%–11% or more in polls in a number of early states, such as Iowa, New Hampshire, Michigan, Nevada—and one recent poll now shows him leading in South Carolina. Historically, a candidate who wins the Iowa caucuses and several of the early primaries benefits from a tremendous amount of national exposure and fundraising momentum.

We know about the Ames Straw Poll. Now let's review the Family Research Council's Values Voter Conference Straw Poll in October 2007.

Attendees of the conference and other campaigns did not realize a little known loophole existed in the voting procedures that would allow non-attendees to vote online. According to the *Politico*, "Romney's campaign had recognized the loophole ahead of time and sent mass email Thursday alerting social conservatives that the FRC was 'allowing people to vote whether or not they attend the conference.'"[423]

The email stated, "Let me tell you how simple this is! Just go to Fraction.org and click on the large banner 'Participate in the 2008 American Values Straw Poll.'"[424]

To become eligible to vote online, voters paid a minimum of one dollar, which went to Family Research Council's FRC Action. According to the *Politico,* FRC's Tony Perkins "said FRC had stuck to the rules of the straw poll … and could not stop candidates from influencing results."[425]

> *As this race heats up and we approach the final stretch of the nominating process, I have three growing concerns:*
>
> *1. Currently, conservatives (whether evangelical or not) are dividing their support among several candidates. In the long run, this only helps Rudy Giuliani, who clearly does not share our values on so many issues.*

At least Rudy Giuliani has authentic qualities and was not muddying his positions on issues to gain votes. Romney, however, is and will become *all things to all people* to achieve his ends. He looks great, he talks a good game by telling us everything we want to hear, banking on the Obama "messiah" strategy to elevate himself to the highest office in the land. If voters fall for the Obama-Romney ploy and strategy, will they not just gain the same old hope and change once again?

> *2. Talk of a possible third party candidate draft movement only helps Giuliani (or, worse yet, Clinton), in my view. While I wholeheartedly agree with Dr. James Dobson that not having a pro-life nominee of either major party presents an unacceptable predicament, I would rather work hard to ensure we do nominate a pro-life candidate than to launch an 11th-hour third party campaign. Mike Huckabee affirmed this concern when he told the Washington Post last week, "I think a third party only helps elect Hillary Clinton."*

Let's review "pro-life" Romney:

- Believes that life begins at conception from a "political perspective," yet supports the destruction of human life because it is going to be "destroyed or discarded anyway."
- Claimed in 2005 that while he was running for governor in 2002 he was "personally pro-life" yet still had a pro-life "conversion" in 2004.

How would we know what Obama-Romney will do once in office regarding life issues or any other issues? Again, we have been down this road with Obama.

3. Perhaps most troubling to me is the idea I keep hearing that electing someone like Hillary Clinton would "actually be good for the conservative movement," since it will "galvanize our forces, enable us to build our mailing lists and raise more money … therefore, I'm not going to vote for anyone this time around." Well, I am not willing to risk negatively changing the Supreme Court, and our entire judicial system, for the next 30 years in exchange for building our conservative mailing lists and operating budgets for the next four or eight years. That, in my opinion, is selfish, short-sighted and dangerous.

Did DeMoss research Romney's record on judicial appointments?

According to the *Boston Globe*, "Governor Mitt Romney, who touts his conservative credentials to out-of-state Republicans, has passed over GOP lawyers for three-quarters of the thirty-six judicial vacancies he has faced, instead tapping registered Democrats or independents—including two gay lawyers who have supported same sex rights …"[426]

Governor Romney also did not fill judicial vacancies when leaving office, wholeheartedly handing his liberal predecessor the appointments. Editor of *Lawyers Weekly* Davis Yas told the *Boston Globe* at the time, "It is a tradition for governors to use that power to appoint judges aggressively in the waning moments of their administration."[427] Apparently judicial appointments meant very little to Romney.

Here is what I believe is at stake in this election:

☐ *Someone is almost certain to appoint two, three, or four justices to the Supreme Court. Do we want that person to be Hillary Clinton, Rudy Giuliani or Mitt Romney?*

☐ *Someone will cast vision and lead Congress on matters of national security, including securing our borders against illegal immigration. Should that be Hillary, Rudy or Mitt?*

☐ *Someone will deal with the definition of marriage in America—and will either defend and model a faithful marriage and strong family, or not. Who should that person be?*

☐ *Someone will either defend unborn life—or defend those who place their rights and desires above those who can't defend themselves. Would we prefer that Clinton, Giuliani or Romney be in that position?*

You have got to be kidding me! From the life issue to defining marriage to appointing judges, Romney has already vividly and emphatically, by his record, shown to be the purveyor of all by his undeniable deeds as governor of the state of Massachusetts. Are we to turn a blind eye to his deeds as the father of what true conservatives stand against and just elect him because he may be "electable"? It is stunning to see DeMoss justify supporting a man with a track record of everything against what the DeMoss family has stood for, for political gain.

[By the way, I am also troubled by skeptical sentiment in some corners about the legitimacy and sincerity of Gov. Romney's "conversion" on the abortion issue. I always thought the pro-life movement existed for the purpose of influencing hearts and minds on the issue of life, and historically, we have celebrated converts to our side. We embraced Ronald Reagan (who signed a liberal abortion law as governor of California), Norma McCorvey ("Jane Roe"), and others—and I am prepared to accept and embrace Mitt Romney. I've also told him he will be held accountable on this if elected.]

How sincere is Romney's "conversion" to pro-life when it is based on stem cell research, which he supports. Let's review what Romney believes a human embryo is after his conversion:

Romney: "I do. I believe from a political perspective that life begins at conception."

Chris Wallace: "But if I may ask you, Governor, specifically, you don't see, as I understand it, the use of these leftover embryos in fertility clinics as destroying life?"

Romney: That's right.

☐ *Someone will need to deal with radical Islamic Jihadists and the threat they pose to our nation. As evangelicals, do we want to entrust Hillary Clinton, Rudy Giuliani or Mitt Romney with that critical assignment?*

I doubt that Hillary Clinton and Rudy Giuliani embrace a common relationship between their faiths and Islam as the Mormons do such as plural marriage, false prophets, plural Gods, "special knowledge," bizarre promises for the afterlife, special "inerrant" books that supersede the Bible, the goal of spreading their religions throughout the world to dominate, works based salvation, little or no authority for women, and more.

Maybe DeMoss has a point. Mitt Romney could probably find more religious common ground with Islamists than Christians.

☐ *Finally, someone will either welcome evangelicals and people of faith into the White House and their administration; or shut them out of deliberations and consideration for various appointments. Would Hillary, Rudy or Mitt be most accepting of evangelicals and people of faith?*

Would you rather have a member of a well-masked cult who has "special knowledge" and superiority through such, as well as divine direction from a false prophet, who yes, may welcome evangelicals, but because of his special knowledge and his relationship with the prophet of the Mormon Church who he *must* follow, would not take council from them in the White House?

Now, I fully recognize some evangelicals take issue with me for supporting a Mormon for the office of president, and I respect their concerns. Indeed, I had to deal with the same concerns in my own heart before offering to help Gov. Romney. But I concluded that I am more concerned that a candidate shares my values than he shares my theology.

Romney's values are his theology, but one needs to know on what these values are based. If DeMoss read the first part of this book, he may be enlightened with the truth.

> *(If I believed similar theology was paramount in a president, I would be writing this memo urging support of Mike Huckabee.) As a Southern Baptist evangelical and political conservative, I am convinced I have more in common with most Mormons than I do with a liberal Southern Baptist, Methodist, Roman Catholic, or a liberal from any other denomination or faith group.*

My question to DeMoss: Are you going to become a God, as Romney believes that Jesus became God, and receive your own planet or kingdom and populate it with spirit children? Will you change your faith to believe that Satan was Jesus' brother in the fairytale pre-existence? Have you decided that the virgin birth was not really a virgin birth, but Jesus/God was made from a physical sexual union with Mary? Do you really have more in common with most Mormons? Seriously?

> *The question shouldn't be, "could I vote for a Mormon," but, "could I vote for this Mormon?" After all, Mitt told me there are Mormons he couldn't vote for (I presume Harry Reid, for example); and there are Southern Baptists I couldn't vote for (Jimmy Carter, Bill Clinton, Al Gore, to name a few).*
>
> *Incidentally, if one-third of "white evangelicals" voted for Bill Clinton the second time (a Southern Baptist who doesn't share our values on most issues), can we not at least consider supporting a Mormon who does share our values? Noted conservative columnist Robert Novak wrote this month that Mitt Romney is "the only Republican candidate unequivocally opposed to marriage and the only one who signed the no tax increase pledge."*

Let's review Romney's record on no tax increase pledges:

- In 2002, Romney refused to sign a no new taxes pledge while running for governor.
- Romney did not support the Bush tax cuts for which *uber* liberal Barney Frank stated he was "very pleased."

- Romney raised taxes and or fees *seven* times as governor of Massachusetts.
- In 2007 Presidential candidate Romney signed a "no new taxes" pledge:
- "Almost five years after he refused to sign a 'no new taxes' pledge during his campaign for governor, Mitt Romney announced yesterday that he had done just that, as his campaign for the 2008 Republican presidential nomination began in earnest" (*Boston Globe*, January 2007).

  On May 17, my friend of nearly 30 years, Jerry Falwell, went to Heaven. In addition to being my first employer and like a second father following the death of my father in 1979, Jerry was my political mentor in many ways. I learned from him, some 25 years ago, the value of working closely with people of other faiths and religions who shared our convictions about the sanctity of life, support for the state of Israel, the sacredness of marriage and the importance of the family unit, the dangers of pornography, and the value of God in public life. Consequently, the Moral Majority (and many subsequent organizations) was built with coalitions of evangelicals and likeminded Roman Catholics, Jews and yes, Mormons.

Catholics and Jews and Evangelicals do not believe that they will become Gods, as Jesus became God.

> *Just about six months before his death, Jerry accepted my invitation to a meeting with Gov. Romney at his home outside Boston. He joined me, and about 15 other evangelicals, for an intimate discussion with the Governor and his wife Ann. Jerry was one of several that day who said, "Governor, I don't have a problem with your being Mormon, but I want to ask you how you would deal with Islamic jihadists ... or with illegal immigration ... or how you would choose justices for the Supreme Court" and so on.*
>
> *While Jerry Falwell never told me how he intended to vote in the upcoming election, I think I know how he would not have voted. I also know he would not have "sat this one out" and given up on the Supreme Court for a generation.*

Let's review how imperative judicial appointments were to Governor Romney. Romney:

- Seventy-five percent of Romney's judicial appointments were registered democrats or independents instead of Republicans. Two appointments were gay lawyers who expressed their support of same sex rights.
- Did not fill judicial vacancies when leaving office, passing his liberal predecessor the appointments, even though "It is a tradition for governors to use that power to appoint judges aggressively in the waning moments of their administration."
- When he did appoint judges, he appointed a pro-choice Democrat as well as a member of the Massachusetts Gay and Lesbian Bar Association.

> *I am wholeheartedly convinced that Mitt Romney can be trusted to uphold the values and principles most important to me as a political conservative and an evangelical Christian. Again, I am not being paid, and I am not interested in a job in a Romney Administration (I would not accept one even if offered, as I'm still raising three teenagers). Neither is my public relations firm involved in any way. I am involved because I believe the stakes are high, perhaps higher than ever before in my life.*

Paul Weyrich, who signed the letter (discussed in an earlier chapter) to then Governor Romney urging him to sign an executive order to rescind gay marriage in Massachusetts, fell under the Romney spell and became a supporter. However, when discovering the truth about Romney, he publically repented. I was in that private meeting room in New Orleans when Weyrich asked for forgiveness to a room full of the top conservative leaders in the country for supporting Romney. Weyrich had a true realization of the deception that had fallen over him and other conservative leaders. However, he was humble enough to apologize and ask for forgiveness. He kept tearfully saying, "I didn't know" over and over again. DeMoss just might learn something from the great cofounder of the Moral Majority, who was humble enough to repent shortly before his death for supporting Romney. DeMoss and Tony Perkins could greatly benefit from a dose of the same humility and repentance.

In closing, I would respectfully urge fellow conservatives and evangelicals to consider doing the following:

1. Pray fervently for this election.

2. Follow the news and the primary calendar; being familiar with the process and aware of the urgency of the schedule.

3. Encourage people to vote and not "sit this one out," merely because they aren't excited about a candidate.

4. Encourage people to support the candidate who best represents their values; whether or not they share your theology.

5. Galvanize support around Mitt Romney, so Rudy Giuliani isn't the unintended beneficiary of our divided support among several other candidates—or, worse yet, so we don't abdicate the presidency (and the future of the Supreme Court) over to Hillary Clinton.

I believe we can make a difference—the difference in this election—and if Mitt Romney should become the 44th president of the United States, I'm confident he won't forget how he got there.

"I'm confident he won't forget how he got there." Do I hear the hint of paybacks?

I hope you'll join me. Thank you for your consideration of these things. /rmd

Unfortunately, too many Christian leaders fell prey to DeMoss' inducements. According to John J. Miller of the *National Review* in December 2006, "Even within the politics of Republican primaries, evangelicals seem more concerned about finding conservatives who can win elections than politicians who are theologically pure."[428] Selecting a candidate solely on his or her electability is why we have the current problem in Washington, D.C. Worse, many Christian leaders not only ignored Romney's anti-Christian faith, but his record on family values that are directly opposed to their own as well.

Let's review. Romney:

- Claimed in 2005 that while he was running for governor in 2002 he was "personally pro-life" yet still had a pro-life "conversion" in 2004.
- After a phony pro-life conversion based on embryonic stem cell research, stated that such research does not destroy human life, even though he believes life begins at conception, and continued to support such Nazi-like research.
- Instituted a health care program in Massachusetts that includes a $50 co-pay for abortion at taxpayer's expense after his "pro-life conversion."
- Gave Planned Parenthood an instrumental role on the policy board in his Massachusetts health care plan after his "pro-life conversion."
- Appointed a pro-choice judge to a lifetime appointment on a Massachusetts court after his "pro-life conversion."
- Altered marriage licenses and ordered judges to perform homosexual marriages in the state of Massachusetts when no law required him to do so; earning him the title of the Father of Gay Marriage in America.
- Awarded a Massachusetts district court judgeship to Stephen Albany, part of the Massachusetts Lesbian and Gay Bar Association and a proponent of the repealing of sodomy laws in the Bay State.
- Increased funding for the homosexual indoctrination of children in Massachusetts schools.
- Did not support the Bush tax cuts for which *uber* liberal Barney Frank stated he was "very pleased."
- Raised taxes and or fees *seven* times as governor of Massachusetts.

Regrettably, many Christian leaders, whether they received donations from DeMoss' father's foundation or not, chose to cross the street to

Romney without looking either way—at his Mormonism or his record—all in the name of winning elections and sacrificing principles.

Lou Sheldon, chairman of the Traditional Values Coalition and a Romney adviser, told the *Telegraph* in 2007, "I've taken an enormous amount of criticism and hate from my fellow evangelicals for supporting Mitt Romney."[429] Perhaps that criticism is warranted.

In 2005 while Romney was governor of Massachusetts, Sheldon himself criticized Romney's own Department of Public Health for taking part in *The Little Black Book: Queer in the 21st Century.* The book, which included graphic homosexual acts such as fisting was distributed to middle and high school students at a Gay, Lesbian and Straight Education Network conference at a Massachusetts high school.[430]

Only after the book encountered a national outcry did Romney state that it was "grossly inappropriate." No Department of Health employees were reprimanded because of the book, and Governor Romney never called for any oversight on how the department used public funds.[431]

In an article Sheldon wrote regarding the book, "If any parent needs a strong argument for opposing the legalization of homosexual marriage in their state, what's happening in Massachusetts should be enough." He went on, "The exposure of ***The Little Black Book*** should serve as a wakeup call to millions of parents who think that homosexual marriage will make little difference in their lives." Sheldon also wrote, "Is sodomy really a 'family value' that should be promoted in public schools? The answer should be obvious—except to the most perverted in our culture."[432]

It is obvious Sheldon knew the Romney administration had a part in the book when he wrote, "*The Little Black Book* was produced by the Boston-based AIDS Action Committee with the help of the Massachusetts Department of Public Health and Boston Public Health Commission."[433] Apparently Romney's lack of action in the matter, as well as his administration's record on pushing the homosexual agenda in schools, and awarding an advocate of repealing sodomy laws a judgeship, did not bother Sheldon.

Incidentally, the original piece written by Sheldon has been scrubbed from the Traditional Values Coalition website, but was found on a Salon.com blog.

Tony Perkins of the Family Research Council told the *National Review* in 2006, "He talks about core values that other Republicans won't touch, which is great, but I am troubled by his changing views on abortion."[434] Perkins told the *Politico* in June 2007 "The 20 years I've been involved in politics, the life issue has been at the very top. How could I turn my back on that?"[435]

In 2006 when a 1994 letter that Romney wrote to Log Cabin Republicans stating "as we seek to establish full equality for America's gay and lesbian citizens, I will provide more effective leadership than my opponent [Ted Kennedy]" was revealed, Perkins again was troubled. Perkins told the *New York Times,* "This is quite disturbing. This type of information is going to create a lot of problems for Governor Romney."[436]

Perkins should have also been troubled by Romney's view on embryonic stem cell research. According to his own Family Research Council website, the FRC "opposes research that destroys, harms or manipulates an embryonic human being."[437]

Yet Perkins chose to turn his back on the life issue as well as the traditional family by calling Romney a "friend of the pro-family movement."[438]

Richard Land of the Southern Baptist Convention also commented on the Log Cabin letter in 2006, telling the Associated Press, "Christians believe in conversion, and so they're open to listen, but when a candidate 12 years ago says he's more of a champion on issues than Ted Kennedy, that needs to be explained."[439] Although Romney's campaign stated that Romney's position on gay marriage had not changed, Land certainly did.

On February 11, 2007, Land told the *Boston Globe*, "If his [Romney's] main competition turns out to be someone who is even more pro-life, then this [his position on embryonic stem cell research] is going to be really problematic. If his main competition is Rudy Giuliani, it won't matter."[440]

Experimenting on and destroying human life "won't matter" if you pick the winning horse?

Land also told the *Washington Post* on February 13, 2007, "Winability is a bigger issue in this campaign because the Darth Vader-like specter of a Hillary Clinton presidency ... [Evangelicals] "want the most socially conservative candidate they can find, who can win."[441]

Dr. John Willke, the founder of the pro-life movement and once president of the National Right to Life Committee, said Romney "is the only candidate who can lead our pro-life and pro-family conservative movement victory in 2008."[442]

According to a 2007 letter sent by the National Right to Life Committee to the US Senate, "Each human being begins as a human embryo, male or female. The government should not fund research that requires the killing of living members of the species homo sapiens."[443] Despite the fact that Romney stated that embryonic stem cell research is not destroying human life, advocated for federal funding of stem cell research and stated that if parents wanted to donate embryos for Frankenstein-like research that was perfectly fine with Dr. Willke.

Focus on the Family's website states, "Focus on the Family opposes stem cell research using human embryos. In order to isolate and culture embryonic stem cells, a living human embryo must be killed. It is never morally or ethically justifiable to kill one human being in order to benefit another. By requiring the destruction of embryos—the tiniest human beings—embryonic stem cell research violates the medical ethic 'Do no harm.'"[444]

The website also states FOF's position on marriage: "We believe that the institution of marriage is a sacred covenant designed by God to model the love of Christ for His people and to serve both the public and private good as the basic building block of human civilization. Marriage is intended by God to be a thriving, lifelong relationship between a man and a woman enduring through trials, sickness, financial crises, and emotional stresses. Therefore, Christians are called to defend and protect God's marriage design and to minister in Christ's name to those who suffer the consequences of its brokenness."[445]

Yet, despite the fact that Romney supports embryonic stem cell research (even though he believes life begins at conception), instituted a health care program in Massachusetts that includes a $50 co-pay for abortion at taxpayer's expense after his "conversion," instituted the first homosexual marriages in the United States with no legal obligation, and increased funding for the homosexual indoctrination of children in Massachusetts schools, Focus on the Family's voter guide praised Romney over Huckabee. As *Time* reported:

> After praising Huckabee's social views, both Perkins and Tom Minnery, a policy expert at Focus on the Family, hammer the former Arkansas governor for his foreign policy views. Minnery suggests that Huckabee does not understand the cause for which American troops are dying in Iraq. Then Perkins suggests that Huckabee lacks the fiscal and national security credentials needed for a conservative presidential candidate. "The conservatives have been successful in electing candidates, and presidents in particular, when they have had a candidate that can address not only the social issues, [but] the fiscal issues and the defense issues,' says Perkins. '[Huckabee] has got to reach out to the fiscal conservatives and the security conservatives.'
>
> Ouch ... So what about Romney? He comes up roses.
>
> 'He has staked out positions on all three of the areas that we have discussed,' says Perkins. 'I think he continues to be solidly conservative.'[446]

Michael Sherer who pointed out the video on *Time's* blog *Swampland*, later noted in an update, "I first viewed the Huckabee video before 11 a.m. eastern time Thursday. When I spoke with Minnery in the afternoon, he said the video had been updated in the morning. As it turns out, the update to the Huckabee video came after I first viewed it. The new version of the video, which you will see if you follow the above link, contains a significantly longer segment of praise for Huckabee's social issue stands than the original post. The criticism of Huckabee appears unchanged. When I asked [Huckabee supporter Mat] Staver what he thought of the new version of the video, he said, 'After their attention was called to this, apparently Focus on the Family Action backtracked and edited the portion on Huckabee to make it appear more objective.'"[447]

Jay Sekulow of the American Center for Law and Justice told the *National Review* in 2006, "I don't think Mormonism will play as an issue ... We're past that. I'm practical, and I'm impressed with him on the things that really matter."[448]

Of the things that really matter to Sekulow, perhaps homosexual marriage is not on the list. A press release by his own American Center for Law and Justice issued in 2004 provides the exact same arguments made in an earlier chapter that Romney was under no legal obligation to institute gay marriage in Massachusetts. According to the press release:

> "It is clear that the Supreme Judicial Court overstepped its authority in the decision in the Goodridge case," said Vincent McCarthy, Senior Counsel of the ACLJ. "The SJC lacked jurisdiction in deciding this case and it is clear that the authority concerning the issue of marriage rests with the Governor and/or legislature according to the Massachusetts Constitution - not the Supreme Judicial Court. We are privileged to represent a bi-partisan group of state legislators who believe the SJC usurped their authority concerning the issue of marriage."
>
> In its filings today at the SJC, the ACLJ contends that the SJC is required under the state constitution to vacate its judgment in the Goodridge case and argues that the constitution grants the Governor and legislature the exclusive authority in cases involving marriage. The constitution states: "All causes of marriage, divorce, and alimony, and all appeals from the Judges of probate shall be heard and determined by the Governor and Council, until the Legislature shall, by law, make other provision."[449]

Sekulow later ironically served on Romney's Faith and Values Steering Committee.

Chuck Colson of Prison Fellowship also told the *Weekly Standard* in 2005, "I could in very good conscience support Romney," and described him as "a first-rate guy in every respect" and "a social conservative on most of the issues we care about."[450]

In 2006, he told the *National Review,* "I would have theological concerns about his soul but not about his competence. I'm looking for someone who shares my values and is capable of governing."[451]

Yet even in 2009, as a drafter of the *Manhattan Declaration: A Call of Christian Conscience*, Colson's declaration states, "A culture of death inevitably cheapens life in all its stages and conditions by promoting the belief that lives that are imperfect, immature or inconvenient are discardable. As predicted by many prescient persons, the cheapening of life that began with abortion has now metastasized. For example, human embryo-destructive research and its public funding are promoted in the name of science and in the cause of developing treatments and cures for diseases and injuries."[452]

He also says, "We confess with sadness that Christians and our institutions have too often scandalously failed to uphold the institution of marriage and to model for the world the true meaning of marriage."[453]

While the declaration also states, "We are Christians who have joined together across historic lines of ecclesial differences to affirm our right—and, more importantly, to embrace our obligation—to speak and act in defense of these truths. We pledge to each other, and to our fellow believers, that *no power on earth, be it cultural or political, will intimidate us into silence or acquiescence.*"[454] [Emphasis mine] Colson appeared to not have been practicing what he is now preaching.

Frank Page, president of the Southern Baptists also told the *Review* in 2006, "I have a deep disagreement with Romney's theology, but I won't rule him out. Among the presidential candidates who have surfaced, he's the closest to the Southern Baptists in his social and moral beliefs."[455]

Richard Lee of First Redeemer Church also commented to the *National Review,* "I didn't know the fortitude of his moral beliefs and I found a kindred spirit on the sanctity of human life and traditional marriage."[456]

Solidly conservative? Shares my values? Closest in social and moral beliefs? Kindred spirit on the sanctity of human life and traditional marriage?

Let's review:

- After a phony pro-life conversion based on embryonic stem cell research, stated that such research does not destroy human life and continued to support such Mengele research.
- Instituted a health care program in Massachusetts that includes a $50 co-pay for abortions at taxpayers' expense after his "pro-life conversion."

- Gave Planned Parenthood an instrumental role on the policy board in his Massachusetts health care plan after his "pro-life conversion."
- Appointed a pro-choice judge to a lifetime appointment on a Massachusetts court after his "pro-life conversion."
- Altered marriage licenses and ordered judges to perform homosexual marriages in the state of Massachusetts when no law required him to do so; earning him the title of the Father of Gay Marriage in America.
- Awarded a Massachusetts district court judgeship to Stephen Albany, part of the Massachusetts Lesbian and Gay Bar Association and a proponent of the repealing of sodomy laws in the Bay State.
- Increased funding for the homosexual indoctrination of children in Massachusetts schools.
- Did not support the Bush tax cuts for which *uber* liberal Barney Frank stated he was "very pleased."
- Raised taxes and or fees *seven* times as Governor of Massachusetts.

Why are these leaders abandoning not only their duty as leaders of the faith to expose the blasphemous religion of Romney but also ignoring his stance on several key issues to which they are diametrically opposed? Are they anticipating a seat at a future table, while the rest of the flock shake their heads in disbelief?

In a 2007 interview, when asked about the "pulse of the evangelical world" with regards to the Romney meeting with Christian leaders, DeMoss replied "I want to be careful not to … translate it as to the evangelical population as a whole. I do think there is some difference in approach to this, between an evangelical leader or pastor, and the average evangelical lay person."[457]

DeMoss recalled a meeting with a "very prominent Southern Baptist pastor" who told him, "You know, I am comfortable with this, but I don't know about my mother and the people that sit in my pews on Sundays."[458]

Perhaps mothers and those who sit in pews on Sundays are not interested in selling out their principles and beliefs for a possible seat at a presidential table.

The Speech

In December 2007 Romney, seeing his support chipped away by the Huckabee candidacy, was forced to deliver his "JFK" speech on his religion. His speech consisted of two directives: pay no attention to my Mormonism (he only mentioned the word "Mormon" one time in the speech) or else you are a bigot, and pay no attention to my record.

In his speech, Romney seemed to be setting the American people up in a way that would make them a bigot to question his strange beliefs in his religion. He likened objections to Mormonism to the "race" theme that is used when people criticize Obama on his radical policies. Instead of addressing the matter, the race card is played in order to shut down credible discussion on the issue or policy at hand.

One of the telling parts of the speech was Romney's statement that "Americans do not respect believers of convenience." Perhaps Romney should look at his own beliefs and the convenience in which he has changed them for political expediency.

As Steve Kornacki of the *New York Observer* pointed out, the location of the speech was no coincidence. Romney delivered the speech at George H. W. Bush's presidential library. Bush 41 also had problems courting the Christian right. Once pro-abortion, Episcopalian, and facing a Christian challenger (Pat Robertson), Bush 41 declared himself a born-again Christian, talked about the sanctity of human life, and advocated for prayer in public schools.[459]

As Kornacki observed, "Both Mr. Bush and Mr. Romney responded to these tough political realities the same way: by reinventing themselves."[460]

Romney's speech was carefully crafted to blur whatever lines exist between Mormonism and Christianity. On the Greta Van Susteren interview with Mitt Romney before his speech, Mitt stated that he would not be talking so much about the religion of Mormonism, but more about the plurality of faith in America. This was code for "there is so much to hide about the Mormon Church that I'll just dance around the Mormon issue by talking about *faith* in general".

Mitt had to pull off the speech of his life, and because he possessed the ability to posture and position issues in such a smooth and eloquent way, he was able to take in the less discerning in the audience.

The Kool-Aid was offered up to America in a slick, flowery speech about faith. When you think about it, in this tolerant era, the creed of tolerance is politically correct; therefore, intolerance of Mitt's religion would be considered bigotry, right? Well, let's see … Mormons emphatically say and believe that The Church of Jesus Christ of Latter-day Saints, the Mormon Church, is the "one and only *true* church" on the face of this earth. Translated (no pun intended), that means all religions other than the Mormon religion are false. Would this not mean that the Mormons are *not* tolerant of all faiths?

Ever the image-conscious Romney, it is important to note that the podium on which Romney delivered his speech happened to display the presidential seal.

Romney's Flip-Flops During the2008 Presidential Campaign

"Hit the phones today, *make all the promises you have to*, and … make sure that we get the funds that we need to keep propelling this campaign forward with power and energy."[461]

Mitt Romney made the above statement to phone bank volunteers in early 2008 as recorded by ABC radio.

Abortion

> Romney in 1994: "I believe that abortion should be safe and legal in this country."[462]

"I have since the time that my mom took that position when she ran in 1970 as a US candidate. I believe that since Roe v. Wade has been the law for 20 years we should sustain and support it."[463]

Planned Parenthood questionnaire in 2002:

Question: Do you support the substance of the Supreme Court decision in Roe v. Wade?

Romney's answer: Yes.[464]

The Mitt Romney record:

- After a phony pro-life conversion based on embryonic stem cell research, stated that such research does not destroy human life, even though he believes life begins at conception, and continued to support such Nazi-like research.
- Instituted a health care program in Massachusetts that includes a $50 co-pay for abortion at taxpayer's expense after his "pro-life conversion."
- Gave Planned Parenthood an instrumental role on the policy board in his Massachusetts health care plan after his "pro-life conversion."
- Appointed a pro-choice judge to a lifetime appointment on a Massachusetts court after his "pro-life conversion."

July 26, 2005 Op-ed in the *Boston Globe*: "I am pro-life. I believe that abortion is the wrong choice except in cases of incest rape and to save the life of the mother … I believe that the states, through the democratic process, should determine their own abortion laws and not have them dictated by judicial mandate." [465]

September 2007 Fox News GOP debate:

Question: Your aides say you see ending abortion as a two-step process: rolling back *Roe v. Wade*, which would leave it legal in some states; and then a constitutional amendment to ban it nationwide. If abortion is murder, how can you live with it being legal in some states?

Romney: "I'd love to have an America that didn't have abortion. But that's not what the American people [want] right now. And so I'd like to see *Roe v. Wade* overturned and allow the states to put in place pro-life legislation. I recognize that for many people, that is considered an act of murder, to have an abortion. It is without question the taking of a human life. And I believe that a civilized society must respect the sanctity of the human life. But we have two lives involved here—a mom, an unborn child. We have to have concern for both lives and show the expression of our compassion and our consideration and work to change hearts and minds, and that's the way in my view we'll ultimately have a society without abortion."[466]

Gay Marriage

Romney in 1994: "When Ted Kennedy speaks on gay rights, he's seen as an extremist, When Mitt Romney speaks on gay rights, he's seen as a centrist and a moderate."[467]

Romney's letter to Log Cabin Republicans: "As we seek to establish full equality for America's gay and lesbian citizens, I will provide more effective leadership than my opponent."[468]

Romney's endorsement from the Log Cabin Republicans was "primarily based on his support for the federal Employment Non-Discrimination Act (EDNA), a pro-gay piece of legislation that at the time had little Republican support."[469]

The record:

- Altered marriage licenses and ordered judges to perform homosexual marriages in the state of Massachusetts when no law required him to do so; earning him the title of the Father of Gay Marriage in America.
- Awarded a Massachusetts district court judgeship to Stephen Albany, part of the Massachusetts Lesbian and Gay Bar Association and a proponent of the repealing of sodomy laws in the Bay State.
- Increased funding for the homosexual indoctrination of children in Massachusetts schools.

December 14, 2006 interview with the *National Review*:

Question "And what about the 1994 letter to Log Cabin Republicans where you indicated you would support the Federal Employment Non-

Discrimination Act (EDNA) and seemed open to changing the 'Don't ask, Don't tell' policy in the military? Are those your positions today?"

Romney: "No, I don't see the need for new or special legislation. My experience over the years as governor has convinced me that EDNA would be an overly broad law that would open a litigation floodgate and unfairly penalize employers at the hands of activist judges ... As for military policy and the 'Don't ask, Don't tell policy,' I trust the counsel of those in uniform who have set these policies over a dozen years ago. I agree with President Bush's decision to maintain this policy and I would do the same."[470]

September 2007 interview with Joe Scarborough of MSNBC:

Scarborough: "Do you support a national constitutional amendment to ban same-sex marriage?"

Romney: "Boy, I sure do ... ultimately we're going to have one standard of marriage in this country and that standard ought to be one man and one woman."[471]

Gun Rights

Romney in 1994, on his support of the Brady Bill and an assault weapons ban: "That's not going to make me the hero of the NRA."[472]

Campaign stop in 1994: "I don't line up with the NRA."[473]

The record:

"But perhaps the most significant gun legislation Romney signed as governor was a 2004 measure instituting a permanent ban on assault weapons. The Legislature mirrored the law after the federal assault weapons ban, which was set to expire. According to activists at the time, the bill made Massachusetts the first state to enact its own such ban, and Romney hailed the move. 'These guns are not made for recreation or self-defense,' he was quoted as saying. 'They are instruments of destruction with the sole purpose of hunting down and killing people'" (*Boston Globe*, January 2007) .[474]

"He now touts his work as governor to ease restrictions on gun owners. He proudly describes himself as a member of the NRA—though his campaign won't say when he joined. And Friday, at his campaign's request, top officials of the NRA and the National Shooting Sports Foundation led him around one of the country's biggest gun shows" (*Boston Globe*, January 2007).[475]

"Romney says he still backs the ban on assault weapons, but he won't say whether he stands by the Brady Bill. And after the gun show tour, his campaign declined to say whether he would still describe himself as a supporter of tough gun laws" (*Boston Globe*, January 2007).[476]

Whether Romney Owns a Gun

On Wednesday, Romney said on an Internet podcast, *The Glenn and Helen Show,* that he hopes states would continue to ease regulations on gun owners, and he expressed enthusiasm for guns and hunting. 'I have a gun of my own. I go hunting myself. I'm a member of the NRA and believe firmly in the right to bear arms,' Romney said" (*Boston Globe*, January 2007).[477]

"Asked by reporters at the gun show Friday whether he personally owned the gun, Romney said he did not. He said one of his sons, Josh, keeps two guns at the family vacation home in Utah, and he uses them 'from time to time.' The guns are a Winchester hunting rifle and a Glock 9mm handgun, which Romney uses for target shooting" (*Boston Globe*, January 2007).[478]

Health Care

In 1994 Romney's own campaign flyer boasted that, while Ted Kennedy supported a government takeover of the health care system, employer mandates, and increased taxes to pay for government-run health care, Romney was adamantly opposed to these.[479]

Conveniently, with no signature issue as governor when gearing up for his presidential run, Romney worked with Senator Kennedy to pass RomneyCare in Massachusetts.

The record:

- "The liberal Commonwealth Fund reports that Massachusetts insurance costs have climbed anywhere from 21 percent to 46 percent faster than the US average since 2005. Employer-sponsored premiums are now the highest in the nation."[480]
- The average premium for family coverage was higher than $15,000 a year in 2009.[481]
- "In the last two years alone, spending on free and subsidized plans for low-income citizens of the bay state has doubled from $630 million in 2007 to an estimated $1.3 billion this year."[482]
- "While Massachusetts' uninsured rate has dropped to around 3%, 68% of the newly insured since 2006 receive coverage that is heavily or completely subsidized by taxpayers. While Mr. Romney insisted that everyone should pay something for coverage, that is not the way his plan has turned out. More than half of the 408,000 newly insured residents pay nothing, according to a February 2010 report by the Massachusetts Health Connector, the state's insurance exchange."[483]
- The average wait to see a primary care physician for new patients in forty-four days. Less than half of Massachusetts internal medicine doctors are accepting new patients. While the average wait time to see a specialist has declined nationally to twenty-one days, it increased to fifty days in Boston.[484]
- "As a result, many patients are insured in name only: they have health coverage, but can't find a doctor." Visits to the emergency room increased seven percent from 2005 to 2007, with half of these visits able to be treated in a doctor's office rather than in the ER.[485]
- Having an abortion under Romney's plan costs a mere $50 co-pay. According to the *Politico*, "Even worse, the plan does not include any exceptions, which means Massachusetts taxpayers are forced to fund abortion-on-demand." RomneyCare also

requires by law that Planned Parenthood plays an instrumental part in naming members to the policy board.[486]

Romney Lauds His Health Care

"Romney's address today to the Florida Medical Association is designed to go beyond his standard stump speech on his healthcare policy in which he lauds the Massachusetts plan as a way to lower premiums and extend coverage to more people without too much government involvement" (*Boston Globe*, August 2007).[487]

Romney Runs From His Health Care Plan

"Romney, a former GOP presidential contender and possible 2012 candidate, has insisted his plan is different from Mr. Obama's, mainly because the Massachusetts plan was state-based. He has even called the implementation of the individual mandate, found in both plans, possibly unconstitutional at the federal level."

"Nevertheless, the White House has called the Massachusetts plan 'the template for what we're trying to do here.' Romney also came under fire during the debate over abortion language in the national health care bill because his plan allowed government-subsidized insurance packages to cover abortion as mandated by state law" (CBS, April 2010).[488]

Campaign Finance Reform

Romney at a 1994 press conference: "These kinds of associations between money and politics in my view are wrong. And for that reason, I would like to have campaign spending limits … I also would abolish PACs … I don't like that kind of influence."[489]

"Back then [since his days as a Senate and gubernatorial candidate in Massachusetts], Romney advocated more stringent measures than McCain-Feingold ultimately included, such as a spending limit for federal elections and a tax on political contributions" (Concord Monitor 2007).[490]

Romney's PAC: "The Commonwealth PACs complied with state rules rather than federal law, allowing some wealthy Romney backers to donate as much as $250,000 to his operation—well above the $2,300 federal cap for individual contributions."[491]

Immigration

Romney in 2005 regarding McCain's amnesty proposal for illegal immigrants: "That's very different from amnesty, where you literally say, 'OK, everybody here gets to stay … It's saying you could work your way into becoming a legal resident of the country by working here without taking benefits and then applying and then paying a fine."[492]

Americans for Border Security statement in 2007:

> In 2006 Governor Romney supported the President's immigration policy as well as the McCain-Kennedy bill. He expressed support for an immigration program that places large numbers of illegal residents on the path toward citizenship and said illegal immigrants should have a chance to obtain citizenship.
>
> Now Presidential Candidate Mitt Romney says he 'strongly opposes' the immigration plan also denounced by conservatives even though his public statements suggest he actually agrees with major aspects of the proposal in Congress.[493]

The record:

The Washington Times, August 2007:

> As governor, Mr. Romney wielded control over a significant budget and oversaw three cities that were proud of their designation as "sanctuary cities:" Cambridge, Somerville and Orleans. Yet as governor, Mr. Romney did not cut their funding. He recommended millions of dollars in state funding of them and made no attempt to force these cities to change their policies.
>
> His immigration bona fides rest on the "deputization" of the state police that would allow them to arrest illegal immigrants—a law signed less than three weeks before he left office and was never implemented.[494]

TARP

Romney to Reuters' James Pethokoukis in March 2009: "The TARP program, while not transparent and not having been used as wisely it should have been, was nevertheless necessary to keep banks from collapsing in a cascade of failures."[495]

Romney at the Values Voters summit in September 2009: "When government is trying to takeover health care, buying car companies, bailing out banks, and giving half the White House staff the title of czar—we have every good reason to be alarmed and to speak our mind!"[496]

Taxes

The record:

- In 2002, Romney refused to sign a "no new taxes" pledge while running for governor.
- Did not support the Bush tax cuts for which *uber* liberal Barney Frank stated he was "very pleased"
- Raised taxes and or fees *seven* times as governor of Massachusetts.

"Almost five years after he refused to sign a 'no new taxes' pledge during his campaign for governor, Mitt Romney announced yesterday that he had done just that, as his campaign for the 2008 Republican presidential nomination began in earnest" (*Boston Globe*, January 2007).[497]

Minimum Wage Laws

2002 Romney campaign website: "The minimum wage is important to our economy and Mitt Romney supports minimum wage increase, at least in line with inflation."[498]

"Governor Mitt Romney yesterday rejected the Legislature's plan to raise the state minimum wage to $8 an hour over two years, angering Democratic lawmakers and advocates who accused him of abandoning a 2002 campaign pledge to significantly boost the pay of low-wage workers" (*Boston Globe*, July 2006).[499]

Fuel Efficiency Standards

"In a speech to business leaders and at an international auto show, he [Romney] was especially critical of new fuel efficiency standards signed into law last month by President Bush. 'Instead of throwing over a life preserver, Washington has dropped yet another anvil on Michigan,' Romney told the Detroit Economic Club. 'And now it's passively sitting back to see if car companies can swim, and the answer is: just barely.'" (*Boston Globe* January 2008)[500]

The record:

"As governor, Romney imposed tough emissions standards in December 2005 that added Massachusetts to a growing list of states seeking to force the auto industry to produce cleaner-burning cars—which automakers considered a back-door attempt to raise fuel standards. Under the rules, cars sold in the state after 2015 must emit 30 percent less carbon dioxide, 20 percent fewer toxic pollutants, and as much as 20 percent fewer smog-causing pollutants than under federal standards" (*Boston Globe*, January 2008).[501]

Marching With Martin Luther King Jr.

Romney to Tim Russert: "I'm very proud of my faith, and it's the faith of my fathers, and I certainly believe that it is a, a faith—well, it's true and I love my faith. And I'm not going to distance myself in any way from my faith. But you can see what I believed and what my family believed by looking at, at our lives. *My dad marched with Martin Luther King.* My mom was a tireless crusader for civil rights."[502]

"He was speaking figuratively, not literally," Eric Fehrnstrom, spokesman for the Romney campaign, said of the candidate (after *Boston Phoenix* found no such documentation that that ever happened).[503]

The record:

According to the *New York Times*, while Romney was attending BYU he stayed "on the sidelines when protests broke out over Brigham Young's all-white sports teams."[504]

With regards to the LDS policies on African-Americans, Romney told the *Times*, "I hoped the time would come when the leaders of the church would receive the inspiration to change the policy."[505]

"But until then, he deferred to church leaders," according to the *Times*. Romney told them, "The way things are achieved in my church, as I believe in other great faiths, is through inspiration from God and not through protests and letters to the editor."[506]

Romney's White Horse Stumbles

After spending more than $40 million of his own money, Romney pulled out of the Republican primary in early February 2008, perhaps realizing that the longer his campaign failed the more he would be labeled damaged goods or a loser. Romney said, "This is not an easy decision for me. I hate to lose. My family, my friends and our supporters ... many of you right here in this room ... have given a great deal to get me where I have a shot at becoming President. If this were only about me, I would go on. But I entered this race because I love America, and because I love America, I feel I must now stand aside, for our party and for our country."[507]

If it were only about him, he "would go on." Romney would go on to allow a failed Barack Obama presidency only help bolster his prospects in 2012, as well as his new book, new PAC, and improved image, carefully crafted once again to fill his and the Mormon church's white horse prophecy.

Chapter 14

Romney Reinvents Himself Yet Again

In July 2010, the *Politico* reported on a poll done by Public Policy Polling that found that disaffected Obama voters view Romney more favorably than any other potential 2012 GOP contender.

According to the *Politico*, "Among the selection of voters who said they voted for Obama but do not now approve of his performance as president, Romney is viewed most favorably of any of the other potential Republican challengers to Obama in 2012."[508]

Thirty-two percent of disappointed Obama voters viewed Romney favorably while only 31 percent viewed him unfavorably, "making the former governor the only Republican with a net positive rating among the group."[509]

Palin received a 63 percent unfavorable rating, while Newt Gingrich and Mike Huckabee received 40 and 39 percent unfavorable ratings respectively among the disaffected Obama voters.[510]

It is easy to see why former Obama voters would support Romney. To Obama voters, Obama was anything they wanted him to be. There was no scrutiny of his ties to Jeremiah Wright and the Weather Underground, his Marxist philosophies or his scant state and Senate records. All Obama had to do was read smartly off of a teleprompter, look good, and promise something different from George Bush.

Now that the economy is in shambles and the country is on a fast track to socialism, these voters are looking for another image machine. Romney can offer himself as an alternative to Obama, but he doesn't have the mainstream media in his corner to gloss over his record, so in order to fool voters he has to once again reinvent himself.

Reinvention Number One: Social Issues—"Nothing to See Here"

During his failed 1994 senate campaign in Massachusetts, Romney was hard pressed to assure Bay State voters that on social issues, he was in lock step with liberals. On his own 1994 campaign flyer, Romney listed "Retain a woman's right to choose" as one of his prominent issues.[511] When asked what were the differences between Romney's and Kennedy's stances on abortion, Romney's political consultant at the time, Charles Manning, stated "it's tiny nuances."[512] In 1994 candidate Romney told *Bay Windows*, New England's largest GLBT newspaper, "When Ted Kennedy speaks on gay rights, he's seen as an extremist, when Mitt Romney speaks on gay rights, he's seen as a centrist and a moderate."[513]

Again, during his gubernatorial campaign in 2002, Romney was still adamant on his liberal stance on social issues. Answering a Planned Parenthood questionnaire in 2002, Romney made his position on abortion well known:

Question: Do you support the substance of the Supreme Court decision in Roe v. Wade?

Romney's answer: Yes.[514]

When asked how Romney's prochoice stance compared to his Democratic opponent Shannon O'Brien, his running mate Kerry Healy stated, "There isn't a dime of difference between Mitt Romney's position on choice and Shannon O'Brien's."[515]

Jonathan Spampinato, a gay Republican activist who served as deputy political director for Romney's gubernatorial campaign, told the *New York Times*, that Romney "explained his position to Log Cabin club members early on by saying, 'Regardless of what you call it, if you look at the benefits I support and the benefits Shannon [his Democrat opponent] supports, there's probably a hair of a difference."[516]

From day one during his governorship, Romney was desperate to convince voters on the national stage that he was a diehard conservative on social issues, which is why he had his fake "conversion" on abortion.

As early as July 26, 2005, Romney penned an op-ed in the *Boston Globe* where he stated:

"I am pro-life. I believe that abortion is the wrong choice except in cases of incest rape and to save the life of the mother … I believe that the states, through the democratic process, should determine their own abortion laws and not have them dictated by judicial mandate."[517]

Romney often cited his fake conversion to pro-life at campaign stops relaying his meeting with a physician regarding embryonic stem cell research. In 2007 at a campaign stop in South Carolina, Romney recalled the meeting. "It struck me very powerfully at that point, that the Roe v. Wade approach so cheapened the value of human life that someone could think that it's not a moral issue to destroy embryos that have been created solely for the purpose of research," he said. "I said to my chief of staff and that's been two and a half years ago, I said to her, 'I want to make it very clear that I'm pro-life.'"[518] Romney did the same with regards to gay marriage even though as governor of Massachusetts he instituted gay marriage in America. In a September 2007 interview with Joe Scarborough of MSNBC, Scarborough asked Romney the following question:

Scarborough: "Do you support a national constitutional amendment to ban same-sex marriage?"

Romney: "Boy, I sure do … ultimately we're going to have one standard of marriage in this country and that standard ought to be one man and one woman."[519]

Realizing his political expediency was showing during the 2008 campaign, Romney decided to reboot. In February 2010 the *Phoenix's* David S. Bernstein wrote, "In retrospect, Team Romney believes their strategy was in error, according to some who are familiar with the campaign's post election brainstorming."[520]

"He was a Massachusetts moderate who tried to be a hard right conservative," Bernstein quoted an unnamed Republican strategist. "It turned out he probably would have been better off sticking with what he was—Mr. Fix It."[521]

"As a result," Bernstein wrote at the time "the new Romney is now deemphasizing social issues like abortion, same-sex marriage and illegal immigration. He has made no public comment, for instance, about last week's announcement that top military leaders intend to end the 'Don't ask, Don't tell' policy, has scrupulously avoided association with the Tea Party movement, and has refrained from backing conservatives that other presidential hopefuls have endorsed, such as Doug Hoffman in New York or Marco Rubio in Florida."[522]

In April 2010, Romney told *Newsweek's* Andrew Romano, "I wish I had been more effective in being able to communicate the central rationale of my campaign, which is strengthening the economy, getting better jobs, raising incomes ... Instead, as a candidate I spent a good deal of time answering questions about social issues."[523]

Romano pointed out, "Note how Romney mixed the past and present tenses. The implication was that he wouldn't make the same mistake twice."[524]

No, he wouldn't. Romney has now given up championing himself as a conservative on social issues, and is simply ignoring them and branding himself as Mr. Fix It. As far as his flip-flops and record on social issues, it is "nothing to see here, move along."

Perhaps social issues are not important to Romney. As Bernstein wrote, close observers of Romney believe he "doesn't care much about social issues, isn't very ideological, and revels in applying management skills to large organizations to help them achieve their goals and functions."[525]

While it is "the economy stupid," do we not want a president to not only care about social issues, but to lead on them as well? The Ground Zero mosque is one example of Romney's lack of credibility and ability to lead on social issues, which are inextricably woven into this nation's fabric.

The planned construction of an Islamic culture center and mosque just two blocks from the hallowed ground of Ground Zero set off a wave of controversy. While several GOP leaders chimed in agreement with almost 70 percent of Americans who oppose the location of the mosque, in a real profile in courage, Romney remained silent.

In late August of 2010, the *Daily Caller* reported, "Noticeably absent from the chest thumping over the mosque issue was Mitt Romney. While others from the GOP poured on and made headlines, Romney sat on the sidelines for weeks, an exercise in calculated restraint that has become his trademark since Obama took office. And when he finally did weigh in, it came through a spokesman, who issued a statement avoiding the more caustic and confrontational tone other 2012 contenders had taken."[526]

The *Boston Globe* was quick to criticize the wishy-washy Romney:

> Romney is a reasonable person who wishes he didn't have to contend with his party's angry base. But rather than stand up to it, even on an issue that speaks directly to his own experiences, he has chosen to take the path of least resistance.
>
> His statements have been mild enough that no one can accuse him of fanning the flames of hatred, but no one in the Republican base can say that Romney disagrees with them, either. The whole episode casts an unflattering light on a man who, just two and a half years ago, said, 'You can be certain of this: Any believer in religious freedom, any person who has knelt in prayer to the Almighty, has a friend and ally in me. And so it is for hundreds of millions of our countrymen: we do not insist on a single strain of religion—rather, we welcome our nation's symphony of faith.[527]

Romney's reaction to the mosque controversy merely highlights his weak principles based solely on political expediency. As Aaron Guerrero wrote in the *Daily Caller,* "The avoidance of the debate surrounding the 'Ground Zero Mosque' is also a firm reminder that the Mitt Romney of 2010 is distinctly different from the Mitt Romney of 2006 and 2007, and that 2012 will be nothing like 2008, when he was essentially forced to morph into a fire-breathing conservative on every issue the base of the GOP cared about."[528]

Yep. Instead of speaking out and leading on the mosque issue, Mr. Fix It wrote an op-ed about the Obama economy instead.

Reinvention Number Two: Anti-spending Tax-cutter

In the midst of the Ground Zero mosque debate, Romney penned an op-ed in the *Boston Globe* titled "Grow Jobs and Shrink Government" on August 18, 2010. In his piece, Romney opined "His [Obama's] policies are anti-investment, anti-jobs, and anti-growth. Raising taxes … new taxes to pay for ObamaCare, and an increase on the dividend tax from 15 percent to nearly 40 percent—depresses new investment throughout the economy … all the while the president's failure to address the looming deficits, national debt …" Romney went on "A pro-job, pro-prosperity government works to create conditions that enable businesses of all sizes to grow and thrive. These should include aligning corporate taxes with those of other developed economies, eliminating special corporate tax breaks that lobbyists have inserted over the years, and preserving the Bush tax cuts."[529]

Romney gets a little credit for actually mentioning ObamaCare, albeit only once, in his op-ed after its twin's disastrous effects in Massachusetts. Let's see how Mr. Fix It felt about spending and taxes while governor of Massachusetts.

Carla Howell, co-founder and president of the Center for Small Government, and sponsor of a 2002 ballot initiative to end the Massachusetts state income tax, explained on the blog LewRockwell.com in 2007: "Each of the four years Romney served as Governor, he raised taxes—while pretending he didn't. He claims he only raised mandatory government 'fees.' But government mandatory fees are nothing but taxes, and taxes are nothing but mandatory government fees."[530]

Writing on the Official Blog of the National Taxpayers Union in 2008, Sam Batkins pointed out "Romney raised taxes or fees seven times in Mass, but only cut taxes three times … Overall, during Romney's four years in office, taxes increased $175 million. This total is nothing compared to some tax-hikers like Jon Corzine (D-NJ), but Romney doesn't have a great record as a tax cutter."[531]

Romney also refused to endorse the Bush tax cuts, another profile in courage, with his spokesman claiming, "It's just not a state matter." When Romney met with an all-Democrat group of House and Senate members in Washington, D.C. in 2003, he reportedly said he would not be a "cheerleader" but that "I have to keep a solid relationship with the White House."[532]

Liberal Democrat Congressman Barney Frank commented at the time, "I was very pleased … Here you have a freshman governor refusing to endorse a tax cut presented by a Republican president at the height of his wartime popularity."[533]

How did Governor Romney deal with spending in Massachusetts?

Romney's claims of cutting the state budget by $2 billion also do not ring true, according to Howell. "These 'cuts' were merely budget games," wrote Howell in 2007. "Spending cuts in one area were simply moved into another area of the budget."[534] According to the National Taxpayers Union, under Romney, spending in the Bay State rose 20.7 percent (from $22,848 billion to $27,588 billion)."[535]

While Romney may blame the primarily liberal state legislature, "when it comes to tax and spend policies, he leads the way," according to Howell. "Each of the four years Romney served as Governor, he started budget negotiations by proposing an increase of about $1 billion. Before the legislation even named a budget figure."[536]

In a typical smoke and mirrors fashion, Romney would accept a few line item budget increases from the legislature. However, when Romney would veto a few other line item increases, "The media helped him out again by making fanfare of his vetoes and portraying him as tough on spending—*after he had already given away the store!*"[537]

How did Mr. Fix It's policies affect citizens of the Bay State?

During Romney's term Massachusetts was in the bottom three of the nation for job creation, only above Michigan and post-Katrina Louisiana.[538] Only 24,400 new jobs were netted during Romney's term, an anemic 0.8 percent increase.[539]

Reinvention Number Three: For Government Run Health Care Before He Was Against It

Scott Brown's senate victory in Massachusetts was touted as the forty-first vote against ObamaCare. Ironically, the person who instituted the precursor in Massachusetts was also working behind the scenes in the Brown campaign. Demonstrating another profile in courage, Romney purposely stayed out of the limelight until the race was won.

Kimberly Strassel wrote in the *Wall Street Journal* on January 21, 2010, "Aware that many voters have mixed views of his governorship, Mr. Romney stayed in the shadows, leaving other notables to stump with Mr. Brown. Behind the scenes was a different story."[540]

Strassel described the behind the scenes operation where Romney would headline fundraisers for the pickup-driving Brown, used his nationwide mailing list to solicit donations, asked supporters to contact others on Brown's behalf and used his own media machine to help with the Brown campaign. Romney's close aides also joined the Brown team. Beth Landstrum, who served in Romney's cabinet, was Brown's campaign manager, Beth Meyers, Romney's presidential campaign manager, also joined the team, and Romney spokesman Eric Fehmstrom helped with television ads.[541]

After the Brown victory, Romney stepped forward to receive praise from Brown and further boost his stature as a winner. Bernstein wrote in the *Phoenix,* "But even in the midst of his moment in the sun, Brown made sure to thank the other handsome, well-coifed man on the stage, Mitt Romney … make no mistake: Romney is in the process of relaunching himself for 2012."[542]

The Brown victory may have inadvertently produced problems for Mr. Fix It. Strassel wrote at the time, "By midweek, the political pundits decreed Mr. Romney the other big winner. Some went so far as to credit him with the 41st vote, potentially saving the nation from ObamaCare. In doing so, they unwittingly touched on the flip side of this week's race. For all the benefits this contest held for the former governor, it also churned up what will prove the biggest obstacle to Romney in 2012."[543]

It is important to remember that in 1994 when HillaryCare was unpopular, Romney's own campaign flyer stated the differences between Senator Kennedy and himself. The flyer proudly boasted that, while Kennedy supported a government takeover of the health care system, employer mandates, and increased taxes to pay for government-run health care, Romney was adamantly opposed to these.[544]

Conveniently, with no signature issue as governor when gearing up for his presidential run, Romney worked with Senator Kennedy to pass RomneyCare in Massachusetts. Now with ObamaCare wildly unpopular, Romney is criticizing Obama's plan while still trying to defend its twin: RomneyCare.

Newsweek's Daniel Gross pointed out in March of 2010, "As countless commentators have noted (Alex Knepper from the right, Brad DeLong from the left, and David Frum from the spurned right), ObamaCare largely is

RomneyCare. The concept of attaining near-universal health insurance in a defined geographic area using a combination of a mandate, subsidies, and cost-control efforts is essentially what Romney did in Massachusetts."[545]

Yet when ObamaCare was passed Romney wrote on the *National Review* blog, "America has just witnessed an unconscionable abuse of power … His health care bill is unhealthy for America. It raises taxes, slashes the more private side of Medicare, installs price controls, and puts a new federal bureaucracy in charge of health care. It will create a new entitlement even as the ones we already have are bankrupt. For these reasons and more, the act should be repealed. That campaign begins today."[546]

Strassel wrote in February 2010 that RomneyCare "shares many elements of Washington's legislation, from an individual mandate, to employer taxes, to subsidized middle-class insurance," yet Romney continues to defend his own plan as somehow vastly different.[547]

According to Strassel, "Mr. Romney has at times put forward selective data suggesting the program's costs aren't exploding. At other times he has complained his state hasn't done enough to control costs. By October of last year he was arguing with CNN that 'We … didn't have any pretense we would somehow be able to change health care costs in Massachusetts.' This, despite promising in 2006 that under his plan 'The costs of health care will be reduced.'"[548]

Health care costs have not been reduced under RomneyCare. According to the *Wall Street Journal*, "The liberal Commonwealth Fund reports that Massachusetts insurance costs have climbed anywhere from 21 percent to 46 percent faster than the US average since 2005. Employer-sponsored premiums are now the highest in the nation."[549] The average premium for family coverage was higher than $15,000 a year in 2009.[550]

It has also been a budget buster. Forbes noted in 2009, "In the last two years alone, spending on free and subsidized plans for low-income citizens of the bay state has doubled from $630 million in 2007 to an estimated $1.3 billion this year."[551]

Romney has tried to defend his plan, even saying, "It isn't a perfect plan," and that "Health care premiums were higher before the law passed." But as Aaron Goldstein points out in the *American Spectator*, in Romney's book *No Apology* "Romney touts the Massachusetts Model as creating an exchange that assists individuals in buying health insurance. He writes on page 177 'The exchange lowers premiums and enables individuals to buy health insurance with pretax dollars, just as companies are able to do.'"[552]

As Goldstein notes, although Romney blames the current Democrat governor of Massachusetts, the legislature and the connector board for rising premiums, "It is worth remembering that Romney signed the plan into law the same year in which he opted not to seek re-election … Is Romney telling us he could not have foreseen that a Democratic governor, a Democratic controlled legislature and a board full of Democratic appointees would have extended RomneyCare coverage once he left office?"[553]

The truth is Romney's signature issue as governor has morphed into an albatross around his presidential aspirations and he will do everything he can to distance himself from it.

Reinvention Number Four: The Regular Joe

In February 2010, Bernstein wrote, "In the battle of Main Street versus Wall Street, there is no question which side Romney represents. Not only did he make a fortune buying companies, stripping them down and selling them in the stock market, his political career has been financed by the very banking and financial executives whose heads the public is demanding on pikes."[554]

Bernstein noted that among the biggest contributors to Romney's 2008 campaign were Goldman Sachs, as well as Morgan Stanley, Citigroup, JP Morgan, and Lehman Brothers.[555]

Now, following on the success of Scott Brown's victory, Romney is trying to portray himself as a regular Joe. According to the *Boston Globe* in late August 2010, "Since losing the 2008 Republican nomination, the former Massachusetts governor has sought to reposition himself with the party, deemphasizing social issues and focusing instead on foreign policy and economic affairs. But the most dramatic reinvention may be a stylistic one: Romney is seeking to come across as more easygoing and accessible than the formerly dressed, perfectly coifed, carefully rehearsed candidate of the last campaign."[556]

In the summer of 2010 Romney was spotted with tousled hair, donning blue jeans, and ... driving an old pickup truck. According to the *Boston Globe,* "In early July, Romney marched in the Wolfeboro's Fourth of July parade in jeans and a checked shirt, his hair tousled, a combination that became something of a uniform on his spring book tour."[557]

According to the Associated Press on August 6, 2010, Romney "drove a beat-up pickup to a New Hampshire fundraiser Thursday night. He's also driven it to other political events as he weighs another run in 2012."[558]

Apparently Romney is trying to emulate the image of the regular guy with a beat-up old pickup that Scott Brown exuded. According to the *Globe,* "When asked if there was anything he could learn from Brown, Romney quipped, 'Where to buy a good barn jacket—I've got a truck.'"[559] Romney, once again, is using a page right out of the Mormon playbook: ignore the facts, the history and the agenda, and focus on how I am just like you.

Romney has also been focusing more on the liberal New Hampshire than conservative Iowa. The Romneys sold their Massachusetts home last year and spent the 2010 summer at their lake house in New Hampshire (they also own an oceanfront home in La Jolla, California). According to the *Globe*, "Romney appears to be paying more attention thus far to New Hampshire than Iowa, which has the first in the nation caucuses that were a focal point of his efforts last time."[560] Perhaps because Romney is more at home in the liberal northeast?

"Romney earlier this month skipped the Iowa state fair, which drew other potential presidential candidates. Instead, Romney has used his New Hampshire summer to further build local relationships in a state *where backers believe the socially moderate Republican electorate allows him a more natural base of support,"* according to the *Globe* in August 2010. [Emphasis mine][561]

Romney may drive a beat-up pickup from his $3.54 million lake house in New Hampshire trying to appeal to voters as a regular guy, but make no mistake about it: his wealth is what is driving his campaign.

Romney Purchases More Votes

Once again, Romney is using his wealth and his PAC to buy influence in key primary states, and is doing it by, as the *Politico* reports, "breaking new ground in testing and besting the limits of state campaign finance laws as well as federal rules."[562]

The *Politico* reported on August 18, 2010, "The maximum donation a person can give a presidential candidate under federal law is $2,400. Yet Edward Conard, a Mitt Romney supporter, has already donated $90,000 to the former Massachusetts governor's campaign apparatus. How is that legal?"[563]

The *Politico* goes on to explain that Romney discovered a loophole in 2006 "when he first established five state political action committees to underwrite the expenses of his federal headquarters and dole out money to local candidates in primary states who could help his presidential quest."[564]

According to the *Politico*, "The Commonwealth PACs complied with state rules rather than federal law, allowing some wealthy Romney backers to donate as much as $250,000 to his operation—well above the $2,300 federal cap for individual contributions."[565] Romney's state PAC affiliates bypassed federal law and served as merely a slush fund for Romney to buy endorsements and influence.

After the 2008 campaign, Romney was able to keep his campaign apparatus intact by renaming his Commonwealth PAC as well has his five state committees (located in primary states Iowa, New Hampshire, South Carolina, Michigan, and Alabama) the Free and Strong America PAC. Each of the state committees are subject to local statues regarding contributions. According to the *Politico,* "That means Romney can collect corporate checks in Alabama, unlimited donations from individual backers in Iowa and regulated donations in South Carolina and New Hampshire. The arrangement provides Romney's most loyal and generous backers with multiple opportunities to grease the gears of his political machine."[566]

According to the *Politico*, from January 1, 2009 to June 30, 2010, just twenty-four individuals accounted for the $486,700 from Romney's state committees.[567] His PAC itself in the first half of 2010 raised $3.5 million, twice the amount of any other potential GOP contender.[568] What is he doing with all his money? The same as last time: purchasing future primary votes.

According to the *Hill*, "A key part of Romney's strategy appears to be building up state candidates and parties in critically early presidential voting states—a move he hopes will help him, in turn, with his own likely presidential bid."[569] But Romney is also being calculating with his money. Another profile in courage, according to the *Politico*, "Romney is mostly waiting until after primaries take place to get involved. After each primary his PAC will issue a statement of support for a state's slate of GOP candidates and cut checks for them individually."[570]

The *Hill* reported in July 2010, that Romney's PAC had already contributed to more than 150 campaigns in 2010, with more than seventy congressional candidates, thirteen senate candidates, and nine gubernatorial candidates. He has also donated to almost sixty legislative candidates in states such as Georgia, South Carolina, and New Hampshire and since 2009 donated over $30,000 to the New Hampshire state GOP with an additional $7,500 to local and state candidates in New Hampshire special elections.[571]

Romney is relying on the backlash against Barack Obama's radical policies to propel him into the presidency. Ever the image master, like Obama, he is positioning himself as the white horse, the savior of the country. He is counting on the American electorate to ignore his record, flip-flops, and insatiable quest for the presidency that began with his father. Where Obama's brand was hope and change and the anti-Bush, Romney's is Mr. Fix It and the anti-Obama.

The only question is: Will we be fooled again?

Conclusion

In conclusion, I want the reader to know that most Mormon churchgoers are some of the nicest people you will ever want to meet. They possess good morals and values and most lean to the conservative side of the political spectrum. They really mean well. However, the church leadership, in my experienced opinion, does not give a flip about its members' well-being. The leadership is more concerned with control, obedience, and money. They accomplish their indoctrination, likened to a technique of mass hypnosis that keeps their victims dutiful to the religion instead of the biblical almighty God.

You see, if the church can keep its membership under deceptive control, the money will continue to flow in to further carry out its agenda, not to mention the wealth of what I call its "corporation" of assets that have absolutely nothing to do with the membership that afforded them the accumulation of it. The Mormon corporation is not accountable to its membership as to where it spends the multi-billions of dollars.

My church, in McLean, Virginia, is completely accountable to its 14,000 members as to where every penny that comes in is spent. The pastor of the church has absolutely nothing to do with the finances, nor does he have a key to the safe. The money that comes into the church goes back to programs that will benefit the membership of the church, the operations of the church, and to the needy. Full disclosure.

Mormons are taught that they do not deserve to know where all the money goes and that they shouldn't ask. So they don't. Is it just me, or to the discerning mind would this not be a huge red flag? There are so many lies, distortions, and secrets in the Mormon Church that it boggles the mind as to why they have any followers at all.

This, coupled with Mitt Romney's political plots, plans, and the truth about his political record, should turn any thinking human being away from the church and away from even considering giving a precious vote to him. On the contrary, the society we live in today tends to turn our eyes to what we want to believe, instead of the facts that we should base our judgment and actions upon.

If you consider Mitt Romney from a conservative or spiritual standpoint, let me ask you point-blank: Can you truly vote for a man who fathered gay marriage, fathered government-run health care, and as a part of this plan offered $50 taxpayer subsidized abortions as a part of the health care benefit? Again, if you are a true conservative and/or Christian, how would God view the support of your vote?

If you consider Mitt Romney from a Republican political standpoint, let me ask you point-blank, again: With our economy in peril, can you truly vote for a man who increased taxes and fees by close to a billion dollars which destroyed the Massachusetts economy and also opposed the Bush tax cuts? In addition, could you vote for a man who supported McCain-Feingold "campaign finance reform," McCain-Kennedy "comprehensive immigration reform" (i.e., amnesty), and parts of the McCain-Lieberman "carbon cap and trade" bill?

If you consider Mitt Romney from a progressive/liberal stand point, would you cast your vote for a president of the United States of America who truly and unequivocally believes that in the next life, he will become a "god" and will call his goddess wife into heaven and be given his own planet to populate with spirit children?

If you have read this book, you know that the aforementioned is just the tip of the iceberg.

Let me leave you with excerpts from *The Mormon Plan for America and the Rise of Mitt Romney.* The book was written by Ed Decker, the founder and international director of Saints Alive in Jesus, a ministry that actively brings the gospel of grace to those lost in the darkness of cultic bondage. Keep in mind that I have experienced in the secret Mormon Temple Ceremony the exact things that he speaks of herewith.

> *According to Mormon Apostle Bruce R. McConkie, "Holy sanctuaries wherein sacred ordinances, rites and ceremonies are performed which*

pertain to salvation and exaltation in the kingdom of God are called temples. They are the most sacred places of worship on earth; each one is literally a House of the Lord, a house of the great Creator, a house where he and his Spirit may dwell, to which he may come, or send his messengers, to confer priesthood and keys and give revelation to his people" (Mormon Doctrine, 1979 ed., pp.779–780).

One of several temple oaths was his oath of Obedience to the Law of Sacrifice, in which he (Mitt Romney) vowed,

"As Jesus Christ has laid down his life for the redemption of mankind, so we should covenant to sacrifice all that we [I] possess, even our [my] own lives [life] if necessary, in sustaining and defending the Kingdom of God."

The "execution of the penalty" for disobedience at the time Mitt Romney took out his "temple Endowments" was demonstrated "by placing the thumb under the left ear, the palm of the hand down, and by drawing the thumb quickly across the throat to the right ear, and dropping the hand to the side."

It is hard to imagine that well-educated Mormon men of such political stature like former Massachusetts Gov. Mitt Romney, Utah Senator Orrin Hatch of Utah or Senator Harry Reid of Nevada could bring their thumbs to their throats and swear a blood oath that they will "suffer" their throats slit from ear to ear should they not "sacrifice all that [they] possess, even [their] own lives if necessary, in sustaining and defending the Kingdom of God, as defined by the Mormon prophet.

These high level temple Mormons clearly know that this Mormon "Kingdom of God" is, in reality, a Mormon one-world government, a theocracy, soon coming to America, that will be run by the strong arm of the Mormon Brethren, headed up by the only true prophet of God on earth. However, it is clear that they did swear such an oath.

The Law of Consecration

The other significant oath Mitt Romney has sworn to obey is the Law of Consecration. In the LDS temple ritual, the officiator says to the temple "patrons,"

We are instructed to give unto you the Law of Consecration as contained in the book of The Doctrine and Covenants, in connection with the Law of the Gospel and the Law of Sacrifice which you have already received. It is that you do consecrate yourselves, your time, talents and everything which the Lord has blessed you, or with which he may bless you, to the Church of Jesus Christ of Latter-day Saints, for the building up of the Kingdom of God on the earth and for the establishment of Zion.

You and each of you covenant and promise before God, angels, and these witnesses at this altar, that you do accept the Law of Consecration as contained in The Doctrine and Covenants, in that you do consecrate yourselves, your time, talents, and everything with which the Lord has blessed you, or with which he may bless you, to the Church of Jesus Christ of Latter-day Saints, for the building up of the Kingdom of God on the earth and for the establishment of Zion.

Works Cited for Part I

1. Smith, Joseph. Joseph Smith—History: Extracts from the History of Joseph Smith, The Prophet, Volume 1. *The Pearl of Great Price.* Salt Lake City,: The Church of Jesus Christ of Latter-day Saints, 1981.

2. Introduction. *The Book of Mormon.* Salt Lake City: The Church of Jesus Christ of Latter-day Saints, 1981.

3. C. Clark Julius, MPS. Joseph Smith. *LDS-Mormon.com.* [Online] August 1987. [Cited: January 3, 2010.] http://www.lds-mormon.com/jsmith.shtml.

4. Introduction. *The Book of Mormon.* Salt Lake City: The Church of Jesus Christ of Latter-day Saints, 1981.

5. Joseph Smith. Joseph Smith—History: Extracts from the History of Joseph Smith, The Prophet, Volume 1. Salt Lake City: The Church of Jesus Christ of Latter-day Saints, 1981, 1:69–72.

6. Porter, Larry C. Aaronic Priesthood:Restoration. Light Planet. [Online] 2008. [Cited: January 5, 2010] http://www.lightplanet.com/mormons/priesthood/aaronic/restoration.htmle]

7. Dudley, Dean A. *Bank Born of Revelation: The Kirtland Safety Society Anti-Banking Company.* 1970.

8. Abanes, Richard. *One Nation Under Gods: A History of the Mormon Church.* New York: Four Walls Eight Windows, 2002.

9. —. *One Nation Under Gods: A History of the Mormon Church.* New York: Four Walls Eight Windows, 2002. pp. 216–217.

10. —. *One Nation Under Gods: A History of the Mormon Church.* New York: Four Walls Eight Windows, 2002. pp. 256–257.

11. —. *One Nation Under Gods: A History of the Mormon Church.* New York: Four Walls Eight Windows, 2002. p. 54.

12. BlackHawk War. *Blackhawkproductions.com.* [Online] 2002. http://www.blackhawkproductions.com.

13. Ibid.

14. Ibid.

15. Hulse, Rocky. *When Salt Lake City Calls.* s.l.: Xulon Press, 2007.

16. *Young, Brigham. The Journal of Discourses. Volume 4:53.[Online] [Cited: January 10, 2010.] http://www.journalofdiscourses.org/.*

17. Tanner, Jerald and Sandra. *Mormonism-Shadow or Reality?* Salt Lake City: Modern Microfilm, 1982. pp. 400–403.

18. The Church of Jesus Christ of Latter Day Saints. [Online] [Cited: January 10, 2010.]).”http://scriptures.lds.org/en/search?type=words&last=Age+of+Accountability+&help=&wo=checked&search=Age+of+eight&do=Search&iw=all&tx=checked&af=checked&hw=checked&sw=checked&bw=1.

19. Tanner, Jerald and Sandra. *Evolution of the Mormon Temple Ceremony: 1842–1990.* Salt Lake City: Lighthouse Ministry, 1990. p. 182.

20. Canon, Stephen F. Personal Freedom Outreach. *Still Wide the Divide: A Critical Analysis of a Mormon and an Evangelical in Dialogue.* [Online] 1997. [Cited: January 10, 2010.] http://www.pfo.org/stilwide.htm.

21. Rocky Hulse. *When Salt Lake City Calls.* Xulon Press. 2007.

22. The Church of Jesus Christ of Latter-day Saints. Newsroom. *Organiztional Structure of the Church.* [Online] [Cited: January 9, 2010.] http://newsroom.lds.org/ldsnewsroom/eng/background-information/organizational-structure-of-the-church.

23. Ibid. [Online]

24. *Doctrine and Covenants.* 1:38, Salt Lake City, Utah: The Church of Jesus Christ of Latter-day Saints, 1981.

25. *Scriptural Index to the Ensign and Improvement Era: LDS General Conference Reports.* Brigham Young University. October 1897. pp. 18–19.

26. Benson, President Ezra Taft. First Presidency Message; Fourteen Fundamentals in Following the Prophets. *LDS.ORG.* [Online] June 1981. [Cited: January 9, 2010.] http://www.lds.org/ldsorg/v/index.jsp?locale=0&sourceId=cc52b4f40c9db010VgnVCM1000004d82620a____&vgnextoid=f318118dd536c010VgnVCM1000004d82620aRCRD.

27. *Doctrine and Covenants 1:14.* Salt Lake City: The Church of Jesus Christ of Latter-day Saints, 1981.

28. Scriptural Index to the Ensign and Improvement Era LDS General Conference Reports. [Online] scriptures.byu.edu/citationspdf.php.

29. Ward Teacher's Message. *Deseret News, Church Section.* May 26, 1945, Vol. section p. 5.

30. Packham, Richard. Mormon Temples and Temple Rituals. [Online] 2007. [Cited: February 4, 2010.] http://home.teleport.com/~packham/temples.htm.

31. Lake, Deborah. *Secret Ceremonies.* s.l.: William Morrow & Co., 1993.

32. *Doctrine and Covenants.* 124:28–36. *Doctrine and Covenants.* Salt Lake City: The Church of Jesus Christ of Latter-day Saints.

33. http://www.facebook.com/note.php?note_id=248461694988

34. Sackett, Chuck. *What's Going On In There?* Thousand Oaks: Sword of the Shepherd Ministries, Inc., 1982. p. 44.

35. Hulse, Rocky. *When Salt Lake City Calls.* s.l.: Xulon Press, 2007. p. 303.

36. Kimball, Heber C. in Hawkins, ed. p. 6:32.

37. Moses 7:22. *The Book of Mormon.* Salt Lake City: The Church of Jesus Christ of Latter-day Saints, 1981.

38. Lee, Harold B. *Decisions for Successful Living.* pp. 164–165.

39. McConkie, Bruce R. *Mormon Doctrine.* First. Salt Lake City: Bookcraft, 1958. pp. 476–477.

40. Young, Brigham. *The Journal of Discourses.* in Watt, ed. Vols. 7:290–291.

41. —. *The Journal of Discouses.* in Watt, ed. Vol. 10:110.

42. McConkie, Bruce R. *Mormon Doctrine.* p. 102.

43. Taylor, Jonh. *The Journal of Discourses.* Vol. 22:304.

44. Young, Brigham. *The Journal of Discourses.* Vols. 7: 290, 1859.

45. Kimball, Spencer W. *The Teachings of Spencer W. Kimball, The Twelfth President of the Church of Jesus Christ of Latter-day Saints.* p. 237.

46. *The Book of Mormon.* Salt Lake City: The Church of Jesus Christ of Latter-day Saints. Vols. Alma 3:6–9.

47. *The Book of Mormon.* Salt Lake City: The Church of Jesus Christ of Latter-day Saints. Vol. Alma 5:6.

48. 1Ibid. Vol. Mormon 5:15.

49. Ibid. Vol. 2 Nephi 5: 21.

50. The Story of Ute Leader Nooch "Black Hawk"1847-1873. [Online] The Story of Ute Leader Nooch "Bl http://www.blackhawkproductions.com/Blackhawk1.htm).

51. Bernstein, David S. Talking Politics - More on My Romney Story. *The Boston Phoenix.* [Online] December 19, 2007. http://thephoenix.com/BLOGS/talkingpolitics/archive/2007/12/19/More-On-My-Romeny-Story.aspx.

52. Ibid. [Online]

53. Young, Brigham. *The Journal of Discourses.* p. 143. Vol. 2.

54. 2008. http://www.youtube.com/watch?v=Q_6ySJVlXb0 (accessed March 2010).

55. *Cult. Dictionary.com., Random House, Inc.,* http://dictionary.reference.com/browse/cult (accessed March 13, 2010).

56. Smith, *Teachings of the Prophet Joseph Smith,* 327.

57. *Articles of Faith.*

58. Hunter, Milton R. *The Gospel Through the Ages.* Salt Lake City, Utah: Stevens and Walls, Inc., 1945.

59. Joseph Fielding Smith, *Doctrines of Salvation.*

60. Young, Brigham. *The Journal of Discourses, 7:334,* 1859.

61. Smith, *Teachings of the Prophet Joseph Smith*

62. —. *Teachings of the Prophet Joseph Smith.*

63. Ibid., 346.

64. Mormon Doctrine, 746

65. Brigham Young in Watt. ed., *The Journal of Discourses, 4:45*

66. Smith, *Doctrines of Salvation,* 1:19

67. *Mormon Doctrine; 5:16,* 1977

68. McConkie, Bruce R. *Mormon Doctrine; 670–671*

69. Articles of Faith, 476

70. Smith, *Doctrines of Salvation*; 1:35

71. *Cult. Dictionary.com., Random House, Inc.,* http://dictionary.reference.com/browse/cult (accessed March 13, 2010).

72. The *Doctrine and Covenants.* Vol. 114. Salt Lake City, Utah: The Church of Jesus Christ of Latter-day Saints, 1981.

73. *History of the Church.* Vol. 2.

74. Ibid.

75. *Journal of Oliver Boardman Huntington.* Vol. 2.

76. *History of the Church.* Vol. 5, 394

77. *Millennial Star.* Vol. 22, 455

78. *History of the Church* , 116 (Note)

79. *History of the Church.* Vol. 2., 456–466

80. *Doctrine and Covenants, Section 111.*

81. Ibid.

82. *Doctrine and Covenants 84:1–5*

83. *Doctrine and Covenants 132:61–62.*

84. Tanner, Jerald Tanner and Sandra. *Mormonis—Shadow or Reality.* Salt Lake City: Modern Microfilm, 1972.

85. Smith, Joseph F. *The Journal of Discourses.* Vol. 18.

86. Ibid. Vol. 6.

87. McConkie, Bruce R. *Mormon Doctrine.* Salt Lake City: Bookcraft, 1979.

88. Shupe, John Heinerman and Anson. *The Mormon Corporate Empire.* Boston: Beacon Press, 1985.

89. *Mormon Quotes (White Horse Prophecy) http://www.ils.unc.edu/~unsworth/mormon/whitehorse.html*

90. Ibid

Works Cited for Part II

1 Heinerman, John, and Anson D. Shupe. *The Mormon Corporate Empire.* Boston: Beacon,1985. Print. p 102

2 "Income of Mormon Church Is Put at $4.7 Billion a Year - NYTimes.com." *NYTimes.com. New York Times,* July 2, 1991. Web. March 20, 2010. <http://www.nytimes.com/1991/07/02/us/income-of-mormon-church-is-put-at–4.7-billion-a-year.html>.

3 Van Biema, David. "Kingdom Come - A Time Magazine Feature Story on the Mormons." *Lds-mormon.com - Tons of Information on Mormonism and the Lds Church.* 4 Aug. 1997. Web. 03 Sept. 2010. <http://www.lds-mormon.com/time.shtml>.

4 Van Biema, David. "Kingdom Come - A Time Magazine Feature Story on the Mormons." *Lds-mormon.com - Tons of Information on Mormonism and the Lds Church.* 4 Aug. 1997. Web. 03 Sept. 2010. <http://www.lds-mormon.com/time.shtml>.

5 Wood LLC, Charles L. *The Mormon Conspiracy.* 2nd ed. San Diego: Black Forest, 2004. Print. P.606Van Biema, David. "Kingdom Come - A Time Magazine Feature Story on the Mormons." *Lds-mormon.com - Tons of Information on Mormonism and the Lds Church.* 4 Aug. 1997. Web. 03 Sept. 2010. <http://www.lds-mormon.com/time.shtml>.

7 Wood LLC, Charles L. *The Mormon Conspiracy.* 2nd ed. San Diego: Black Forest, 2004. Print. P.100

8 "How Much Money Does the Church Have?" *MormonThink.com.* Web. 14 Nov. 2010. <http://webcache.googleusercontent.com/search?q=cache:4r0r7c0pOREJ:www.mormonthink.com/tithing.

htm PBS special, mormon assets 80 billion&cd=2&hl=en&ct=clnk&gl=us>.

9 Wood LLC, Charles L. *The Mormon Conspiracy*. 2nd ed. San Diego: Black Forest, 2004. Print. P.100

10 Wood LLC, Charles L. *The Mormon Conspiracy*. 2nd ed. San Diego: Black Forest, 2004. Print. P.98

11 Heinerman, John, and Anson D. Shupe. *The Mormon Corporate Empire*. Boston: Beacon, 1985. Print. P. 74

12 Wood LLC, Charles L. *The Mormon Conspiracy*. 2nd ed. San Diego: Black Forest, 2004. Print. P.107

13 Heinerman, John, and Anson D. Shupe. *The Mormon Corporate Empire*. Boston: Beacon, 1985. Print. P. 29

14 "Bonneville Markets." *Bonneville International*. Web. 22 Mar. 2010. <http://www.bonneville.com/?nid=3>.

15 Hutchinson, Janis. "Strategies of the Mormon Church." *Www.janishutchinson.com*. Web. 14 Oct. 2010. <http://www.janishutchinson.com/strategies.html>.

16 Decker, Joshua. "Marketing and the Mormon Church." *Home | Saints Alive in Jesus*. 26 Aug. 2009. Web. 03 Sept. 2010. <http://saintsalive.com/resourcelibrary/mormonism/marketing-and-the-mormon-chuirch>

17 Walden, David M. "Bonneville International Corporation: Information from Answers.com." *Answers.com*. Web. 22 Mar. 2010. <http://www.answers.com/topic/bonneville-international-corporation>.

18 Chapman, Anne E., and Kenneth C. Petress. *The Mormon Church and Image Advertising: Appeals for Family Unity and Community Responsibility*. Thesis. University of Maine at Presque Isle, 1991. Web. 10 Mar. 2010. <http://webcache.googleusercontent.com/search?q=cache:http://www.umpi.maine.edu/~petress/>.

19 Feldman, Noah. "What Is It about Mormonism?" *NYTimes.com. New York Times*, 6 Jan. 2008. Web. 12 Mar. 2010. <http://www.nytimes.com/2008/01/06/magazine/06mormonism-t.html>.

20 Van Biema, David. "KINGDOM COME - A Time Magazine Feature Story on the Mormons." *Lds-mormon.com - Tons of Information on Mormonism and the Lds Church*. 4 Aug. 1997. Web. 03 Sept. 2010. <http://www.lds-mormon.com/time.shtml>.

21 Feldman, Noah. "What Is It about Mormonism?" *NYTimes.com. New York Times*, 6 Jan. 2008. Web. 12 Mar. 2010. <http://www.nytimes.com/2008/01/06/magazine/06mormonism-t.html>.

22 "History of Mormon Tabernacle Choir." *Utah Information and Resource Guide*. Web. 03 Sept. 2010. <http://onlineutah.com/choirhistory.shtml>.

23 Moody, John. *Kiss It Good-Bye*. Fairfield: Shadow Mountain, 2010. Print. P 24

24 Moody, John. *Kiss It Good-Bye*. Fairfield: Shadow Mountain, 2010. Print. P 23

25 Surround Yourself With Greatness. Advertisement. *Shadow Mountain Publishing | The Official Site of Shadow Mountain Publishing*. Web. 15 Oct. 2010. <http://www.shadowmountain.com/products-page/nonfiction/surround-yourself-with-greatness/>.

26 Astle, Randy. "LDS Living - Mormons and Film: 100 Years on the Silver Screen." *LDSLiving.com*. LDS Living Magazine, 20 Mar. 2009. Web. 15 Oct. 2010. <http://www.ldsliving.com/story/4478-mormons-and-film–100-years-on-the-silver-screen>.

27 Astle, Randy. "LDS Living - Mormons and Film: 100 Years on the Silver Screen." *LDSLiving.com*. LDS Living Magazine, 20 Mar. 2009. Web. 15 Oct. 2010. <http://www.ldsliving.com/story/4478-mormons-and-film–100-years-on-the-silver-screen>.

28 Winder, Michael K. *Presidents and Prophets*. American Fork: Covenant Communications, 2007. Print

29 Solomon, John. "Romney's Old Ties To Firm Pay Off." *Washington Post*. 14 Aug. 2007. Web. 25 Nov. 2009. <http://www.washingtonpost.com/wp dyn/content/article/2007/08/13/AR2007081301171.html>.

30 Drogin, Bob. "To Assess Romney, Look beyond the Bottom Line - Los Angeles Times." *Featured Articles From The Los Angeles Times*. 16 Dec. 2007. Web. 03 Sept. 2010. <http://articles.latimes.com/2007/dec/16/nation/na-mittbain16>.

31 Drogin, Bob. "To Assess Romney, Look beyond the Bottom Line - Los Angeles Times." *Featured Articles From The Los Angeles Times*. 16 Dec. 2007. Web. 03 Sept. 2010. <http://articles.latimes.com/2007/dec/16/nation/na-mittbain16>.

32 Drogin, Bob. "To Assess Romney, Look beyond the Bottom Line - Los Angeles Times." *Featured Articles From The Los Angeles Times*. 16 Dec. 2007. Web. 03 Sept. 2010. <http://articles.latimes.com/2007/dec/16/nation/na-mittbain16>.

33 Drogin, Bob. "To Assess Romney, Look beyond the Bottom Line - Los Angeles Times." *Featured Articles From The Los Angeles Times*. 16 Dec. 2007. Web. 03 Sept. 2010. <http://articles.latimes.com/2007/dec/16/nation/na-mittbain16>.

34 Drogin, Bob. "To Assess Romney, Look beyond the Bottom Line - Los Angeles Times." *Featured Articles From The Los Angeles Times*. 16 Dec. 2007. Web. 03 Sept. 2010. <http://articles.latimes.com/2007/dec/16/nation/na-mittbain16>.

35 Drogin, Bob. "To Assess Romney, Look beyond the Bottom Line - Los Angeles Times." *Featured Articles From The Los Angeles Times*. 16 Dec. 2007. Web. 03 Sept. 2010. <http://articles.latimes.com/2007/dec/16/nation/na-mittbain16>.

36 Drogin, Bob. "To Assess Romney, Look beyond the Bottom Line - Los Angeles Times." *Featured Articles From The Los Angeles Times*. 16 Dec. 2007. Web. 03 Sept. 2010. <http://articles.latimes.com/2007/dec/16/nation/na-mittbain16>.

37 Drogin, Bob. "To Assess Romney, Look beyond the Bottom Line - Los Angeles Times." *Featured Articles From The Los Angeles*

Times. 16 Dec. 2007. Web. 03 Sept. 2010. <http://articles.latimes.com/2007/dec/16/nation/na-mittbain16>.

38 Drogin, Bob. "To Assess Romney, Look beyond the Bottom Line - Los Angeles Times." *Featured Articles From The Los Angeles Times*. 16 Dec. 2007. Web. 03 Sept. 2010. <http://articles.latimes.com/2007/dec/16/nation/na-mittbain16>.

39 Gavin, Robert. "Reaping Profit in Study, Sweat - The *Boston Globe*." *Boston.com*. 26 June 2007. Web. 03 Sept. 2010. <http://www.boston.com/news/politics/2008/specials/romney/articles/part3_main/>.

40 Drogin, Bob. "To Assess Romney, Look beyond the Bottom Line - Los Angeles Times." *Featured Articles From The Los Angeles Times*. 16 Dec. 2007. Web. 03 Sept. 2010. <http://articles.latimes.com/2007/dec/16/nation/na-mittbain16>.

41 Drogin, Bob. "To Assess Romney, Look beyond the Bottom Line - Los Angeles Times." *Featured Articles From The Los Angeles Times*. 16 Dec. 2007. Web. 03 Sept. 2010. <http://articles.latimes.com/2007/dec/16/nation/na-mittbain16>.

42 Gavin, Robert. "Reaping Profit in Study, Sweat - The *Boston Globe*." *Boston.com*. 26 June 2007. Web. 03 Sept. 2010. <http://www.boston.com/news/politics/2008/specials/romney/articles/part3_main/>.43 Feldman, Noah. "What Is It about Mormonism?" *NYTimes.com*. *New York Times*, 6 Jan. 2008. Web. 12 Mar. 2010. <http://www.nytimes.com/2008/01/06/magazine/06mormonism-t.html>.

44 Goldberg, Michelle. "Proposition 8, The Mormon Coming Out Party | Politics." *Religion Dispatches*. 21 Nov. 2008. Web. 28 May 2010. <http://www.religiondispatches.org/archive/politics/766/>.

45 Goldberg, Michelle. "Proposition 8, The Mormon Coming Out Party | Politics." *Religion Dispatches*. 21 Nov. 2008. Web. 28 May 2010. <http://www.religiondispatches.org/archive/politics/766/>.

46 Jordan, Mary. "The New Face of Global Mormonism." *Washington Post* 19 Nov. 2007. *Washingtonpost.com - Nation, World, Technology and Washington Area News and Headlines.* 19 Nov. 2007. Web. 2 June 2010. <http://www.washingtonpost.com/wp-dyn/content/article/2007/11/18/AR2007111801392.html>.

47 "CHURCH AND STATE; Mormons in Utah wield plenty of conservative clout in politics.(PAGE ONE)(SPECIAL REPORT)." The Washington Times (Washington, DC). 2003. *HighBeam Research.* (September 13, 2010). http://www.highbeam.com/doc/1G1–101952580.html

48 Bernick Jr., Bob, and Deborah Bulkeley. "Lawmakers, LDS Church Brainstorm | Deseret News." *Salt Lake City and Utah Breaking News, Sports, Entertainment and News Headlines - Deseret News.* 19 Jan. 2008. Web. 10 Mar. 2010. <http://www.deseretnews.com/article/695245489/Lawmakers-LDS-Church-brainstorm.html>.

49 "CHURCH AND STATE; Mormons in Utah wield plenty of conservative clout in politics. (PAGE ONE) (SPECIAL REPORT)." The Washington Times (Washington, DC). 2003. *HighBeam Research.* (September 13, 2010). http://www.highbeam.com/doc/1G1–101952580.html

50 Carpenter, Amanda B. "Romney's Mormon Money Paradox." *Human Events.com.* Human Events, 18 Apr. 2007. Web. 1 Dec. 2009. <http://www.humanevents.com/article.php?id=20307>.

51 Dougherty, Michael Brendan. "Mormons at the Door." *The American Conservative.* 23 Feb. 2009. Web. 28 May 2010. <http://www.amconmag.com/article/2009/feb/23/00014/>.

52 Fletcher Stack, Peggy, and Robert Gehrke. "LDS Take Capital Steps." *Salt Lake Tribune.* Religion News Blog, 10 Apr. 2005. Web. 24 May 2010. <http://www.religionnewsblog.com/10859/lds-take-capital-steps>.

53 Fletcher Stack, Peggy, and Robert Gehrke. "LDS Take Capital Steps." *Salt Lake Tribune.* Religion News Blog, 10 Apr. 2005.

Web. 24 May 2010. <http://www.religionnewsblog.com/10859/lds-take-capital-steps>.

54 Feldman, Noah. "What Is It about Mormonism?" *NYTimes.com. New York Times*, 6 Jan. 2008. Web. 12 Mar. 2010. <http://www.nytimes.com/2008/01/06/magazine/06mormonism-t.html>.

55 Winder, Michael K. *Presidents and Prophets*. American Fork: Covenant Communications, 2007. Print P.273

56 Winder, Michael K. *Presidents and Prophets*. American Fork: Covenant Communications, 2007. Print P.273

57 Fletcher Stack, Peggy, and Robert Gehrke. "LDS Take Capital Steps." *Salt Lake Tribune*. Religion News Blog, 10 Apr. 2005. Web. 24 May 2010. <http://www.religionnewsblog.com/10859/lds-take-capital-steps>.

58 Fletcher Stack, Peggy, and Robert Gehrke. "LDS Take Capital Steps." *Salt Lake Tribune*. Religion News Blog, 10 Apr. 2005. Web. 24 May 2010. <http://www.religionnewsblog.com/10859/lds-take-capital-steps>.

59 Fletcher Stack, Peggy, and Robert Gehrke. "LDS Take Capital Steps." *Salt Lake Tribune*. Religion News Blog, 10 Apr. 2005. Web. 24 May 2010. <http://www.religionnewsblog.com/10859/lds-take-capital-steps>.

60 Whitley, Jared. *Washington, D.C. Is a "Mormon Mecca"* UtahPolicy.com, 2 Oct. 2009. Web. 28 May 2010

61 Fletcher Stack, Peggy, and Robert Gehrke. "LDS Take Capital Steps." *Salt Lake Tribune*. Religion News Blog, 10 Apr. 2005. Web. 24 May 2010. <http://www.religionnewsblog.com/10859/lds-take-capital-steps>.

62 Whitley, Jared. *Washington, D.C. Is a "Mormon Mecca"* UtahPolicy.com, 2 Oct. 2009. Web. 28 May 2010

63 Fletcher Stack, Peggy, and Robert Gehrke. "LDS Take Capital Steps." *Salt Lake Tribune*. Religion News Blog, 10 Apr. 2005. Web. 24 May 2010. <http://www.religionnewsblog.com/10859/lds-take-capital-steps>.

64 Fletcher Stack, Peggy, and Robert Gehrke. "LDS Take Capital Steps." *Salt Lake Tribune.* Religion News Blog, 10 Apr. 2005. Web. 24 May 2010. <http://www.religionnewsblog.com/10859/lds-take-capital-steps>.

65 Fletcher Stack, Peggy, and Robert Gehrke. "LDS Take Capital Steps." *Salt Lake Tribune.* Religion News Blog, 10 Apr. 2005. Web. 24 May 2010. <http://www.religionnewsblog.com/10859/lds-take-capital-steps>.

66 Fletcher Stack, Peggy, and Robert Gehrke. "LDS Take Capital Steps." *Salt Lake Tribune.* Religion News Blog, 10 Apr. 2005. Web. 24 May 2010. <http://www.religionnewsblog.com/10859/lds-take-capital-steps>.

67 Clark, Drew. "The Mormon Stem-Cell Choir." *Slate.com.* Slate Magazine, 3 Aug. 2001. Web. 12 Mar. 2010. <http://www.slate.com/id/112974/>.

68 Anderson, Donna. "CIA? Nope, Just Missionaries." *Associated Press* 1 Oct. 1981. *BYU NewsNet.* Web. 28 May 2010. <http://nn.byu.edu/print/story.cfm/57673>.

69 Wood LLC, Charles L. *The Mormon Conspiracy.* 2nd ed. San Diego: Black Forest, 2004. Print. P.232

70 Kranish, Michael. "Mormon Church Obtained Vietnam Draft Deferrals for Romney, Other Missionaries - The *Boston Globe.*" *Boston.com.* 24 June 2007. Web. 15 Mar. 2010. <http://www.boston.com/news/politics/2008/specials/romney/articles/part1_side_2/>.

71 Kranish, Michael. "Mormon Church Obtained Vietnam Draft Deferrals for Romney, Other Missionaries - The *Boston Globe.*" *Boston.com.* 24 June 2007. Web. 15 Mar. 2010. <http://www.boston.com/news/politics/2008/specials/romney/articles/part1_side_2/>.

72 Kranish, Michael. "Mormon Church Obtained Vietnam Draft Deferrals for Romney, Other Missionaries - The *Boston Globe.*" *Boston.com.* 24 June 2007. Web. 15 Mar. 2010. <http://www.boston.com/news/politics/2008/specials/romney/articles/part1_side_2/>.

73 Conroy, Scott. "Romney: Sons Serve Country By Campaigning." *CBSNews.com*. CBS News, 8 Aug. 2007. Web. 15 Oct. 2010. <http://www.cbsnews.com/stories/2007/08/08/politics/main3147321.shtml?source=RSSattr=Politics_3147321>.

74 Reilly, Adam. "News & Features | Onward, Mormon Soldiers." *Boston Phoenix*. 18–24 Mar. 2005. Web. 3 June 2010. <http://www.bostonphoenix.com/boston/news_features/other_stories/multi-page/documents/04538494.asp>.

75 Riccardi, Nicholas. "Mormons Feel the Backlash over Their Support of Prop. 8 - Los Angeles Times." *LATimes.com*. Los Angeles Times, 17 Nov. 2008. Web. 10 Mar. 2010. <http://articles.latimes.com/2008/nov/17/nation/na-mormons17>.

76 Fletcher Stack, Peggy. "Prop 8 Involvement a P.R. Fiasco for LDS Church." *Salt Lake Tribune* 22 Nov. 2008. *Monterey County Weekly*. 10 Feb. 2010. Web. 10 Mar. 2010. <http://.monterey.montereycountyweekly.com/LegalServices/slc-approves-gay-rights-measu…>.

77 Reilly, Adam. "News & Features | Onward, Mormon Soldiers." *Boston Phoenix*. 18–24 Mar. 2005. Web. 3 June 2010. <http://www.bostonphoenix.com/boston/news_features/other_stories/multi-page/documents/04538494.asp>.

78 Fletcher Stack, Peggy. "Prop 8 Involvement a P.R. Fiasco for LDS Church." *Salt Lake Tribune* 22 Nov. 2008. *Monterey County Weekly*. 10 Feb. 2010. Web. 10 Mar. 2010. <http://.monterey.montereycountyweekly.com/LegalServices/slc-approves-gay-rights-measu…>.

79 McKinley, Jesse, and Kirk Johnson. "Mormons Tipped Scale in Ban on Gay Marriage." *NYTimes.com*. The *New York Times*, 15 Nov. 2008. Web. 1 June 2010. <http://www.nytimes.com/2008/11/15/us/politics/15marriage.html>.

80 Schoofs, Mark. "Mormons Boost Antigay Marriage Effort - WSJ.com." *WSJ.com*. The Wall Street Journal, 20 Sept. 2008. Web. 26 Nov. 2009. <http://online.wsj.com/article/NA_WSJ_PUB:SB122186063716658279.html>.

81 Van Biema, David. "The Church and Gay Marriage: Are Mormons Misunderstood?" *Time. Time.com.* Time, 22 June 2009. Web. 10 Mar. 2010. <http://www.time.com/time/magazine/article/0,9171,1904146,00.html>.

82 Schoofs, Mark. "Mormons Boost Antigay Marriage Effort - WSJ.com." *WSJ.com.* The Wall Street Journal, 20 Sept. 2008. Web. 26 Nov. 2009. <http://online.wsj.com/article/NA_WSJ_PUB:SB122186063716658279.html>.

83 Van Biema, David. "The Church and Gay Marriage: Are Mormons Misunderstood? - *Time.*" *Time.com.* Time, 22 June 2009. Web. 10 Mar. 2010. <http://www.time.com/time/magazine/article/0,9171,1904146,00.html>.

84 Van Biema, David. "The Church and Gay Marriage: Are Mormons Misunderstood? - *Time.*" *Time.com.* Time, 22 June 2009. Web. 10 Mar. 2010. <http://www.time.com/time/magazine/article/0,9171,1904146,00.html>.

85 McKinley, Jesse, and Kirk Johnson. "Mormons Tipped Scale in Ban on Gay Marriage." *NYTimes.com.* The *New York Times,* 15 Nov. 2008. Web. 1 June 2010. <http://www.nytimes.com/2008/11/15/us/politics/15marriage.html>.

86 Pulliam, Sarah. "A Latter-day Alliance." *ChristianityToday.* Christianity Today Magazine, 2 Dec. 2008. Web. 28 May 2010. <http://www.christianitytoday.com/ct/2008/decemberweb-only/149–22.0.html>.

87 Perkins, Tony. "Grateful for LDS Support on Prop 8." Editorial. *Deseret News* 11 Dec. 2008. *FRC.org.* Family Research Council. Web. 15 Oct. 2010. <http://www.frc.org/op-eds/grateful-for-lds-support-on-prop–8>.

88 Canham, Matt, Derek P. Jensen, and Rosemary Winters. "Salt Lake City Adopts Pro-gay Statutes—with LDS Church Support." *Salt Lake Tribune* 11 Nov. 2009. *Sltrib.com.* Salt Lake Tribune, 11 Nov. 2009. Web. 26 Nov. 2009. <http://www.sltrib.com/article/html/articleId=13758070>.

89 Canham, Matt, Derek P. Jensen, and Rosemary Winters. "Salt Lake City Adopts Pro-gay Statutes—with LDS Church Support." *Salt Lake Tribune* 11 Nov. 2009. *Sltrib.com*. Salt Lake Tribune, 11 Nov. 2009. Web. 26 Nov. 2009. <http://www.sltrib.com/article/html/articleId=13758070>.

90 Jordan, Mary. "The New Face of Global Mormonism." *Washington Post* 19 Nov. 2007. *Washingtonpost.com - Nation, World, Technology and Washington Area News and Headlines*. 19 Nov. 2007. Web. 2 June 2010. <http://www.washingtonpost.com/wp-dyn/content/article/2007/11/18/AR2007111801392.html>.

91 Goldberg, Michelle. "Proposition 8, The Mormon Coming Out Party | Politics." *Religion Dispatches*. 21 Nov. 2008. Web. 28 May 2010. <http://www.religiondispatches.org/archive/politics/766/>.

92 Goldberg, Michelle. "Proposition 8, The Mormon Coming Out Party | Politics." *Religion Dispatches*. 21 Nov. 2008. Web. 28 May 2010. <http://www.religiondispatches.org/archive/politics/766/>.

93 Goldberg, Michelle. "Proposition 8, The Mormon Coming Out Party | Politics." *Religion Dispatches*. 21 Nov. 2008. Web. 28 May 2010. <http://www.religiondispatches.org/archive/politics/766/>.

94 Wilkins, Richard. "Istanbul: Defending the Family." Speech. *World Family Policy Center*. Web. 28 May 2010. <http://www.law2.byu.edu/wfpc/history.htm>.

95 Wilkins, Richard. "Istanbul: Defending the Family." Speech. *World Family Policy Center*. Web. 28 May 2010. <http://www.law2.byu.edu/wfpc/history.htm>.

96 Carlson, PhD, Allan. "On the World Congress of Families." Speech. Presentation to the Charismatic Leaders Fellowship. Jacksonville. 12 Jan. 2005. *WorldCongress.org*. The Howard Center. Web. 28 May 2010. <http://profam.org/docs/acc/thc.acc.020112.wcf.htm>.

97 Butler, Jennifer. "300 Religious Right Participants Attend Beijing PrepCom." Web log post. *GlobalPolicy.org.* 1 June 2000. Web. 28 May 2010. <http://www.globalpolicy.org/component/content/article/177-un/31727.html?tmpl=compon...>.

98 Carlson, PhD, Allan. "On the World Congress of Families." Speech. Presentation to the Charismatic Leaders Fellowship. Jacksonville. 12 Jan. 2005. *WorldCongress.org.* The Howard Center. Web. 28 May 2010. <http://profam.org/docs/acc/thc.acc.020112.wcf.htm>.

99 Butler, Jennifer. "300 Religious Right Participants Attend Beijing PrepCom." Web log post. *GlobalPolicy.org.* 1 June 2000. Web. 28 May 2010. <http://www.globalpolicy.org/component/content/article/177-un/31727.html?tmpl=compon...>.

100 Carlson, PhD, Allan. "On the World Congress of Families." Speech. Presentation to the Charismatic Leaders Fellowship. Jacksonville. 12 Jan. 2005. *WorldCongress.org.* The Howard Center. Web. 28 May 2010. <http://profam.org/docs/acc/thc.acc.020112.wcf.htm>.

101 "World Congress of Families V Convenes in the Netherlands." *LDS Church News The Jesus Christ of Latter-day Saints.* The Jesus Christ of Latter-day Saints, 12 Aug. 2009. Web. 15 Oct. 2010. <http://www.ldschurchnews.com/articles/57740/World-Congress-of-Families-V-convenes-in-the-Netherlands.html>.

102 World Congress of Families. *Become A World Congress of Families Partner.* World Congress of Families. *WorldCongress.org.* World Congress of Families. Web. 15 Oct. 2010. <http://www.worldcongress.org/Special/wcf.partfly.0912.pdf>.

103 Goldberg, Michelle. "Proposition 8, The Mormon Coming Out Party | Politics." *Religion Dispatches.* 21 Nov. 2008. Web. 28 May 2010. <http://www.religiondispatches.org/archive/politics/766/>.

104 Martelle, Scott. "Romney's Running Mate - Los Angeles Times." *Featured Articles From The Los Angeles Times.* 25 Dec. 2007. Web. 13 Apr. 2010. <http://articles.latimes.com/2007/dec/25/nation/na-romneydadson25>.

105 STEVE LeBLANC. "For Republican presidential hopeful Mitt Romney, his life is his father's legacy." AP Worldstream. 2007. *HighBeam Research.* (September 13, 2010). http://www.highbeam.com/doc/1A1-D8SML88O2.html

106 STEVE LeBLANC. "For Republican presidential hopeful Mitt Romney, his life is his father's legacy." AP Worldstream. 2007. *HighBeam Research.* (September 13, 2010). http://www.highbeam.com/doc/1A1-D8SML88O2.html

107 Bringhurst, Newell G., and Craig L. Foster. *The Mormon Quest for the Presidency.* Independence, MO: John Whitmer, 2008. Print. Pp.55–56

108 Bringhurst, Newell G., and Craig L. Foster. *The Mormon Quest for the Presidency.* Independence, MO: John Whitmer, 2008. Print. P.56

109 Romney, Mitt. *No Apology: the Case for American Greatness.* New York: St. Martin's, 2010. Print. Pp. 5–6

110 David D. Kirkpatrick The New York Times Media Group. "Father's ghost haunts Romney campaign ELECTIONS 2008." International Herald Tribune. 2007. *HighBeam Research.* (September 13, 2010). http://www.highbeam.com/doc/1P1-147257119.html

111 David D. Kirkpatrick The New York Times Media Group. "Father's ghost haunts Romney campaign ELECTIONS 2008." International Herald Tribune. 2007. *HighBeam Research.* (September 13, 2010). http://www.highbeam.com/doc/1P1-147257119.html

112 Bringhurst, Newell G., and Craig L. Foster. *The Mormon Quest for the Presidency.* Independence, MO: John Whitmer, 2008. Print. P.58

113 David D. Kirkpatrick The New York Times Media Group. "Father's ghost haunts Romney campaign ELECTIONS 2008." International Herald Tribune. 2007. *HighBeam Research.* (September 13, 2010). http://www.highbeam.com/doc/1P1-147257119.html

114 Bringhurst, Newell G., and Craig L. Foster. *The Mormon Quest for the Presidency.* Independence, MO: John Whitmer, 2008. Print. P.59

115 Romney, Mitt. *No Apology: the Case for American Greatness.* New York: St. Martin's, 2010. Print. P. 7116 David D. Kirkpatrick The New York Times Media Group. "Father's ghost haunts Romney campaign ELECTIONS 2008." International Herald Tribune. 2007. *HighBeam Research.* (September 13, 2010). http://www.highbeam.com/doc/1P1–147257119.html

117 Bachelder, Chris. "Crashing the party: the ill-fated 1968 presidential campaign of Governor George Romney." Michigan Historical Review. 2007. *HighBeam Research.* (September 13, 2010). http://www.highbeam.com/doc/1G1–172597476.html

118 Bringhurst, Newell G., and Craig L. Foster. *The Mormon Quest for the Presidency.* Independence, MO: John Whitmer, 2008. Print. Pp. 60–61

119 Bringhurst, Newell G., and Craig L. Foster. *The Mormon Quest for the Presidency.* Independence, MO: John Whitmer, 2008. Print. P.61

120 Bringhurst, Newell G., and Craig L. Foster. *The Mormon Quest for the Presidency.* Independence, MO: John Whitmer, 2008. Print. P.62

121 Bringhurst, Newell G., and Craig L. Foster. *The Mormon Quest for the Presidency.* Independence, MO: John Whitmer, 2008. Print. P.66

122 ALEX BEAM. "WHO WAS GEORGE ROMNEY?." The *Boston Globe* (Boston, MA). 2004. *HighBeam Research.* (September 13, 2010). http://www.highbeam.com/doc/1P2–7878001.html

123 Bachelder, Chris. "Crashing the party: the ill-fated 1968 presidential campaign of Governor George Romney." Michigan Historical Review. 2007. *HighBeam Research.* (September 13, 2010). http://www.highbeam.com/doc/1G1–172597476.html

124 Bringhurst, Newell G., and Craig L. Foster. *The Mormon Quest for the Presidency*. Independence, MO: John Whitmer, 2008. Print. P.64

125 Bringhurst, Newell G., and Craig L. Foster. *The Mormon Quest for the Presidency*. Independence, MO: John Whitmer, 2008. Print. P.66

126 Bringhurst, Newell G., and Craig L. Foster. *The Mormon Quest for the Presidency*. Independence, MO: John Whitmer, 2008. Print. P.72

127 Bringhurst, Newell G., and Craig L. Foster. *The Mormon Quest for the Presidency*. Independence, MO: John Whitmer, 2008. Print. P.66

128 Bringhurst, Newell G., and Craig L. Foster. *The Mormon Quest for the Presidency*. Independence, MO: John Whitmer, 2008. Print. P.69 129 "Republicans: The Brainwashed Candidate - *Time*." Editorial. *Time* 15 Sept. 1967. *Time.com*. Time. Web. 14 Oct. 2010. <http://www.time.com/time/magazine/article/0,9171,941126,00.html>.

130 "Republicans: The Brainwashed Candidate - *Time*." Editorial. *Time* 15 Sept. 1967. *Time.com*. Time. Web. 14 Oct. 2010. <http://www.time.com/time/magazine/article/0,9171,941126,00.html>.

131 Bringhurst, Newell G., and Craig L. Foster. *The Mormon Quest for the Presidency*. Independence, MO: John Whitmer, 2008. Print. P.75

132 Bachelder, Chris. "Crashing the party: the ill-fated 1968 presidential campaign of Governor George Romney." Michigan Historical Review. 2007. *HighBeam Research*. (September 13, 2010). http://www.highbeam.com/doc/1G1–172597476.html

133 David D. Kirkpatrick The New York Times Media Group. "Father's ghost haunts Romney campaign ELECTIONS 2008." International Herald Tribune. 2007. *HighBeam Research*. (September 13, 2010). http://www.highbeam.com/doc/1P1–147257119.html

134 David D. Kirkpatrick The New York Times Media Group. "Father's ghost haunts Romney campaign ELECTIONS 2008." International Herald Tribune. 2007. *HighBeam Research.* (September 13, 2010). http://www.highbeam.com/doc/1P1–147257119.html

135 Bringhurst, Newell G., and Craig L. Foster. *The Mormon Quest for the Presidency.* Independence, MO: John Whitmer, 2008. Print. P.74

136 Bringhurst, Newell G., and Craig L. Foster. *The Mormon Quest for the Presidency.* Independence, MO: John Whitmer, 2008. Print. P.76

137 Bringhurst, Newell G., and Craig L. Foster. *The Mormon Quest for the Presidency.* Independence, MO: John Whitmer, 2008. Print. P.77

138 Martelle, Scott. "Romney's Running Mate - Los Angeles Times." *Featured Articles From The Los Angeles Times.* 25 Dec. 2007. Web. 13 Apr. 2010. <http://articles.latimes.com/2007/dec/25/nation/na-romneydadson25>.

139 Martelle, Scott. "Romney's Running Mate - Los Angeles Times." *Featured Articles From The Los Angeles Times.* 25 Dec. 2007. Web. 13 Apr. 2010. <http://articles.latimes.com/2007/dec/25/nation/na-romneydadson25>.

140 David D. Kirkpatrick The New York Times Media Group. "Father's ghost haunts Romney campaign ELECTIONS 2008." International Herald Tribune. 2007. *HighBeam Research.* (September 13, 2010). http://www.highbeam.com/doc/1P1–147257119.html

141 Murdock, Deroy. "Mitt Romney's Swett Problem." *HumanEvents.com.* Human Events, 6 Mar. 2007. Web. 12 Apr. 2010. <www.humanevents.com>.

142 Murdock, Deroy. "Mitt Romney's Swett Problem." *HumanEvents.com.* Human Events, 6 Mar. 2007. Web. 12 Apr. 2010. <www.humanevents.com>.

143 Murdock, Deroy. "Mitt Romney's Swett Problem." *HumanEvents.com*. Human Events, 6 Mar. 2007. Web. 12 Apr. 2010. <www.humanevents.com>.

144 Murdock, Deroy. "Mitt Romney's Swett Problem." *HumanEvents.com*. Human Events, 6 Mar. 2007. Web. 12 Apr. 2010. <www.humanevents.com>.

145 Swidey, Neil, and Stephanie Ebbert. "Journeys of a Shared Life - The *Boston Globe*." *Boston.com*. 27 June 2007. Web. 03 Sept. 2010. <http://www.boston.com/news/politics/2008/specials/romney/articles/part4_main/>.

146 Swidey, Neil, and Stephanie Ebbert. "Journeys of a Shared Life - The *Boston Globe*." *Boston.com*. 27 June 2007. Web. 03 Sept. 2010. <http://www.boston.com/news/politics/2008/specials/romney/articles/part4_main/>.

147 Balz, Dan, and Shailagh Murray. "Mass. Governor's Rightward Shift Raises Questions - Washingtonpost.com." *Washingtonpost.com*. 21 Dec. 2006. Web. 12 Apr. 2010. <http://www.washingtonpost.com/wp-dyn/content/article/2006/12/20/AR2006122002046.html>.

148 York, Byron. "Will They Believe Romney?" Editorial. *National Review* 18 Dec. 2006. *LogCabin.org*. 18 Dec. 2006. Web. 25 Nov. 2009. <http://online.logcabin.org/will-they-believe-romney.html>. 149 Balz, Dan, and Shailagh Murray. "Mass. Governor's Rightward Shift Raises Questions - Washingtonpost.com." *Washingtonpost.com*. 21 Dec. 2006. Web. 12 Apr. 2010. <http://www.washingtonpost.com/wp-dyn/content/article/2006/12/20/AR2006122002046.html>.

150 "The Mitt Romney Deception." *MassResistance!* Web. 4 May 2010. <http://www.massresistance.org/docs/marriage/romney/record/>.

151 "Mitt Romney's Flip-Flops." *Log Cabin Republicans*. Web. 25 Nov. 2009. <http://online.logcabin.org/mitt-romneys-flip-flops.html>.

152 Swidey, Neil, and Stephanie Ebbert. "Journeys of a Shared Life - The *Boston Globe*." *Boston.com*. 27 June 2007. Web. 03 Sept. 2010.

<http://www.boston.com/news/politics/2008/specials/romney/articles/part4_main/>.

153 "The Mitt Romney Deception." *MassResistance!* Web. 4 May 2010. <http://www.massresistance.org/docs/marriage/romney/record/>.

154 "Romney Attended Planned Parenthood Fundraiser in 1994 - Political Radar." *Political Punch.* 18 Dec. 2007. Web. 03 Sept. 2010. <http://blogs.abcnews.com/politicalradar/2007/12/romney-attended.html>.

155 "Romney Attended Planned Parenthood Fundraiser in 1994 - Political Radar." *Political Punch.* 18 Dec. 2007. Web. 03 Sept. 2010. <http://blogs.abcnews.com/politicalradar/2007/12/romney-attended.html>.

156 Romney for US Senate. Romney for US Senate, 1994. *Politico.com.* Web. 14 Oct. 2010. <http://www.politico.com/pdf/wmr_1994_senate_flier_side_1.pdf>.157 Swidey, Neil, and Stephanie Ebbert. "Journeys of a Shared Life - The *Boston Globe.*" *Boston.com.* 27 June 2007. Web. 03 Sept. 2010. <http://www.boston.com/news/politics/2008/specials/romney/articles/part4_main/>.

158 York, Byron. "Will They Believe Romney?" Editorial. *National Review* 18 Dec. 2006. *LogCabin.org.* 18 Dec. 2006. Web. 25 Nov. 2009. <http://online.logcabin.org/will-they-believe-romney.html>.

159 Balz, Dan, and Shailagh Murray. "Mass. Governor's Rightward Shift Raises Questions - Washingtonpost.com." *Washingtonpost.com.* 21 Dec. 2006. Web. 12 Apr. 2010. <http://www.washingtonpost.com/wp-dyn/content/article/2006/12/20/AR2006122002046.html>.

160 "The Mitt Romney Deception." *MassResistance!* Web. 4 May 2010. <http://www.massresistance.org/docs/marriage/romney/record/>.

161 "The Mitt Romney Deception." *MassResistance!* Web. 4 May 2010. <http://www.massresistance.org/docs/marriage/romney/record/>.

162 "The Mitt Romney Deception." *MassResistance!* Web. 4 May 2010. <http://www.massresistance.org/docs/marriage/romney/record/>.

163 "The Mitt Romney Deception." *MassResistance!* Web. 4 May 2010. <http://www.massresistance.org/docs/marriage/romney/record/>.

164 "Mitt Romney's Flip-Flops." *Log Cabin Republicans*. Web. 25 Nov. 2009. <http://online.logcabin.org/mitt-romneys-flip-flops.html>.

165 "The Mitt Romney Deception." *MassResistance!* Web. 4 May 2010. <http://www.massresistance.org/docs/marriage/romney/record/>.

166 "Mitt Romney's Flip-Flops." *Log Cabin Republicans*. Web. 25 Nov. 2009. <http://online.logcabin.org/mitt-romneys-flip-flops.html>.

167 "The Mitt Romney Deception." *MassResistance!* Web. 4 May 2010. <http://www.massresistance.org/docs/marriage/romney/record/>.

168 "Mitt Romney's Flip-Flops." *Log Cabin Republicans*. Web. 25 Nov. 2009. <http://online.logcabin.org/mitt-romneys-flip-flops.html>.

169 Romney for US Senate. Romney for US Senate, 1994. *Politico.com*. Web. 14 Oct. 2010. <http://www.politico.com/pdf/wmr_1994_senate_flier_side_1.pdf>.

170 David D. Kirkpatrick The New York Times Media Group. "Father's ghost haunts Romney campaign ELECTIONS 2008." International Herald Tribune. 2007. *HighBeam Research*. (September 13, 2010). http://www.highbeam.com/doc/1P1–147257119.html

171 "Romney: Ban PACs, Tax Campaign Contributions A History of Support for Campaign Finance Reform." Targeted News Service. 2007. *HighBeam Research*. (September 13, 2010). http://www.highbeam.com/doc/1P3–1364476891.html

172 "Romney: Ban PACs, Tax Campaign Contributions A History of Support for Campaign Finance Reform." Targeted News Service. 2007. *HighBeam Research*. (September 13, 2010). http://www.highbeam.com/doc/1P3–1364476891.html

173 Pindell, James. "Rival Campaigns Remind That Romney Was against Flat Tax." *Boston.com. Boston Globe*, 28 May 2007. Web. 15 Oct. 2010. <http://www.boston.com/news/local/politics/primarysource/romney/>.

174 Lunt, David J. "Mormon and the Olympics: Constructing an Olympic Identity." *Olympika* XVI (2007): 1–17. Print.

175 Lunt, David J. "Mormon and the Olympics: Constructing an Olympic Identity." *Olympika* XVI (2007): 1–17. Print.

176 Lunt, David J. "Mormon and the Olympics: Constructing an Olympic Identity." *Olympika* XVI (2007): 1–17. Print.

177 Lunt, David J. "Mormon and the Olympics: Constructing an Olympic Identity." *Olympika* XVI (2007): 1–17. Print.

178 Lunt, David J. "Mormon and the Olympics: Constructing an Olympic Identity." *Olympika* XVI (2007): 1–17. Print.

179 Lunt, David J. "Mormon and the Olympics: Constructing an Olympic Identity." *Olympika* XVI (2007): 1–17. Print.

180 Lunt, David J. "Mormon and the Olympics: Constructing an Olympic Identity." *Olympika* XVI (2007): 1–17. Print.

181 Lunt, David J. "Mormon and the Olympics: Constructing an Olympic Identity." *Olympika* XVI (2007): 1–17. Print.

182 Lunt, David J. "Mormon and the Olympics: Constructing an Olympic Identity." *Olympika* XVI (2007): 1–17. Print.

183 Lunt, David J. "Mormon and the Olympics: Constructing an Olympic Identity." *Olympika* XVI (2007): 1–17. Print.

184 Lunt, David J. "Mormon and the Olympics: Constructing an Olympic Identity." *Olympika* XVI (2007): 1–17. Print.

185 Lunt, David J. "Mormon and the Olympics: Constructing an Olympic Identity." *Olympika* XVI (2007): 1–17. Print.

186 Hohler, Bob. "In Games, a Showcase for Future Races." *Boston.com. Boston Globe*, 28 June 2007. Web. 26 Nov. 2009. <http://www.boston.com/news/politics/2008/specials/romney/articles/part5_main/>.

187 Lunt, David J. "Mormon and the Olympics: Constructing an Olympic Identity." *Olympika* XVI (2007): 1–17. Print.

188 Hohler, Bob. "In Games, a Showcase for Future Races." *Boston. com. Boston Globe*, 28 June 2007. Web. 26 Nov. 2009. <http://www.boston.com/news/politics/2008/specials/romney/articles/part5_main/>.

189 Hohler, Bob. "In Games, a Showcase for Future Races." *Boston. com. Boston Globe*, 28 June 2007. Web. 26 Nov. 2009. <http://www.boston.com/news/politics/2008/specials/romney/articles/part5_main/>.

190 Hohler, Bob. "In Games, a Showcase for Future Races." *Boston. com. Boston Globe*, 28 June 2007. Web. 26 Nov. 2009. <http://www.boston.com/news/politics/2008/specials/romney/articles/part5_main/>.

191 Hohler, Bob. "In Games, a Showcase for Future Races." *Boston. com. Boston Globe*, 28 June 2007. Web. 26 Nov. 2009. <http://www.boston.com/news/politics/2008/specials/romney/articles/part5_main/>.

192 Hohler, Bob. "In Games, a Showcase for Future Races." *Boston. com. Boston Globe*, 28 June 2007. Web. 26 Nov. 2009. <http://www.boston.com/news/politics/2008/specials/romney/articles/part5_main/>.

193 Hohler, Bob. "In Games, a Showcase for Future Races." *Boston. com. Boston Globe*, 28 June 2007. Web. 26 Nov. 2009. <http://www.boston.com/news/politics/2008/specials/romney/articles/part5_main/>.

194 Hohler, Bob. "In Games, a Showcase for Future Races." *Boston. com. Boston Globe*, 28 June 2007. Web. 26 Nov. 2009. <http://www.boston.com/news/politics/2008/specials/romney/articles/part5_main/>.

195 Riley Roche, Lisa. "Romney Used Olympics for Political Gain, Article Says." *Deseret News*. DeseretNews.com, 29 June 2007. Web. 19 Mar. 2010. <https://secure.deseretnews.com/article/680194893/Romney-used-Olympics-for-political-gain-article-says.html>.

196 Hohler, Bob. "In Games, a Showcase for Future Races." *Boston.com. Boston Globe*, 28 June 2007. Web. 26 Nov. 2009. <http://www.boston.com/news/politics/2008/specials/romney/articles/part5_main/>.

197 Hohler, Bob. "In Games, a Showcase for Future Races." *Boston.com. Boston Globe*, 28 June 2007. Web. 26 Nov. 2009. <http://www.boston.com/news/politics/2008/specials/romney/articles/part5_main/>.

198 Hohler, Bob. "In Games, a Showcase for Future Races." *Boston.com. Boston Globe*, 28 June 2007. Web. 26 Nov. 2009. <http://www.boston.com/news/politics/2008/specials/romney/articles/part5_main/>.

199 Baumann, David. "Romney Helped Salvage Olympics." *St. Petersburg Times*. SPTimes.com, 27 Sept. 2007. Web. 12 Mar. 2010. <http://www.sptimes.com/2007/09/27/Worldandnation/Romney_helped_salvage.shtml>.

200 Baumann, David. "Romney Helped Salvage Olympics." *St. Petersburg Times*. SPTimes.com, 27 Sept. 2007. Web. 12 Mar. 2010. <http://www.sptimes.com/2007/09/27/Worldandnation/Romney_helped_salvage.shtml>.

201 Hohler, Bob. "In Games, a Showcase for Future Races." *Boston.com. Boston Globe*, 28 June 2007. Web. 26 Nov. 2009. <http://www.boston.com/news/politics/2008/specials/romney/articles/part5_main/>.

202 Foy, Paul. "Olympic Budget Highlights Big Costs." 11 Jan. 2002. Web. 14 Oct. 2010. <http://iocc.ca/documents/OlympicBudgetBigCosts.pdf>.

203 Barlett, Donald L., and James B. Steele. "Snow Job." *SI.com*. CNN/Sports Illustrated, 10 Dec. 2001. Web. 25 Apr. 2010. <http://sportsillustrated.cnn.com/vault/article/magazine/MAG1024516/index.htm>.

204 Barlett, Donald L., and James B. Steele. "Snow Job." *SI.com*. CNN/Sports Illustrated, 10 Dec. 2001. Web. 25 Apr. 2010. <http://

sportsillustrated.cnn.com/vault/article/magazine/MAG1024516/ index.htm>.

205 Barlett, Donald L., and James B. Steele. "Snow Job." *SI.com*. CNN/ Sports Illustrated, 10 Dec. 2001. Web. 25 Apr. 2010. <http:// sportsillustrated.cnn.com/vault/article/magazine/MAG1024516/ index.htm>.

206 Barlett, Donald L., and James B. Steele. "Snow Job." *SI.com*. CNN/ Sports Illustrated, 10 Dec. 2001. Web. 25 Apr. 2010. <http:// sportsillustrated.cnn.com/vault/article/magazine/MAG1024516/ index.htm>.

207 Barlett, Donald L., and James B. Steele. "Snow Job." *SI.com*. CNN/ Sports Illustrated, 10 Dec. 2001. Web. 25 Apr. 2010. <http:// sportsillustrated.cnn.com/vault/article/magazine/MAG1024516/ index.htm>.

208 Grigg, William Norman. "Going for the (Taxpayers') Gold: The Olympic Games have produced a gold rush of federal subsidies — and some of the nation's wealthiest corporate leaders are among the biggest winners. (Olympics).(United States)(Statistical Data Included)." The New American. 2002. *HighBeam Research.* (September 13, 2010). http://www.highbeam.com/doc/1G1–82394276.html

209 Grigg, William Norman. "Going for the (Taxpayers') Gold: The Olympic Games have produced a gold rush of federal subsidies — and some of the nation's wealthiest corporate leaders are among the biggest winners. (Olympics).(United States)(Statistical Data Included)." The New American. 2002. *HighBeam Research.* (September 13, 2010). http://www.highbeam.com/doc/1G1–82394276.html

210 Barlett, Donald L., and James B. Steele. "Snow Job." *SI.com*. CNN/ Sports Illustrated, 10 Dec. 2001. Web. 25 Apr. 2010. <http:// sportsillustrated.cnn.com/vault/article/magazine/MAG1024516/ index.htm>.

211 Barlett, Donald L., and James B. Steele. "Snow Job." *SI.com*. CNN/ Sports Illustrated, 10 Dec. 2001. Web. 25 Apr. 2010. <http://

sportsillustrated.cnn.com/vault/article/magazine/MAG1024516/index.htm>.

212 Drogin, Bob. "GOP Spat Began with Olympics." *LATimes.com.* Los Angeles Times, 03 Feb. 2008. Web. 24 Nov. 2009. <http://articles.latimes.com/2008/feb/03/nation/na-olympics3>.

213 Schlussel, Debbie. "What's So Great About the Olympics? Part II." Web log post. *DebbieSchlussel.com.* 12 Feb. 2002. Web. 10 Mar. 2010. <http://www.debbieschlussel.com/78/whats-so-great-about-the-olympics-part-ii>.

214 Barlett, Donald L., and James B. Steele. "Snow Job." *SI.com.* CNN/Sports Illustrated, 10 Dec. 2001. Web. 25 Apr. 2010. <http://sportsillustrated.cnn.com/vault/article/magazine/MAG1024516/index.htm>.

215 Grigg, William Norman. "Going for the (Taxpayers') Gold: The Olympic Games have produced a gold rush of federal subsidies — and some of the nation's wealthiest corporate leaders are among the biggest winners. (Olympics).(United States)(Statistical Data Included)." The New American. 2002. *HighBeam Research.* (September 13, 2010). http://www.highbeam.com/doc/1G1–82394276.html

216 Grigg, William Norman. "Going for the (Taxpayers') Gold: The Olympic Games have produced a gold rush of federal subsidies — and some of the nation's wealthiest corporate leaders are among the biggest winners. (Olympics).(United States)(Statistical Data Included)." The New American. 2002. *HighBeam Research.* (September 13, 2010). http://www.highbeam.com/doc/1G1–82394276.html

217 Barlett, Donald L., and James B. Steele. "Snow Job." *SI.com.* CNN/Sports Illustrated, 10 Dec. 2001. Web. 25 Apr. 2010. <http://sportsillustrated.cnn.com/vault/article/magazine/MAG1024516/index.htm>.

218 Barlett, Donald L., and James B. Steele. "Snow Job." *SI.com.* CNN/Sports Illustrated, 10 Dec. 2001. Web. 25 Apr. 2010. <http://

sportsillustrated.cnn.com/vault/article/magazine/MAG1024516/index.htm>.

219 Grigg, William Norman. "Going for the (Taxpayers') Gold: The Olympic Games have produced a gold rush of federal subsidies — and some of the nation's wealthiest corporate leaders are among the biggest winners. (Olympics).(United States)(Statistical Data Included)." The New American. 2002. *HighBeam Research.* (September 13, 2010). http://www.highbeam.com/doc/1G1-82394276.html

220 Grigg, William Norman. "Going for the (Taxpayers') Gold: The Olympic Games have produced a gold rush of federal subsidies — and some of the nation's wealthiest corporate leaders are among the biggest winners. (Olympics).(United States)(Statistical Data Included)." The New American. 2002. *HighBeam Research.* (September 13, 2010). http://www.highbeam.com/doc/1G1-82394276.html

221 Joanna Weiss, Globe Staff. "ROMNEY FRIEND BUILT OLYMPIC PARK, WON TAX BREAKS SOME IN SALT LAKE QUESTION SITING IN SHOPPING MALL." The *Boston Globe* (Boston, MA). 2002. *HighBeam Research.* (September 13, 2010). http://www.highbeam.com/doc/1P2-7707903.html

222 Hohler, Bob. "In Games, a Showcase for Future Races." *Boston.com. Boston Globe,* 28 June 2007. Web. 26 Nov. 2009. <http://www.boston.com/news/politics/2008/specials/romney/articles/part5_main/>.

223 Lunt, David J. "Mormon and the Olympics: Constructing an Olympic Identity." *Olympika* XVI (2007): 1–17. Print.

224 Hohler, Bob. "In Games, a Showcase for Future Races." *Boston.com. Boston Globe,* 28 June 2007. Web. 26 Nov. 2009. <http://www.boston.com/news/politics/2008/specials/romney/articles/part5_main/>.

225 Hohler, Bob. "In Games, a Showcase for Future Races." *Boston.com. Boston Globe,* 28 June 2007. Web. 26 Nov. 2009. <http://

www.boston.com/news/politics/2008/specials/romney/articles/part5_main/>.

226 Hohler, Bob. "In Games, a Showcase for Future Races." *Boston.com. Boston Globe*, 28 June 2007. Web. 26 Nov. 2009. <http://www.boston.com/news/politics/2008/specials/romney/articles/part5_main/>.

227 Lunt, David J. "Mormon and the Olympics: Constructing an Olympic Identity." *Olympika* XVI (2007): 1–17. Print.

228 Fletcher Stack, Peggy. "Mormons Are Game for Rio Olympics." *Salt Lake Tribune. Sltrib.com.* Salt Lake Tribune, 9 Oct. 2009. Web. 26 Nov. 2009. <http://www.sltrib.com/portlet/article/html/jsp?articleId=13518320>.

229 Hohler, Bob. "In Games, a Showcase for Future Races." *Boston.com. Boston Globe*, 28 June 2007. Web. 26 Nov. 2009. <http://www.boston.com/news/politics/2008/specials/romney/articles/part5_main/>.

230 Lunt, David J. "Mormon and the Olympics: Constructing an Olympic Identity." *Olympika* XVI (2007): 1–17. Print.

231 Lunt, David J. "Mormon and the Olympics: Constructing an Olympic Identity." *Olympika* XVI (2007): 1–17. Print.

232 Van Biema, David. "The Man Who Made Romney Possible - *Time*." *Time* Jan. 2008. *Breaking News, Analysis, Politics, Blogs, News Photos, Video, Tech Reviews - Time.com*. 29 Jan. 2008. Web. 17 Mar. 2010. <http://www.time.com/time/nation/article/0,8599,1707753,00.html>.

233 Hohler, Bob. "Romney's Olympic Ties Helped Him Reap Campaign Funds." *Boston.com. Boston Globe*, 28 June 2007. Web. 25 Nov. 2009. <http://www.boston.com/news/politics/2008/specials/romney/articles/part5_side/>.

234 Hohler, Bob. "Romney's Olympic Ties Helped Him Reap Campaign Funds." *Boston.com. Boston Globe*, 28 June 2007. Web. 25 Nov. 2009. <http://www.boston.com/news/politics/2008/specials/romney/articles/part5_side/>.

235 Hohler, Bob. "Romney's Olympic Ties Helped Him Reap Campaign Funds." *Boston.com. Boston Globe*, 28 June 2007. Web. 25 Nov. 2009. <http://www.boston.com/news/politics/2008/specials/romney/articles/part5_side/>.

236 Hohler, Bob. "Romney's Olympic Ties Helped Him Reap Campaign Funds." *Boston.com. Boston Globe*, 28 June 2007. Web. 25 Nov. 2009. <http://www.boston.com/news/politics/2008/specials/romney/articles/part5_side/>.

237 Hohler, Bob. "Romney's Olympic Ties Helped Him Reap Campaign Funds." *Boston.com. Boston Globe*, 28 June 2007. Web. 25 Nov. 2009. <http://www.boston.com/news/politics/2008/specials/romney/articles/part5_side/>.

238 Hohler, Bob. "Romney's Olympic Ties Helped Him Reap Campaign Funds." *Boston.com. Boston Globe*, 28 June 2007. Web. 25 Nov. 2009. <http://www.boston.com/news/politics/2008/specials/romney/articles/part5_side/>.

239 Hohler, Bob. "Romney's Olympic Ties Helped Him Reap Campaign Funds." *Boston.com. Boston Globe*, 28 June 2007. Web. 25 Nov. 2009. <http://www.boston.com/news/politics/2008/specials/romney/articles/part5_side/>.

240 Stephanie Ebbert, Globe Staff. "ROMNEY BEGAN SPENDING EARLY BIG PUSH SEEN BEFORE DECLARATION." *The Boston Globe* (Boston, MA). 2002. *HighBeam Research.* (September 13, 2010). http://www.highbeam.com/doc/1P2–7714537.html

241 Zernike, Kate. "Olympics: The Man in Charge; Romney's Future After Salt Lake A Guessing Game." *NYTimes.com. New York Times*, 12 Feb. 2002. Web. 19 Mar. 2010. <http://www.nytimes.com/2002/02/12/sports/olympics-thc-man-in-chargc-romncy-s-future-after-salt-lake-a-guessing-game.html>.

242 Zernike, Kate. "Olympics: The Man in Charge; Romney's Future After Salt Lake A Guessing Game." *NYTimes.com. New York Times*, 12 Feb. 2002. Web. 19 Mar. 2010. <http://www.nytimes.com/2002/02/12/sports/olympics-the-man-in-charge-romney-s-future-after-salt-lake-a-guessing-game.html>.

243 Janofsky, Michael. "Games Behind Him, Olympics Leader Considers Political Run." *NYTimes.com. New York Times*, 25 Feb. 2002. Web. 19 Mar. 2010. <http://www.nytimes.com/2002/02/25/us/games-behind-him-olympics-leader-considers-political-run.html>.

244 Zernike, Kate. "Olympics: The Man in Charge; Romney's Future After Salt Lake A Guessing Game." *NYTimes.com. New York Times*, 12 Feb. 2002. Web. 19 Mar. 2010. <http://www.nytimes.com/2002/02/12/sports/olympics-the-man-in-charge-romney-s-future-after-salt-lake-a-guessing-game.html>.

245 Mooney, Brian. "Taking Office, Remaining an Outsider." *Boston.com. Boston Globe*, 29 June 2007. Web. 15 Mar. 2010. <http://www.boston.com/news/politics/2008/specials/romney/articles/part6_main/>.

246 Mooney, Brian. "Taking Office, Remaining an Outsider." *Boston.com. Boston Globe*, 29 June 2007. Web. 15 Mar. 2010. <http://www.boston.com/news/politics/2008/specials/romney/articles/part6_main/>.

247 Mooney, Brian. "Taking Office, Remaining an Outsider." *Boston.com. Boston Globe*, 29 June 2007. Web. 15 Mar. 2010. <http://www.boston.com/news/politics/2008/specials/romney/articles/part6_main/>.

248 Mooney, Brian. "Taking Office, Remaining an Outsider." *Boston.com. Boston Globe*, 29 June 2007. Web. 15 Mar. 2010. <http://www.boston.com/news/politics/2008/specials/romney/articles/part6_main/>.

249 Mooney, Brian. "Taking Office, Remaining an Outsider." *Boston.com. Boston Globe*, 29 June 2007. Web. 15 Mar. 2010. <http://www.boston.com/news/politics/2008/specials/romney/articles/part6_main/>.

250 Mooney, Brian. "Taking Office, Remaining an Outsider." *Boston.com. Boston Globe*, 29 June 2007. Web. 15 Mar. 2010. <http://www.boston.com/news/politics/2008/specials/romney/articles/part6_main/>.

251 Mooney, Brian. "Taking Office, Remaining an Outsider." *Boston.com. Boston Globe*, 29 June 2007. Web. 15 Mar. 2010. <http://www.boston.com/news/politics/2008/specials/romney/articles/part6_main/>.

252 Mooney, Brian. "Taking Office, Remaining an Outsider." *Boston.com. Boston Globe*, 29 June 2007. Web. 15 Mar. 2010. <http://www.boston.com/news/politics/2008/specials/romney/articles/part6_main/>.

253 Mooney, Brian. "Taking Office, Remaining an Outsider." *Boston.com. Boston Globe*, 29 June 2007. Web. 15 Mar. 2010. <http://www.boston.com/news/politics/2008/specials/romney/articles/part6_main/>.

254 Mooney, Brian. "Taking Office, Remaining an Outsider." *Boston.com. Boston Globe*, 29 June 2007. Web. 15 Mar. 2010. <http://www.boston.com/news/politics/2008/specials/romney/articles/part6_main/>.

255 "The Mitt Romney Deception." *MassResistance!* Web. 4 May 2010. <http://www.massresistance.org/docs/marriage/romney/record/>.

256 "Mitt Romney's Flip-Flops." *Log Cabin Republicans*. Web. 25 Nov. 2009. <http://online.logcabin.org/mitt-romneys-flip-flops.html>.

257 "The Mitt Romney Deception." *MassResistance!* Web. 4 May 2010. <http://www.massresistance.org/docs/marriage/romney/record/>.

258 "The Mitt Romney Deception." *MassResistance!* Web. 4 May 2010. <http://www.massresistance.org/docs/marriage/romney/record/>.

259 "A Report on the Pro-life Views of Governor Mitt Romney." *MassResistance!* Web. 17 May 2010. <http://www.massresistance.org/profile.html>.

260 "Mitt Romney's Flip-Flops." *Log Cabin Republicans*. Web. 25 Nov. 2009. <http://online.logcabin.org/mitt-romneys-flip-flops.html>.

261 "The Mitt Romney Deception." *MassResistance!* Web. 4 May 2010. <http://www.massresistance.org/docs/marriage/romney/record/>.

262 "Romney's Tone on Gay Rights Seen as Shift." *NYTimes. New York Times*, 8 Sept. 2007. Web. 17 May 2010. <http://www.nytimes.com/2007/09/08/us/politics/08romney.html>.

263 "Romney's Tone on Gay Rights Seen as Shift." *NYTimes. New York Times*, 8 Sept. 2007. Web. 17 May 2010. <http://www.nytimes.com/2007/09/08/us/politics/08romney.html>.

264 Mooney, Brian. "Taking Office, Remaining an Outsider." *Boston.com. Boston Globe*, 29 June 2007. Web. 15 Mar. 2010. <http://www.boston.com/news/politics/2008/specials/romney/articles/part6_main/>.

265 Kirkpatrick, David D. "Romney Used His Wealth to Enlist Richest Donors." *The New York Times*. 6 Apr. 2007. Web. 1 Dec. 2009. <http://www.nytimes.com/2007/04/06/us/politics/06romney.html>.

266 Kirkpatrick, David D. "Romney Used His Wealth to Enlist Richest Donors." The *New York Times*. 6 Apr. 2007. Web. 1 Dec. 2009. <http://www.nytimes.com/2007/04/06/us/politics/06romney.html>.

267 Mooney, Brian C., Stephanie Ebbert, and Scott Helman. "Ambitious Goals; Shifting Stances." *Boston.com. Boston Globe*, 30 June 2007. Web. 15 Mar. 2010. <http://www.boston.com/news/politics/2008/specials/romney/articles/part7_main/>.

268 Mooney, Brian C., Stephanie Ebbert, and Scott Helman. "Ambitious Goals; Shifting Stances." *Boston.com. Boston Globe*, 30 June 2007. Web. 15 Mar. 2010. <http://www.boston.com/news/politics/2008/specials/romney/articles/part7_main/>.

269 Mooney, Brian C., Stephanie Ebbert, and Scott Helman. "Ambitious Goals; Shifting Stances." *Boston.com. Boston Globe*, 30 June 2007. Web. 15 Mar. 2010. <http://www.boston.com/news/politics/2008/specials/romney/articles/part7_main/>.

270 Mooney, Brian C., Stephanie Ebbert, and Scott Helman. "Ambitious Goals; Shifting Stances." *Boston.com. Boston Globe*, 30 June 2007. Web. 15 Mar. 2010. <http://www.boston.com/news/politics/2008/specials/romney/articles/part7_main/>.

271 Szep, Jason. "Mitt Romney's Economic Record Questioned| Reuters." *Reuters.com*. 20 Jan. 2008. Web. 24 Nov. 2009. <http://www.reuters.com/article/idUSN2033704120080120>.

272 Szep, Jason. "Mitt Romney's Economic Record Questioned| Reuters." *Reuters.com*. 20 Jan. 2008. Web. 24 Nov. 2009. <http://www.reuters.com/article/idUSN2033704120080120>.

273 Mooney, Brian. "Taking Office, Remaining an Outsider." *Boston.com*. *Boston Globe*, 29 June 2007. Web. 15 Mar. 2010. <http://www.boston.com/news/politics/2008/specials/romney/articles/part6_main/>.

274 "Romney Used Fee Hikes to Trim Budget." AP Online. 2007. *HighBeam Research*. (October 14, 2010). http://www.highbeam.com/doc/1Y1–109837189.html

275 Howell, Carla. "Mitt Romney: Champion of Big Government." *LewRockwell.com*. 31 May 2007. Web. 03 Sept. 2010. <http://www.lewrockwell.com/orig4/howell5.html>.

276 Eddlem, Thomas. "Mitt Romney and the Wreckage of GOP Leadership." *Examiner.com*. 17 Aug. 2009. Web. 03 Sept. 2010. <http://www.examiner.com/gop-in-hartford>.

277 Mooney, Brian. "Taking Office, Remaining an Outsider." *Boston.com*. *Boston Globe*, 29 June 2007. Web. 15 Mar. 2010. <http://www.boston.com/news/politics/2008/specials/romney/articles/part6_main/>. 278 Howell, Carla. "Mitt Romney: Champion of Big Government." *LewRockwell.com*. 31 May 2007. Web. 03 Sept. 2010. <http://www.lewrockwell.com/orig4/howell5.html>.

279 Batkins, Sam. "New Budget Data: Romney's Mediocre Record." Web log post. *Government Bytes*. National Taxpayers Union, 26 June 2008. Web. 25 Nov. 2009. <http://blog.ntu.org/main/post.php?post_id=3541>.

280 Dayton, Soren. "Romney Lying about His Tax Record (update)." *SorenDayton.com*. 7 Feb. 2007. Web. 30 Nov. 2009. <http://sorendayton.com/2007/02/07/romney-lying-about-his-tax-record>.

281 Dayton, Soren. "Romney Lying about His Tax Record (update)." *SorenDayton.com*. 7 Feb. 2007. Web. 30 Nov. 2009. <http://sorendayton.com/2007/02/07/romney-lying-about-his-tax-record>.

282 Howell, Carla. "Mitt Romney: Champion of Big Government." *LewRockwell.com*. 31 May 2007. Web. 03 Sept. 2010. <http://www.lewrockwell.com/orig4/howell5.html>.

283 Batkins, Sam. "New Budget Data: Romney's Mediocre Record." Web log post. *Government Bytes*. National Taxpayers Union, 26 June 2008. Web. 25 Nov. 2009. <http://blog.ntu.org/main/post.php?post_id=3541>.

284 Howell, Carla. "Mitt Romney: Champion of Big Government." *LewRockwell.com*. 31 May 2007. Web. 03 Sept. 2010. <http://www.lewrockwell.com/orig4/howell5.html>.

285 Howell, Carla. "Mitt Romney: Champion of Big Government." *LewRockwell.com*. 31 May 2007. Web. 03 Sept. 2010. <http://www.lewrockwell.com/orig4/howell5.html>.

286 Szep, Jason. "Mitt Romney's Economic Record Questioned| Reuters." *Reuters.com*. 20 Jan. 2008. Web. 24 Nov. 2009. <http://www.reuters.com/article/idUSN2033704120080120>.

287 Szep, Jason. "Mitt Romney's Economic Record Questioned| Reuters." *Reuters.com*. 20 Jan. 2008. Web. 24 Nov. 2009. <http://www.reuters.com/article/idUSN2033704120080120>.

288 Mooney, Brian C., Stephanie Ebbert, and Scott Helman. "Ambitious Goals; Shifting Stances." *Boston.com*. *Boston Globe*, 30 June 2007. Web. 15 Mar. 2010. <http://www.boston.com/news/politics/2008/specials/romney/articles/part7_main/>.

289 Szep, Jason. "Mitt Romney's Economic Record Questioned| Reuters." *Reuters.com*. 20 Jan. 2008. Web. 24 Nov. 2009. <http://www.reuters.com/article/idUSN2033704120080120>.

290 Szep, Jason. "Mitt Romney's Economic Record Questioned| Reuters." *Reuters.com*. 20 Jan. 2008. Web. 24 Nov. 2009. <http://www.reuters.com/article/idUSN2033704120080120>.

291 Szep, Jason. “Mitt Romney's Economic Record Questioned| Reuters.” *Reuters.com*. 20 Jan. 2008. Web. 24 Nov. 2009. <http://www.reuters.com/article/idUSN20337041200801 20>.

292 JOAN VENNOCHI. “ROMNEY'S REAL GOAL IN GAY CAMPAIGN.” The *Boston Globe* (Boston, MA). 2004. *HighBeam Research*. (September 13, 2010). http://www.highbeam.com/doc/1P2–7838392.html

293 JENNIFER PETER, Associated Press Writer. “Gay Marriage a Quandary for Romney.” AP Online. 2004. *HighBeam Research*. (September 13, 2010). http://www.highbeam.com/doc/1P1–94809477.html294 JENNIFER PETER, Associated Press Writer. “Gay Marriage a Quandary for Romney.” AP Online. 2004. *HighBeam Research*. (September 13, 2010). http://www.highbeam.com/doc/1P1–94809477.html

295 JENNIFER PETER, Associated Press Writer. “Gay Marriage a Quandary for Romney.” AP Online. 2004. *HighBeam Research*. (September 13, 2010). http://www.highbeam.com/doc/1P1–94809477.html

296 Arkes, Hadley. “The Missing Governor.” *National Review Online*. 17 May 2004. Web. 4 May 2010. <http://old.nationalreview.com/arkes/arkes200405170901.asp>.

297 “The Mitt Romney Deception.” *MassResistance!* Web. 4 May 2010. <http://www.massresistance.org/docs/marriage/romney/record/>.

298 Zezima, Katie. “Obey Same-Sex Marriage Law, Officials Told.” *NYTimes.com*. *New York Times*, 26 Apr. 2004. Web. 4 May 2010. <http://www.nytimes.com/2004/04/26/us/obey-same-sex-marriage-law-officials-told.html>.

299 “The Mitt Romney Deception.” *MassResistance!* Web. 4 May 2010. <http://www.massresistance.org/docs/marriage/romney/record/>.

300 “Gov. Mitt Romney and Same-sex Marriage in Massachusetts - Here's What Happened.” *MassResistance!* Web. 13 Sept. 2010. <http://www.massresistance.org/docs/marriage/romney>.

301 "Joint Letter to Governor Romney from Pro-Family Leaders." Letter to Governor W. Mitt Romney. 20 Dec. 2006. *MassResistance.org.* Web. 4 May 2010. <www.massresistance.org/docs/marriage/romney/dec_letter/letter.pdf>.

302 "Joint Letter to Governor Romney from Pro-Family Leaders." Letter to Governor W. Mitt Romney. 20 Dec. 2006. *MassResistance.org.* Web. 4 May 2010. <www.massresistance.org/docs/marriage/romney/dec_letter/letter.pdf>.

303 "Joint Letter to Governor Romney from Pro-Family Leaders." Letter to Governor W. Mitt Romney. 20 Dec. 2006. *MassResistance.org.* Web. 4 May 2010. <www.massresistance.org/docs/marriage/romney/dec_letter/letter.pdf>.

304 "Joint Letter to Governor Romney from Pro-Family Leaders." Letter to Governor W. Mitt Romney. 20 Dec. 2006. *MassResistance.org.* Web. 4 May 2010. <www.massresistance.org/docs/marriage/romney/dec_letter/letter.pdf>.

305 "Joint Letter to Governor Romney from Pro-Family Leaders." Letter to Governor W. Mitt Romney. 20 Dec. 2006. *MassResistance.org.* Web. 4 May 2010. <www.massresistance.org/docs/marriage/romney/dec_letter/letter.pdf>.

306 "The Mitt Romney Deception." *MassResistance!* Web. 4 May 2010. <http://www.massresistance.org/docs/marriage/romney/record/>.

307 "The Mitt Romney Deception." *MassResistance!* Web. 4 May 2010. <http://www.massresistance.org/docs/marriage/romney/record/>.

308 "The Mitt Romney Deception." *MassResistance!* Web. 4 May 2010. <http://www.massresistance.org/docs/marriage/romney/record/>.

309 "The Mitt Romney Deception." *MassResistance!* Web. 4 May 2010. <http://www.massresistance.org/docs/marriage/romney/record/>.

310 "The Mitt Romney Deception." *MassResistance!* Web. 4 May 2010. <http://www.massresistance.org/docs/marriage/romney/record/>.

311 "The Mitt Romney Deception." *MassResistance!* Web. 4 May 2010. <http://www.massresistance.org/docs/marriage/romney/record/>.

312 Mooney, Brian. "Taking Office, Remaining an Outsider." *Boston.com. Boston Globe*, 29 June 2007. Web. 15 Mar. 2010. <http://www.boston.com/news/politics/2008/specials/romney/articles/part6_main/>.

313 (Mooney, Brian. "Taking Office, Remaining an Outsider." *Boston.com. Boston Globe*, 29 June 2007. Web. 15 Mar. 2010. <http://www.boston.com/news/politics/2008/specials/romney/articles/part6_main/>.

314 "The Mitt Romney Deception." *MassResistance!* Web. 4 May 2010. <http://www.massresistance.org/docs/marriage/romney/record/>.

315 Broder, David S. "Romney Leaving Mass. With Mixed Record - Washingtonpost.com." *Washingtonpost.com*. Washington Post, 26 Nov. 2006. Web. 30 Nov. 2009. <http://www.washingtonpost.com/wp-dyn/content/article/2006/11/25/AR2006112500736.html>.

316 Mooney, Brian C., Stephanie Ebbert, and Scott Helman. "Ambitious Goals; Shifting Stances." *Boston.com. Boston Globe*, 30 June 2007. Web. 15 Mar. 2010. <http://www.boston.com/news/politics/2008/specials/romney/articles/part7_main/>.

317 Mooney, Brian C., Stephanie Ebbert, and Scott Helman. "Ambitious Goals; Shifting Stances." *Boston.com. Boston Globe*, 30 June 2007. Web. 15 Mar. 2010. <http://www.boston.com/news/politics/2008/specials/romney/articles/part7_main/>.

318 Mooney, Brian C., Stephanie Ebbert, and Scott Helman. "Ambitious Goals; Shifting Stances." *Boston.com. Boston Globe*, 30 June 2007. Web. 15 Mar. 2010. <http://www.boston.com/news/politics/2008/specials/romney/articles/part7_main/>.

319 Mooney, Brian C., Stephanie Ebbert, and Scott Helman. "Ambitious Goals; Shifting Stances." *Boston.com. Boston Globe*, 30 June 2007. Web. 15 Mar. 2010. <http://www.boston.com/news/politics/2008/specials/romney/articles/part7_main/>.

320 Mooney, Brian C., Stephanie Ebbert, and Scott Helman. "Ambitious Goals; Shifting Stances." *Boston.com. Boston Globe*,

30 June 2007. Web. 15 Mar. 2010. <http://www.boston.com/news/politics/2008/specials/romney/articles/part7_main/>.

321 Mooney, Brian C., Stephanie Ebbert, and Scott Helman. "Ambitious Goals; Shifting Stances." *Boston.com. Boston Globe*, 30 June 2007. Web. 15 Mar. 2010. <http://www.boston.com/news/politics/2008/specials/romney/articles/part7_main/>.

322 Tanner, Michael. *Lessons from the Fall of RomneyCare*. Rep. Cato Institute. The Cato Institute. Web. 30 Nov. 2009. <http://www.cato.org/pubs/policy_report/v30n1/cpr30n1–1.html>.

323 Tanner, Michael. *No Miracle in Massachusetts: Why Governor Romney's Health Care Reform Won't Work*. Issue brief no. 97. *The Cato Institute*. 6 June 2006. Web. 30 Nov. 2009. <http://www.cato.org/pub_display.php?pub_id=6407>.

324 "RomneyCare Revisited." Editorial. *Wall Street Journal* Jan. 2010, Review & Outlook sec. *WSJ.com*. 21 Jan. 2010. Web. 30 Nov. 2009. <http://online.wsj.com/article/SB10001424052748703837004575013080421218008.html>.

325 Cheplick, Thomas, and Joe Emanuel. "Massachusetts Slashes Funding, Rations Care - by Thomas Cheplick and Joe Emanuel - Health Care News." *Health Care News* 6 Aug. 2009. *The Heartland Institute*. Web. 30 Nov. 2009. <http://www.heartland.org/publications/health care/article/25810/Massachusetts_Slashes_Funding_Rations_Care.html>.

326 Robinson, Peter. "Mitt Romney's Big-Government Health Care Plan - Forbes.com." Editorial. *Forbes. Forbes.com*. 7 Aug. 2009. Web. 30 Nov. 2009. <http://www.forbes.com/2009/08/06/mitt-romney-health-care-gop-opinions-columnists-peter-robinson.html>.

327 Romano, Andrew. "Mitt Romney on RomneyCare." *Newsweek* 19 Apr. 2010. *Newsweek.com*. 19 Apr. 2010. Web. 07 Sept. 2010. <http://www.newsweek.com/2010/04/18/mitt-romney-on-romneycare.html>.

328 Turner, Grace-Marie. "The Failure of RomneyCare - WSJ.com." *Wall Street Journal* 17 Mar. 2007. *WSJ.com*. Wall Street Journal,

16 Mar. 2010. Web. 14 Oct. 2010. <http://online.wsj.com/article/SB10001424052748703625304575115691871093652.html>.

329 Tanner, Michael. *Lessons from the Fall of RomneyCare*. Rep. Cato Institute. The Cato Institute. Web. 30 Nov. 2009. <http://www.cato.org/pubs/policy_report/v30n1/cpr30n1–1.html>.

330 Robinson, Peter. "Mitt Romney's Big-Government Health Care Plan - Forbes.com." Editorial. *Forbes. Forbes.com.* 7 Aug. 2009. Web. 30 Nov. 2009. <http://www.forbes.com/2009/08/06/mitt-romney-health-care-gop-opinions-columnists-peter-robinson.html>.

331 "The Massachusetts Health Mess." Editorial. *Wall Street Journal*, Review & Outlook sec. *WSJ.com.* 11 July 2009. Web. 30 Nov. 2009. <http://online.wsj.com/article/SB124726287099225209.html>.

332 "Review & Outlook: Back to the ObamaCare Future with Massachusetts - WSJ.com." *Wall Street Journal. WSJ.com.* Wall Street Journal, 1 Mar. 2010. Web. 14 Oct. 2010. <http://online.wsj.com/article/SB1000142405274870344480457507129413928 6892.html>.

333 Turner, Grace-Marie. "The Failure of RomneyCare - WSJ.com." *Wall Street Journal* 17 Mar. 2007. *WSJ.com.* Wall Street Journal, 16 Mar. 2010. Web. 14 Oct. 2010. <http://online.wsj.com/article/SB10001424052748703625304575115691871093652.html>.

334 "National Health Preview: The Massachusetts Debacle, Coming Soon to Your Neighborhood." Editorial. *The Wall Street Journal* 27 Mar. 2009, Review & Outlook sec.: A12. *WSJ.com.* 27 Mar. 2009. Web. 30 Nov. 2009. <http://online.wsj.com/article/SB123811121310853037.html>.

335 Turner, Grace-Marie. "The Failure of RomneyCare - WSJ.com." *Wall Street Journal* 17 Mar. 2007. *WSJ.com.* Wall Street Journal, 16 Mar. 2010. Web. 14 Oct. 2010. <http://online.wsj.com/article/SB10001424052748703625304575115691871093652.html>.

336 Cannon, Michael F. "Romney's Folly - Health-Care Mandates Are a Middle-Class Tax | Michael F. Cannon | Cato Institute:

Commentary." Editorial. *National Review* 24 July 2009. *The Cato Institute.* 24 July 2009. Web. 30 Nov. 2009. <http://www.cato.org/pub_display.php?pub_id=10381>.

337 Turner, Grace-Marie. "The Failure of RomneyCare - WSJ.com." *Wall Street Journal* 17 Mar. 2007. *WSJ.com.* Wall Street Journal, 16 Mar. 2010. Web. 14 Oct. 2010. <http://online.wsj.com/article/SB10001424052748703625304575115691871093652.html>.

338 Allott, Daniel. "Romney, Get Real about Your Abortion Record - Daniel Allott - POLITICO.com." Editorial. *POLITICO.com.* 20 Dec. 2007. Web. 15 Oct. 2010. <http://www.politico.com/news/stories/1207/7482.html>.

339 Mooney, Brian C., Stephanie Ebbert, and Scott Helman. "Ambitious Goals; Shifting Stances." *Boston.com. Boston Globe,* 30 June 2007. Web. 15 Mar. 2010. <http://www.boston.com/news/politics/2008/specials/romney/articles/part7_main/>.

340 Mooney, Brian C., Stephanie Ebbert, and Scott Helman. "Ambitious Goals; Shifting Stances." *Boston.com. Boston Globe,* 30 June 2007. Web. 15 Mar. 2010. <http://www.boston.com/news/politics/2008/specials/romney/articles/part7_main/>.

341 Mooney, Brian C., Stephanie Ebbert, and Scott Helman. "Ambitious Goals; Shifting Stances." *Boston.com. Boston Globe,* 30 June 2007. Web. 15 Mar. 2010. <http://www.boston.com/news/politics/2008/specials/romney/articles/part7_main/>.

342 Allen, Mike. "A Mormon as President?" *Time. Time.com.* 26 Nov. 2006. Web. 11 Mar. 2010. <http://www.time.com/time/magazine/article/0,9171,1562941,00.html>.

343 Allen, Mike. "A Mormon as President?" *Time. Time.com.* 26 Nov. 2006. Web. 11 Mar. 2010. <http://www.time.com/time/magazine/article/0,9171,1562941,00.html>.

344 "Can LDS Film Director Mitch Davis Help Mitt Romney Get in the White House?" Interview by Meridian Magazine. *MeridianMagazine.com.* Meridian Magazine, 2006. Web. 28 May 2010. <http://www.meridianmagazine.com/article/1138?ac=1>.

345 "Can LDS Film Director Mitch Davis Help Mitt Romney Get in the White House?" Interview by Meridian Magazine. *MeridianMagazine.com*. Meridian Magazine, 2006. Web. 28 May 2010. <http://www.meridianmagazine.com/article/1138?ac=1>.

346 "Can LDS Film Director Mitch Davis Help Mitt Romney Get in the White House?" Interview by Meridian Magazine. *MeridianMagazine.com*. Meridian Magazine, 2006. Web. 28 May 2010. <http://www.meridianmagazine.com/article/1138?ac=1>.

347 Helman, Scott, and Michael Levenson. "Romney Camp Consulted with Mormon Leaders." *Boston Globe. Boston.com. Boston Globe*, 19 Oct. 2006. Web. 1 Dec. 2009. <http://www.boston.com/news/nation/articles/2006/10/19/romney_camp_consulted_with_mormon_leaders/>.

348 Helman, Scott, and Michael Levenson. "Romney Camp Consulted with Mormon Leaders." *Boston Globe. Boston.com. Boston Globe*, 19 Oct. 2006. Web. 1 Dec. 2009. <http://www.boston.com/news/nation/articles/2006/10/19/romney_camp_consulted_with_mormon_leaders/>.

349 Helman, Scott, and Michael Levenson. "Romney Camp Consulted with Mormon Leaders." *Boston Globe. Boston.com. Boston Globe*, 19 Oct. 2006. Web. 1 Dec. 2009. <http://www.boston.com/news/nation/articles/2006/10/19/romney_camp_consulted_with_mormon_leaders/>.

350 Helman, Scott, and Michael Levenson. "Romney Camp Consulted with Mormon Leaders." *Boston Globe. Boston.com. Boston Globe*, 19 Oct. 2006. Web. 1 Dec. 2009. <http://www.boston.com/news/nation/articles/2006/10/19/romney_camp_consulted_with_mormon_leaders/>.

351 Helman, Scott, and Michael Levenson. "Romney Camp Consulted with Mormon Leaders." *Boston Globe. Boston.com. Boston Globe*, 19 Oct. 2006. Web. 1 Dec. 2009. <http://www.boston.com/news/nation/articles/2006/10/19/romney_camp_consulted_with_mormon_leaders/>.

352 Helman, Scott, and Michael Levenson. "Romney Camp Consulted with Mormon Leaders." *Boston Globe. Boston.com. Boston Globe*, 19 Oct. 2006. Web. 1 Dec. 2009. <http://www.boston.com/news/nation/articles/2006/10/19/romney_camp_consulted_with_mormon_leaders/>.

353 Helman, Scott, and Michael Levenson. "Romney Camp Consulted with Mormon Leaders." *Boston Globe. Boston.com. Boston Globe*, 19 Oct. 2006. Web. 1 Dec. 2009. <http://www.boston.com/news/nation/articles/2006/10/19/romney_camp_consulted_with_mormon_leaders/>.

354 Helman, Scott, and Michael Levenson. "Romney Camp Consulted with Mormon Leaders." *Boston Globe. Boston.com. Boston Globe*, 19 Oct. 2006. Web. 1 Dec. 2009. <http://www.boston.com/news/nation/articles/2006/10/19/romney_camp_consulted_with_mormon_leaders/>.

355 Helman, Scott, and Michael Levenson. "Romney Camp Consulted with Mormon Leaders." *Boston Globe. Boston.com. Boston Globe*, 19 Oct. 2006. Web. 1 Dec. 2009. <http://www.boston.com/news/nation/articles/2006/10/19/romney_camp_consulted_with_mormon_leaders/>.

356 Helman, Scott, and Michael Levenson. "Romney Camp Consulted with Mormon Leaders." *Boston Globe. Boston.com. Boston Globe*, 19 Oct. 2006. Web. 1 Dec. 2009. <http://www.boston.com/news/nation/articles/2006/10/19/romney_camp_consulted_with_mormon_leaders/>.

357 Helman, Scott, and Michael Levenson. "Romney Camp Consulted with Mormon Leaders." *Boston Globe. Boston.com. Boston Globe*, 19 Oct. 2006. Web. 1 Dec. 2009. <http://www.boston.com/news/nation/articles/2006/10/19/romney_camp_consulted_with_mormon_leaders/>.

358 Helman, Scott, and Michael Levenson. "Romney Camp Consulted with Mormon Leaders." *Boston Globe. Boston.com. Boston Globe*, 19 Oct. 2006. Web. 1 Dec. 2009. <http://www.boston.com/news/nation/articles/2006/10/19/romney_camp_consulted_with_mormon_leaders/>.

359 Helman, Scott, and Michael Levenson. "Romney Camp Consulted with Mormon Leaders." *Boston Globe. Boston.com. Boston Globe*, 19 Oct. 2006. Web. 1 Dec. 2009. <http://www.boston.com/news/nation/articles/2006/10/19/romney_camp_consulted_with_mormon_leaders/>.

360 Helman, Scott, and Michael Levenson. "Romney Camp Consulted with Mormon Leaders." *Boston Globe. Boston.com. Boston Globe*, 19 Oct. 2006. Web. 1 Dec. 2009. <http://www.boston.com/news/nation/articles/2006/10/19/romney_camp_consulted_with_mormon_leaders/>.

361 Helman, Scott, and Michael Levenson. "Romney Camp Consulted with Mormon Leaders." *Boston Globe. Boston.com. Boston Globe*, 19 Oct. 2006. Web. 1 Dec. 2009. <http://www.boston.com/news/nation/articles/2006/10/19/romney_camp_consulted_with_mormon_leaders/>.

362 Helman, Scott, and Michael Levenson. "Romney Camp Consulted with Mormon Leaders." *Boston Globe. Boston.com. Boston Globe*, 19 Oct. 2006. Web. 1 Dec. 2009. <http://www.boston.com/news/nation/articles/2006/10/19/romney_camp_consulted_with_mormon_leaders/>.

363 Helman, Scott, and Michael Levenson. "Romney Camp Consulted with Mormon Leaders." *Boston Globe. Boston.com. Boston Globe*, 19 Oct. 2006. Web. 1 Dec. 2009. <http://www.boston.com/news/nation/articles/2006/10/19/romney_camp_consulted_with_mormon_leaders/>.

364 "Romney's candidacy stirs interest in Mormons: Church bolsters its outreach efforts, adds media guide." The Tribune (Mesa, AZ). 2007. *HighBeam Research.* (October 14, 2010). http://www.highbeam.com/doc/1G1-168723577.html

365 Murray, Matthew. "Mormon Political Donors Helped Fund PBS Series." *Roll Call.* 2 May 2007. Web. 28 May 2010. <http://www.rollcall.com/issues/52_118/news/18285-1.html>.

366 Murray, Matthew. “Mormon Political Donors Helped Fund PBS Series.” *Roll Call.* 2 May 2007. Web. 28 May 2010. <http://www.rollcall.com/issues/52_118/news/18285–1.html>.

367 “Romney Taps Donors Through Mormon Church.” AP Online. 2007. *HighBeam Research.* (September 13, 2010). http://www.highbeam.com/doc/1Y1–105379616.html

368 Carpenter, Amanda B. “Romney’s Mormon Money Paradox.” *Human Events.com*. Human Events, 18 Apr. 2007. Web. 1 Dec. 2009. <http://www.humanevents.com/article.php?id=20307>.

369 Carpenter, Amanda B. “Romney’s Mormon Money Paradox.” *Human Events.com*. Human Events, 18 Apr. 2007. Web. 1 Dec. 2009. <http://www.humanevents.com/article.php?id=20307>.

370 Romney Taps Donors Through Mormon Church.” AP Online. 2007. *HighBeam Research.* (September 13, 2010). http://www.highbeam.com/doc/1Y1–105379616.html

371 Romney Taps Donors Through Mormon Church.” AP Online. 2007. *HighBeam Research.* (September 13, 2010). http://www.highbeam.com/doc/1Y1–105379616.html

372 Carpenter, Amanda B. “Romney’s Mormon Money Paradox.” *Human Events.com*. Human Events, 18 Apr. 2007. Web. 1 Dec. 2009. <http://www.humanevents.com/article.php?id=20307>.

373 Cummings, Jeanne. “Minding Business Pays off for Romney.” *POLITICO.com*. 25 Oct. 2007. Web. 28 Mar. 2010. <http://www.politico.com/news/stories/1007/6535.html>.

374 Cummings, Jeanne. “Minding Business Pays off for Romney.” *POLITICO.com*. 25 Oct.2007. Web. 28 Mar. 2010. <http://www.politico.com/news/stories/1007/6535.html>.

375 Mooney, Brian C. “Romney Left Mass. on 212 Days in ‘06 - The *Boston Globe*.” *Boston.com*. *Boston Globe*, 24 Dec. 2006. Web. 16 June 2010. <http://www.boston.com/news/local/articles/2006/12/24/romney_left_mass_on_212_days_in_06/>.

376 Mooney, Brian C. “Romney Left Mass. on 212 Days in ‘06 - The *Boston Globe*.” *Boston.com*. *Boston Globe*, 24 Dec. 2006.

Web. 16 June 2010. <http://www.boston.com/news/local/articles/2006/12/24/romney_left_mass_on_212_days_in_06/>.

377 Mooney, Brian C. "Romney Left Mass. on 212 Days in '06 - The *Boston Globe*." *Boston.com. Boston Globe*, 24 Dec. 2006. Web. 16 June 2010. <http://www.boston.com/news/local/articles/2006/12/24/romney_left_mass_on_212_days_in_06/>.

378 Kirkpatrick, David D. "In Romney's Bid, His Wallet Opens to the Right." *NYTimes.com*. The *New York Times*, 11 Mar. 2007. Web. 28 Mar. 2010. <http://www.nytimes.com/2007/03/11/us/politics/11romney.html>.

379 "The Mitt Romney Deception." *MassResistance!* Web. 4 May 2010. <http://www.massresistance.org/docs/marriage/romney/record/>.

380 Kirkpatrick, David D. "In Romney's Bid, His Wallet Opens to the Right." *NYTimes.com*. The *New York Times*, 11 Mar. 2007. Web. 28 Mar. 2010. <http://www.nytimes.com/2007/03/11/us/politics/11romney.html>.

381 Kirkpatrick, David D. "In Romney's Bid, His Wallet Opens to the Right." *NYTimes.com*. The *New York Times*, 11 Mar. 2007. Web. 28 Mar. 2010. <http://www.nytimes.com/2007/03/11/us/politics/11romney.html>.

382 Hudson, Deal W. "The Problem with Mitt Romney's Pro-Life Conversion." *InsideCatholic.com*. 27 Dec. 2007. Web. 21 June 2010. <http://www.insidecatholic.com/index2.php?option=com_content&task=view&id=2024&...>.

383 Silverstein, Ken. "Making Mitt Romney: How to Fabricate a Conservative (Harper's Magazine)." Editorial. *Harpers.org*. Harper's Magazine, Nov. 2007. Web. 15 Mar. 2010. <http://www.harpers.org/archive/2007/11/0081773>.

384 *Premier Radio Networks. Clear Channel Communications, Inc.* Web. 15 Oct. 2010. <http://www.clearchannel.com/radio/pressrelease.aspx?pressreleaseID=1599&p hidde>.

385 Clear Channel Communications, Inc. *Clear Channel Communications, Inc. Enters into Merger Agreement with*

Private Equity Group Co-Led By Bain Capital Partners, LLC and Thomas H. Lee Partners, L.P. ClearChannel.com. Clear Channel Communications, Inc., 16 Nov. 2006. Web. 26 Nov. 2009. <http://www.clearchannel.com/Corporate/PressRelease.aspx?PressReleaseID=1824>.

386 Harris, Marlys. "Millionaires-in-Chief." *CNNMoney.com*. 12 July 2007. Web. 27 Mar. 2010. <http://money.cnn.com/galleries/2007/moneymag/0712/gallery.candidates.moneymag/index.html>.

387 Heslam, Jessica. "WRKO Bumps Rush Limbaugh for Charley Manning - BostonHerald.com." *BostonHerald.com*. Boston Herald, 02 Mar. 2010. Web. 17 Mar. 2010. <http://www.bostonherald.com/news/regional/view.bg?articleid=1236534>.

388 "The Mitt Romney Deception." *MassResistance!* Web. 4 May 2010. <http://www.massresistance.org/docs/marriage/romney/record/>.

389 "The Mitt Romney Deception." *MassResistance!* Web. 4 May 2010. <http://www.massresistance.org/docs/marriage/romney/record/>.

390 "The Mitt Romney Deception." *MassResistance!* Web. 4 May 2010. <http://www.massresistance.org/docs/marriage/romney/record/>.

391 Allott, Daniel. "Romney, Get Real about Your Abortion Record - Daniel Allott - POLITICO.com." Editorial. *POLITICO.com*. 20 Dec. 2007. Web. 15 Oct. 2010. <http://www.politico.com/news/stories/1207/7482.html>.

392 Ruth Marcus. "Mitt Romney's Extreme Makeover." The Washington Post. 2007. *HighBeam Research*. (September 13, 2010). http://www.highbeam.com/doc/1P2–5806022.html

393 Ruth Marcus. "Mitt Romney's Extreme Makeover." The Washington Post. 2007. *HighBeam Research*. (September 13, 2010). http://www.highbeam.com/doc/1P2–5806022.html

394 Ruth Marcus. "Mitt Romney's Extreme Makeover." The Washington Post. 2007. *HighBeam Research*. (September 13, 2010). http://www.highbeam.com/doc/1P2–5806022.html

395 Rubin, Jennifer. "Mitt Romney's Conversion." *Weekly Standard.com*. Weekly Standard, 5 Feb. 2007. Web. 21 June 2010. <http://

www.weeklystandard.com/content/public/articles/000/000/013 /222htyos.asp>.

396 Klein, Rick. "Romney's Pro-Life Conversion: Myth or Reality? - ABC News." *ABCNews.com*. ABC New Internet Ventures, 14 June 2007. Web. 21 June 2010. <http://abcnews.go.com/Politics/story?id=3279653&page=1>.

397 Rubin, Jennifer. "Mitt Romney's Conversion." *Weekly Standard.com*. Weekly Standard, 5 Feb. 2007. Web. 21 June 2010. <http://www.weeklystandard.com/content/public/articles/000/000/013/222htyos.asp>.

398 Klein, Rick. "Romney's Pro-Life Conversion: Myth or Reality? - ABC News." *ABCNews.com*. ABC New Internet Ventures, 14 June 2007. Web. 21 June 2010. <http://abcnews.go.com/Politics/story?id=3279653&page=1>.

399 Belluck, Pam. "Massachusetts Democrats Object to Stem Cell Research Ban." *NYTimes.com*. The *New York Times*, 11 Feb. 2005. Web. 21 June 2010. <http://www.nytimes.com/2005/02/11/national/11stem.html>.

400 Belluck, Pam. "Massachusetts Democrats Object to Stem Cell Research Ban." *NYTimes.com*. The *New York Times*, 11 Feb. 2005. Web. 21 June 2010. <http://www.nytimes.com/2005/02/11/national/11stem.html>.

401 Mooney, Brian C., Stephanie Ebbert, and Scott Helman. "Ambitious Goals; Shifting Stances." *Boston.com*. *Boston Globe*, 30 June 2007. Web. 15 Mar. 2010. <http://www.boston.com/news/politics/2008/specials/romney/articles/part7_main/>.

402 Klein, Rick. "Romney's Pro-Life Conversion: Myth or Reality? - ABC News." *ABCNews.com*. ABC New Internet Ventures, 14 June 2007. Web. 21 June 2010. <http://abcnews.go.com/Politics/story?id=3279653&page=1>.

403 "Transcript: Stem Cell Debate on 'FNS' - FOX News Sunday | Chris Wallace - FOXNews.com." Interview by Chris Wallace. *FOXNews.com*. 22 May 2005. Web. 15 Oct. 2010. <http://www.foxnews.com/story/0,2933,157293,00.html>.

404 Hudson, Deal W. "The Problem with Mitt Romney's Pro-Life Conversion." *InsideCatholic.com.* 27 Dec. 2007. Web. 21 June 2010. <http://www.insidecatholic.com/index2.php?option=com_content&task=view&id=2024&...>.

405 Hudson, Deal W. "The Problem with Mitt Romney's Pro-Life Conversion." *InsideCatholic.com.* 27 Dec. 2007. Web. 21 June 2010. <http://www.insidecatholic.com/index2.php?option=com_content&task=view&id=2024&...>.

406 "Mitt Romney on Abortion." *OnTheIssues.org - Candidates on the Issues.* Web. 15 Oct. 2010. <http://www.ontheissues.org/governor/Mitt_Romney_Abortion.htm>.

407 *Arthur S DeMoss Foundation.* Rep. GuideStar Nonprofit Reports and Forms 990 for Donors, Grantmakers and Businesses. Web. 27 June 2010. <http://www.guidestar.org/pqShowGsReport.do?partner=iwave&grantType=grant&npoId=>.

408 DeMoss, Mark. "Article VI Blog Interview - Mark DeMoss." Interview by John Schroeder and Lowell Brown. Web log post. *Article6Blog.com.* 3 May 2007. Web. 30 June 2010. <http://www.article6blog.com/2007/05/03/article-vi-blog-interview-mark-demoss/>.

409 Miller, John J. "Evangelicals for Romney?" *National Review Online.* National Review, 18 Dec. 2006. Web. 15 June 2010. <http://nrd.nationalreview.com/article/?q=YWNjMzE2MGMzZGFlZmNjZGZiNDA3YjYyMmFjOWY1NTc=>.

410 DeMoss, Mark. "Article VI Blog Interview - Mark DeMoss." Interview by John Schroeder and Lowell Brown. Web log post. *Article6Blog.com.* 3 May 2007. Web. 30 June 2010. <http://www.article6blog.com/2007/05/03/article-vi-blog-interview-mark-demoss/>.

411 Miller, John J. "Evangelicals for Romney?" *National Review Online.* National Review, 18 Dec. 2006. Web. 15 June 2010. <http://nrd.nationalreview.com/article/?q=YWNjMzE2MGMzZGFlZmNjZGZiNDA3YjYyMmFjOWY1NTc=>.

412 DeMoss, Mark. "Article VI Blog Interview - Mark DeMoss." Interview by John Schroeder and Lowell Brown. Web log post. *Article6Blog.com*. 3 May 2007. Web. 30 June 2010. <http://www.article6blog.com/2007/05/03/article-vi-blog-interview-mark-demoss/>.

413 Miller, John J. "Evangelicals for Romney?" *National Review Online*. National Review, 18 Dec. 2006. Web. 15 June 2010. <http://nrd.nationalreview.com/article/?q=YWNjMzE2MGMzZGFlZmNjZGZiNDA3YjYyMmFjOWY1NTc=>.

414 DeMoss, Mark. "The 2008 Presidential Election." Letter to Conservative & Evangelical Leaders. 9 Oct. 2007. *NYTimes.com*. *New York Times*, 10 Oct. 2007. Web. 14 Oct. 2010. <http://graphics8.nytimes.com/packages/pdf/politics/demoss_memo.pdf>.

415 Silverstein, Ken. "Making Mitt Romney: How to Fabricate a Conservative (Harper's Magazine)." Editorial. *Harpers.org*. Harper's Magazine, Nov. 2007. Web. 15 Mar. 2010. <http://www.harpers.org/archive/2007/11/0081773>.

416 Silverstein, Ken. "Making Mitt Romney: How to Fabricate a Conservative (Harper's Magazine)." Editorial. *Harpers.org*. Harper's Magazine, Nov. 2007. Web. 15 Mar. 2010. <http://www.harpers.org/archive/2007/11/0081773>.

417 Shear, Michael D., and Alec MacGillis. "Romney's Cash Beckons Iowans To Straw Poll - Washingtonpost.com." *Washingtonpost.com*. Washington Post, 10 Aug. 2007. Web. 15 June 2010. <http://www.washingtonpost.com/wp-dyn/content/article/2007/08/09/AR2007080902379.html>.

418 Shear, Michael D., and Alec MacGillis. "Romney's Cash Beckons Iowans To Straw Poll - Washingtonpost.com." *Washingtonpost.com*. Washington Post, 10 Aug. 2007. Web. 15 June 2010. <http://www.washingtonpost.com/wp-dyn/content/article/2007/08/09/AR2007080902379.html>.

419 Silverstein, Ken. "Making Mitt Romney: How to Fabricate a Conservative (Harper's Magazine)." Editorial. *Harpers.org*.

Harper's Magazine, Nov. 2007. Web. 15 Mar. 2010. <http://www.harpers.org/archive/2007/11/0081773>.

420 Shear, Michael D., and Alec MacGillis. "Romney's Cash Beckons Iowans To Straw Poll - Washingtonpost.com." *Washingtonpost.com.* Washington Post, 10 Aug. 2007. Web. 15 June 2010. <http://www.washingtonpost.com/wp-dyn/content/article/2007/08/09/AR2007080902379.html>.

421 Overby, Peter. "NPR: Election 2008: Candidates' Cash Flow Ahead of Super Tuesday." *NPR : National Public Radio.* 4 Feb. 2008. Web. 15 Oct. 2010. <http://www.npr.org/news/specials/election2008/cashfeb5.html>.

422 Cummings, Jeanne. "Minding Business Pays off for Romney." *POLITICO.com.* 25 Oct. 2007. Web. 28 Mar. 2010. <http://www.politico.com/news/stories/1007/6535.html>.

423 Allen, Mike. "Romney Wins Online, Huckabee Wins Room - Mike Allen - POLITICO.com." *POLITICO.com.* 20 Oct. 2007. Web. 15 June 2010. <http://www.politico.com/news/stories/1007/6465.html>.

424 Allen, Mike. "Romney Wins Online, Huckabee Wins Room - Mike Allen - POLITICO.com." *POLITICO.com.* 20 Oct. 2007. Web. 15 June 2010. <http://www.politico.com/news/stories/1007/6465.html>.

425 Allen, Mike. "Romney Wins Online, Huckabee Wins Room - Mike Allen - POLITICO.com." *POLITICO.com.* 20 Oct. 2007. Web. 15 June 2010. <http://www.politico.com/news/stories/1007/6465.html>.

426 "The Mitt Romney Deception." *MassResistance!* Web. 4 May 2010. <http://www.massresistance.org/docs/marriage/romney/record/>.

427 "The Mitt Romney Deception." *MassResistance!* Web. 4 May 2010. <http://www.massresistance.org/docs/marriage/romney/record/>.

428 Miller, John J. "Evangelicals for Romney?" *National Review Online.* National Review, 18 Dec. 2006. Web. 15 June 2010.

<http://nrd.nationalreview.com/article/?q=YWNjMzE2MGMzZGFlZmNjZGZiNDA3YjYyMmFjOWY1NTc=>.

429 Harnden, Toby. "Romney Strives to Win over Evangelicals." *Telegraph.co.uk*. London Telegraph, 6 Dec. 2007. Web. 30 Aug. 2010. <http://www.telegraph.co.uk/news/worldnews/1571753/Mitt-Romney-strives-to-win-over-evangelicals.html>.

430 "The Mitt Romney Deception." *MassResistance!* Web. 4 May 2010. <http://www.massresistance.org/docs/marriage/romney/record/>.

431 "The Mitt Romney Deception." *MassResistance!* Web. 4 May 2010. <http://www.massresistance.org/docs/marriage/romney/record/>.

432 "It's All About the Butt Sex." Web log post. *World O'Crap*. 19 May 2005. Web. 15 Oct. 2010. <http://blogs.salon.com/0002874/2005/05/19.html>.

433 "It's All About the Butt Sex." Web log post. *World O'Crap*. 19 May 2005. Web. 15 Oct. 2010. <http://blogs.salon.com/0002874/2005/05/19.html>.

434 Miller, John J. "Evangelicals for Romney?" *National Review Online*. National Review, 18 Dec. 2006. Web. 15 June 2010. <http://nrd.nationalreview.com/article/?q=YWNjMzE2MGMzZGFlZmNjZGZiNDA3YjYyMmFjOWY1NTc=>.

435 Kuhn, David Paul. "Conservatives Would Bolt GOP over Rudy - POLITICO.com Print View." *POLITICO.com*. 7 June 2007. Web. 15 Oct. 2010. <http://dyn.politico.com/printstory.cfm?uuid=1C61FCFB–3048–5C12–00ABDC8E6A0C594B>.

436 Nagourney, Adam, and David D. Kirkpatrick. "Romney's Gay Rights Stance Draws Ire." *NYTimes.com*. *New York Times*, 9 Dec. 2006. Web. 12 July 2010. <http://www.nytimes.com/2006/12/09/us/politics/09romney.html>.

437 "Stem Cells and Biotechnology." *FRC.org*. Family Research Council. Web. 15 June 2010. <http://www.frc.org/life--bioethics#stem_cells>.

438 Family Research Council. "Values Voter Summit Adds More Star Power." 22 July 2008. E-mail.

439 Johnson, Glen. "Romney Urged To Explain Gay Rights Remark - December 13, 2006." *NYsun.com*. The New York Sun, 13 Dec. 2006. Web. 12 July 2010. <http://www.nysun.com/national/romney-urged-to-explain-gay-rights-remark/45109/>.

440 Helman, Scott. "Romney's Stem Cell View May Upset the Right - The *Boston Globe*." *Boston.com. Boston Globe*, 11 Feb. 2007. Web. 09 Sept. 2010. <http://www.boston.com/news/nation/articles/2007/02/11/romneys_stem_cell_view_may_upset_the_right/>.

441 Cooperman, Alan, and Chris Cillizza. "McCain, Romney Vying for Support Of Conservatives - Washingtonpost.com." *Washingtonpost.com*. Washington Post, 13 Feb. 2007. Web. 15 June 2010. <http://www.washingtonpost.com/wp-dyn/content/article/2007/02/12/AR2007021201642.html>.

442 *Dr. John Willke, A Founder of the Pro-Life Movement Nationally & Internationally, Endorses Gov. Romney. National Review Online.* 9 Oct. 2007. Web. 15 Oct. 2010. <http://www.nationalreview.com/corner/150728/romney-catches-big-pro-life-fish/kathryn-jean-lopez>.

443 O'Steen, David N. "NRLC Letter to U.S. Senate regarding Senate Bills S. 5 and S. 30." Letter to The United States Senate. 2 Apr. 2007. *NRLC.org*. National Right to Life, 2 Apr. 2007. Web. 15 Oct. 2010. <http://www.nrlc.org/killing_embryos/NRLCLettertoSenateS5andS30.html>.

444 "Our Position (Stem Cells) - Focus on the Family." *FocusontheFamily.com*. Focus on the Family. Web. 15 Oct. 2010. <http://www.focusonthefamily.com/socialissues/sanctity-of-life/stem-cell-research/our-position.aspx>.

445 "Focus on the Family's Foundational Values - Focus on the Family." *FocusontheFamily.com*. Focus on the Family. Web. 15 Oct. 2010. <http://www.focusonthefamily.com/about_us/guiding-principles.aspx>.

446 Scherer, Michael. "A Stealth Mitt Romney Endorsement from the Religious Right's Powerbrokers? - Swampland - *Time*.com." Web

log post. *Swampland.* Time, 24 Jan. 2008. Web. 15 Oct. 2010. <http://swampland.blogs.time.com/2008/01/24/a_stealth_mitt_romney_endorsem/>.

447 Scherer, Michael. "A Stealth Mitt Romney Endorsement from the Religious Right's Powerbrokers? - Swampland - *Time*.com." Web log post. *Swampland.* Time, 24 Jan. 2008. Web. 15 Oct. 2010. <http://swampland.blogs.time.com/2008/01/24/a_stealth_mitt_romney_endorsem/>.

448 Miller, John J. "Evangelicals for Romney?" *National Review Online*. National Review, 18 Dec. 2006. Web. 15 June 2010. <http://nrd.nationalreview.com/article/?q=YWNjMzE2MGMzZGFlZmNjZGZiNDA3YjYyMmFjOWY1NTc=>.

449 American Center for Law and Justice. *ACLJ Files Legal Challenge on Behalf of a Group of Massachusetts Legislators to Stop the Mass. Supreme Judicial Court Decision Allowing Same-Sex Marriage. ACLJ.org.* 27 Apr. 2004. Web. 7 Sept. 2010. <http://www.aclj.org/news/Read.aspx?ID=273>.

450 Eastland, Terry. "In 2008, Will It Be Mormon in America?" *WeeklyStandard.com*. The Weekly Standard, 6 June 2005. Web. 15 Oct. 2010. <http://www.weeklystandard.com/Content/Public/Articles/000/000/005/672kwvro.asp>.

451 Miller, John J. "Evangelicals for Romney?" *National Review Online*. National Review, 18 Dec. 2006. Web. 15 June 2010. <http://nrd.nationalreview.com/article/?q=YWNjMzE2MGMzZGFlZmNjZGZiNDA3YjYyMmFjOWY1NTc=>.

452 George, Robert, Timothy George, and Chuck Colson. "Manhattan Declaration: A Call of Christian Conscience." *ManhattanDeclaration.org.* The Manhattan Declaration, 20 Nov. 2009. Web. 15 Oct. 2010. <http://www.manhattandeclaration.org/the-declaration/read.aspx>.

453 George, Robert, Timothy George, and Chuck Colson. "Manhattan Declaration: A Call of Christian Conscience." *ManhattanDeclaration.org.* The Manhattan Declaration, 20 Nov.

2009. Web. 15 Oct. 2010. <http://www.manhattandeclaration.org/the-declaration/read.aspx>.

454 George, Robert, Timothy George, and Chuck Colson. "Manhattan Declaration: A Call of Christian Conscience." *ManhattanDeclaration.org.* The Manhattan Declaration, 20 Nov. 2009. Web. 15 Oct. 2010. <http://www.manhattandeclaration.org/the-declaration/read.aspx>.

455 Miller, John J. "Evangelicals for Romney?" *National Review Online.* National Review, 18 Dec. 2006. Web. 15 June 2010. <http://nrd.nationalreview.com/article/?q=YWNjMzE2MGMzZGFlZmNjZGZiNDA3YjYyMmFjOWY1NTc=>.

456 Miller, John J. "Evangelicals for Romney?" *National Review Online.* National Review, 18 Dec. 2006. Web. 15 June 2010. <http://nrd.nationalreview.com/article/?q=YWNjMzE2MGMzZGFlZmNjZGZiNDA3YjYyMmFjOWY1NTc=>.

457 DeMoss, Mark. "Article VI Blog Interview - Mark DeMoss." Interview by John Schroeder and Lowell Brown. Web log post. *Article6Blog.com.* 3 May 2007. Web. 30 June 2010. <http://www.article6blog.com/2007/05/03/article-vi-blog-interview-mark-demoss/>.

458 DeMoss, Mark. "Article VI Blog Interview - Mark DeMoss." Interview by John Schroeder and Lowell Brown. Web log post. *Article6Blog.com.* 3 May 2007. Web. 30 June 2010. <http://www.article6blog.com/2007/05/03/article-vi-blog-interview-mark-demoss/>.

459 Kornacki, Steve. "Romney More G.H.W.B. Than J.F.K." Editorial. *Observer.com.* New York Observer, 6 Dec. 2007. Web. 16 June 2010. <http://www.observer.com/2007/romney-more-ghwb-jfk>.

460 Kornacki, Steve. "Romney More G.H.W.B. Than J.F.K." Editorial. *Observer.com.* New York Observer, 6 Dec. 2007. Web. 16 June 2010. <http://www.observer.com/2007/romney-more-ghwb-jfk>.

461 I, Mark. “Romney in Seven Words.” *RedState.com*. 11 Jan. 2008. Web. 15 June 2010. <http://redstate.com/blog/mark_i/2008/jan/11/romney_in_seven_words>.

462 “The Mitt Romney Deception.” *MassResistance!* Web. 4 May 2010. <http://www.massresistance.org/docs/marriage/romney/record/>.

463 “Mitt Romney’s Flip-Flops.” *Log Cabin Republicans*. Web. 25 Nov. 2009. <http://online.logcabin.org/mitt-romneys-flip-flops.html>.

464 “The Mitt Romney Deception.” *MassResistance!* Web. 4 May 2010. <http://www.massresistance.org/docs/marriage/romney/record/>.

465 “Mitt Romney’s Flip-Flops.” *Log Cabin Republicans*. Web. 25 Nov. 2009. <http://online.logcabin.org/mitt-romneys-flip-flops.html>.

466 “Mitt Romney on Abortion.” *OnTheIssues.org - Candidates on the Issues*. Web. 15 Oct. 2010. <http://www.ontheissues.org/governor/Mitt_Romney_Abortion.htm>.

467 Balz, Dan, and Shailagh Murray. “Mass. Governor’s Rightward Shift Raises Questions - Washingtonpost.com.” *Washingtonpost.com*. 21 Dec. 2006. Web. 12 Apr. 2010. <http://www.washingtonpost.com/wp-dyn/content/article/2006/12/20/AR2006122002046.html>.

468 “The Mitt Romney Deception.” *MassResistance!* Web. 4 May 2010. <http://www.massresistance.org/docs/marriage/romney/record/>.

469 “The Mitt Romney Deception.” *MassResistance!* Web. 4 May 2010. <http://www.massresistance.org/docs/marriage/romney/record/>.

470 “Mitt Romney’s Flip-Flops.” *Log Cabin Republicans*. Web. 25 Nov. 2009. <http://online.logcabin.org/mitt-romneys-flip-flops.html>.

471 “Mitt Romney’s Flip-Flops.” *Log Cabin Republicans*. Web. 25 Nov. 2009. <http://online.logcabin.org/mitt-romneys-flip-flops.html>.

472 “Mitt Romney’s Flip-Flops.” *Log Cabin Republicans*. Web. 25 Nov. 2009. <http://online.logcabin.org/mitt-romneys-flip-flops.html>.

473 “Mitt Romney’s Flip-Flops.” *Log Cabin Republicans*. Web. 25 Nov. 2009. <http://online.logcabin.org/mitt-romneys-flip-flops.html>.

474 Helman, Scott. "Romney Retreats on Gun Control." *Boston.com. Boston Globe*, 14 Jan. 2007. Web. 14 Oct. 2010. <http://www.boston.com/news/local/articles/2007/01/14/romney_retreats_on_gun_control/>.

475 Helman, Scott. "Romney Retreats on Gun Control." *Boston.com. Boston Globe*, 14 Jan. 2007. Web. 14 Oct. 2010. <http://www.boston.com/news/local/articles/2007/01/14/romney_retreats_on_gun_control/>.

476 Helman, Scott. "Romney Retreats on Gun Control." *Boston.com. Boston Globe*, 14 Jan. 2007. Web. 14 Oct. 2010.<http://www.boston.com/news/local/articles/2007/01/14/romney_retreats_on_gun_control/>.

477 Helman, Scott. "Romney Retreats on Gun Control." *Boston.com. Boston Globe*, 14 Jan. 2007. Web. 14 Oct. 2010. <http://www.boston.com/news/local/articles/2007/01/14/romney_retreats_on_gun_control/>.

478 Helman, Scott. "Romney Retreats on Gun Control." *Boston.com. Boston Globe*, 14 Jan. 2007. Web. 14 Oct. 2010. <http://www.boston.com/news/local/articles/2007/01/14/romney_retreats_on_gun_control/>.

479 Romney for US Senate. Romney for US Senate, 1994. *Politico.com.* Web. 14 Oct. 2010. <http://www.politico.com/pdf/wmr_1994_senate_flier_side_1.pdf>.

480 "RomneyCare Revisited." Editorial. *Wall Street Journal* Jan. 2010, Review & Outlook sec. *WSJ.com.* 21 Jan. 2010. Web. 30 Nov. 2009. <http://online.wsj.com/article/SB10001424052748703837004575013080421218008.html>.

481 Cheplick, Thomas, and Joe Emanuel. "Massachusetts Slashes Funding, Rations Care - by Thomas Cheplick and Joe Emanuel - Health Care News." *Health Care News* 6 Aug. 2009. *The Heartland Institute.* Web. 30 Nov. 2009. <http://www.heartland.org/publications/health care/article/25810/Massachusetts_Slashes_Funding_Rations_Care.html>.

482 Robinson, Peter. "Mitt Romney's Big-Government Health Care Plan - Forbes.com." Editorial. *Forbes. Forbes.com.* 7 Aug. 2009. Web. 30 Nov. 2009. <http://www.forbes.com/2009/08/06/mitt-romney-health-care-gop-opinions-columnists-peter-robinson.html>.

483 Turner, Grace-Marie. "The Failure of RomneyCare - WSJ.com." *Wall Street Journal* 17 Mar. 2007. *WSJ.com.* Wall Street Journal, 16 Mar. 2010. Web. 14 Oct. 2010. <http://online.wsj.com/article/SB10001424052748703625304575115691871093652.html>.

484 Cannon, Michael F. "Romney's Folly - Health-Care Mandates Are a Middle-Class Tax | Michael F. Cannon | Cato Institute: Commentary." Editorial. *National Review* 24 July 2009. *The Cato Institute.* 24 July 2009. Web. 30 Nov. 2009. <http://www.cato.org/pub_display.php?pub_id=10381>.

485 Turner, Grace-Marie. "The Failure of RomneyCare - WSJ.com." *Wall Street Journal* 17 Mar. 2007. *WSJ.com.* Wall Street Journal, 16 Mar. 2010. Web. 14 Oct. 2010. <http://online.wsj.com/article/SB10001424052748703625304575115691871093652.html>.

486 Allott, Daniel. "Romney, Get Real about Your Abortion Record - Daniel Allott - POLITICO.com." Editorial. *POLITICO.com.* 20 Dec. 2007. Web. 15 Oct. 2010. <http://www.politico.com/news/stories/1207/7482.html>.

487 Wangsness, Lisa. "Romney to Detail His Healthcare Rx." *Boston.com. Boston Globe*, 24 Aug. 2007. Web. 15 Oct. 2010. <http://www.boston.com/news/nation/articles/2007/08/24/romney_to_detail_his_healthcare_rx/>

488 Condon, Stephanie. "Romney's Health Care Administrator Moves to ObamaCare." *CBSNews.com.* CBS News, 14 Apr. 2010. Web. 15 Oct. 2010. <http://www.cbsnews.com/8301–503544_162–20002705–503544.html>.

489 "Romney: Ban PACs, Tax Campaign Contributions A History of Support for Campaign Finance Reform." Targeted News Service. 2007. *HighBeam Research.* (September 13, 2010). http://www.highbeam.com/doc/1P3–1364476891.html

490 "Romney: Ban PACs, Tax Campaign Contributions A History of Support for Campaign Finance Reform." Targeted News Service. 2007. *HighBeam Research.* (September 13, 2010). http://www.highbeam.com/doc/1P3–1364476891.html

491 Cummings, Jeanne. "Minding Business Pays off for Romney." *POLITICO.com*. 25 Oct. 2007. Web. 28 Mar. 2010. <http://www.politico.com/news/stories/1007/6535.html>.

492 "Mitt Romney's Flip-Flops." *Log Cabin Republicans*. Web. 25 Nov. 2009. <http://online.logcabin.org/mitt-romneys-flip-flops.html>.

493 Dayton, Soren. "Border Security Group Attacks Romney for Flip-flopping on Immigration." *SorenDayton.com*. 30 May 2007. Web. 30 Nov. 2009. <http://sorendayton.com/2007/05/30/border-security-group-attacks-romney-for-flip-floppi…>.

494 "The two Mitt Romneys; A serious flip-flop on illegal immigration. (OPED)." The Washington Times (Washington, DC). 2007. *HighBeam Research.* (September 13, 2010). http://www.highbeam.com/doc/1G1–167666556.html

495 Pethokoukis, James. "Did Romney Filp-flop on TARP?" Web log post. *Reuters.com*. Reuters, 21 Sept. 2009. Web. 30 Nov. 2009. <http://blogs.reuters.com/james-pethokoukis/2010/01/19/mass-u-s-senate-showdown-brown-vs-coakley-live-blogging/>.

496 Pethokoukis, James. "Did Romney Filp-flop on TARP?" Web log post. *Reuters.com*. Reuters, 21 Sept. 2009. Web. 30 Nov. 2009. <http://blogs.reuters.com/james-pethokoukis/2010/01/19/mass-u-s-senate-showdown-brown-vs-coakley-live-blogging/>.

497 "Mitt Romney's Flip-Flops." *Log Cabin Republicans*. Web. 25 Nov. 2009. <http://online.logcabin.org/mitt-romneys-flip-flops.html>.

498 "The Mitt Romney Deception." *MassResistance!* Web. 4 May 2010. <http://www.massresistance.org/docs/marriage/romney/record/>.

499 "Mitt Romney's Flip-Flops." *Log Cabin Republicans*. Web. 25 Nov. 2009. <http://online.logcabin.org/mitt-romneys-flip-flops.html>.

500 Levenson, Michael, and Robert Gavin. "Romney Singing New Tune, Sweeter to Detroit's Ears." *Boston.com. Boston Globe*, 15

Jan. 2008. Web. 30 Nov. 2009. <http://www.boston.com/news/nation/articles/2008/01/15/romney_singing_new_tune_sweeter_to_detroits_ears/>.

501 Levenson, Michael, and Robert Gavin. "Romney Singing New Tune, Sweeter to Detroit's Ears." *Boston.com. Boston Globe*, 15 Jan. 2008. Web. 30 Nov. 2009. <http://www.boston.com/news/nation/articles/2008/01/15/romney_singing_new_tune_sweeter_to_detroits_ears/>.

502 McLaughlin, Dan. "George Romney, Martin Luther King and Mitt Romney's Recovered Memory." *Redstate.com*. 2008. Web. 15 Oct. 2010. <http://archive.redstate.com/blogs/dan_mclaughlin/2007/dec/20/george_romney_martin_luther_king_and_mitt_romneys_recovered_memory>.

503 McLaughlin, Dan. "George Romney, Martin Luther King and Mitt Romney's Recovered Memory." *Redstate.com*. 2008. Web. 15 Oct. 2010. <http://archive.redstate.com/blogs/dan_mclaughlin/2007/dec/20/george_romney_martin_luther_king_and_mitt_romneys_recovered_memory>.

504 Kirkpatrick, David D. "Romney, Searching and Earnest, Set His Path in '60s." *NYTimes.com. New York Times*, 15 Nov. 2007. Web. 1 Dec. 2009. <http://www.nytimes.com/2007/11/15/us/politics/15romney.html>.

505 Kirkpatrick, David D. "Romney, Searching and Earnest, Set His Path in '60s." *NYTimes.com. New York Times*, 15 Nov. 2007. Web. 1 Dec. 2009. <http://www.nytimes.com/2007/11/15/us/politics/15romney.html>.

506 Kirkpatrick, David D. "Romney, Searching and Earnest, Set His Path in '60s." *NYTimes.com. New York Times*, 15 Nov. 2007. Web. 1 Dec. 2009. <http://www.nytimes.com/2007/11/15/us/politics/15romney.html>.

507 Allen, Mike, and Jonathan Martin. "Romney Ends Bid, Eyeing 2012." *POLITICO.com*. 7 Feb. 2008. Web. 15 Oct. 2010. <http://www.politico.com/news/stories/0208/8386.html>.

508 Barr, Andy. “Poll: Ex-Obama Voters like Romney.” *POLITICO.com*. 15 July 2010. Web. 15 Oct. 2010. <http://www.politico.com/news/stories/0710/39779.html>.

509 Barr, Andy. “Poll: Ex-Obama Voters like Romney.” *POLITICO.com*. 15 July 2010. Web. 15 Oct. 2010. <http://www.politico.com/news/stories/0710/39779.html>.

510 Barr, Andy. “Poll: Ex-Obama Voters like Romney.” *POLITICO.com*. 15 July 2010. Web. 15 Oct. 2010. <http://www.politico.com/news/stories/0710/39779.html>.

511 Romney for US Senate. Romney for US Senate, 1994. *Politico.com*. Web. 14 Oct. 2010. <http://www.politico.com/pdf/wmr_1994_senate_flier_side_1.pdf>.

512 Swidey, Neil, and Stephanie Ebbert. “Journeys of a Shared Life - The *Boston Globe*.” *Boston.com*. 27 June 2007. Web. 03 Sept. 2010. <http://www.boston.com/news/politics/2008/specials/romney/articles/part4_main/>.

513 Balz, Dan, and Shailagh Murray. “Mass. Governor’s Rightward Shift Raises Questions - Washingtonpost.com.” *Washingtonpost.com*. 21 Dec. 2006. Web. 12 Apr. 2010. <http://www.washingtonpost.com/wp-dyn/content/article/2006/12/20/AR2006122002046.html>.

514 “The Mitt Romney Deception.” *MassResistance!* Web. 4 May 2010. <http://www.massresistance.org/docs/marriage/romney/record/>.

515 “The Mitt Romney Deception.” *MassResistance!* Web. 4 May 2010. <http://www.massresistance.org/docs/marriage/romney/record/>.

516 Luo, Michael. “Romney’s Tone on Gay Rights Is Seen as Shift.” *NYTimes.com*. *New York Times*, 8 Sept. 2007. Web. 17 May 2010. <http://www.nytimes.com/2007/09/08/us/politics/08romney.html>.

517 “Mitt Romney’s Flip-Flops.” *Log Cabin Republicans*. Web. 25 Nov. 2009. <http://online.logcabin.org/mitt-romneys-flip-flops.html>.

518 (Klein, Rick. “Romney’s Pro-Life Conversion: Myth or Reality? - ABC News.” *ABCNews.com*. ABC New Internet Ventures, 14

June 2007. Web. 21 June 2010. <http://abcnews.go.com/Politics/story?id=3279653&page=1>.

519 "Mitt Romney's Flip-Flops." *Log Cabin Republicans.* Web. 25 Nov. 2009. <http://online.logcabin.org/mitt-romneys-flip-flops.html>.

520 Bernstein, David S. "New and Improved Romney." *ThePhoenix.com*. 12 Feb. 2010. Web. 24 Aug. 2010. <http://thephoenix.com/boston/news/96976-new-and-improved-romney/>.

521 Bernstein, David S. "New and Improved Romney." *ThePhoenix.com*. 12 Feb. 2010. Web. 24 Aug. 2010. <http://thephoenix.com/boston/news/96976-new-and-improved-romney/>.

522 Bernstein, David S. "New and Improved Romney." *ThePhoenix.com*. 12 Feb. 2010. Web. 24 Aug. 2010. <http://thephoenix.com/boston/news/96976-new-and-improved-romney/>.

523 Romano, Andrew. "How Mitt Romney Is Taking Advantage of the Mosque Controversy." *Newsweek.com*. Newsweek, 19 Aug. 2010. Web. 24 Aug. 2010. <http://www.newsweek.com/blogs/the-gaggle/2010/08/19/how-mitt-romney-is-taking-advantage-of-the-mosque-controversy.html>.

524 Romano, Andrew. "How Mitt Romney Is Taking Advantage of the Mosque Controversy." *Newsweek.com*. Newsweek, 19 Aug. 2010. Web. 24 Aug. 2010. <http://www.newsweek.com/blogs/the-gaggle/2010/08/19/how-mitt-romney-is-taking-advantage-of-the-mosque-controversy.html>.

525 Bernstein, David S. "New and Improved Romney." *ThePhoenix.com*. 12 Feb. 2010. Web. 24 Aug. 2010. <http://thephoenix.com/boston/news/96976-new-and-improved-romney/>.

526 Guerrero, Aaron. "Mitt Romney Chooses the Economy over the Mosque." *DailyCaller.com*. 24 Aug. 2010. Web. 24 Aug. 2010. <http://dailycaller.com/2010/08/24/mitt-romney-chooses-the-economy-over-the-mosque/>.

527 "Romney's Cave-in on Mosque Violates His Own Principles - The *Boston Globe*." Editorial. *Boston.com*. *Boston Globe*, 25 Aug.

2010. Web. 14 Oct. 2010. <http://www.boston.com/bostonglobe/editorial_opinion/editorials/articles/2010/08/25/romneys_cave_in_on_mosque_violates_his_own_principles/>.

528 Guerrero, Aaron. "Mitt Romney Chooses the Economy over the Mosque." *DailyCaller.com*. 24 Aug. 2010. Web. 24 Aug. 2010. <http://dailycaller.com/2010/08/24/mitt-romney-chooses-the-economy-over-the-mosque/>.

529 Romney, Mitt. "Grow Jobs and Shrink Government." Editorial. *Boston.com. Boston Globe*, 18 Aug. 2010. Web. 24 Aug. 2010. <http://www.boston.com/bostonglobe/editorial_opinion/oped/articles/2010/08/18/grow_jobs_and_shrink_government/>.

530 Howell, Carla. "Mitt Romney: Champion of Big Government." *LewRockwell.com*. 31 May 2007. Web. 03 Sept. 2010. <http://www.lewrockwell.com/orig4/howell5.html>.

531 Batkins, Sam. "New Budget Data: Romney's Mediocre Record." Web log post. *Government Bytes*. National Taxpayers Union, 26 June 2008. Web. 25 Nov. 2009. <http://blog.ntu.org/main/post.php?post_id=3541>.

532 Dayton, Soren. "Romney Lying about His Tax Record (update)." *SorenDayton.com*. 7 Feb. 2007. Web. 30 Nov. 2009. <http://sorendayton.com/2007/02/07/romney-lying-about-his-tax-record>.

533 Dayton, Soren. "Romney Lying about His Tax Record (update)." *SorenDayton.com*. 7 Feb. 2007. Web. 30 Nov. 2009. <http://sorendayton.com/2007/02/07/romney-lying-about-his-tax-record>.

534 Howell, Carla. "Mitt Romney: Champion of Big Government." *LewRockwell.com*. 31 May 2007. Web. 03 Sept. 2010. <http://www.lewrockwell.com/orig4/howell5.html>.

535 Batkins, Sam. "New Budget Data: Romney's Mediocre Record." Web log post. *Government Bytes*. National Taxpayers Union, 26 June 2008. Web. 25 Nov. 2009. <http://blog.ntu.org/main/post.php?post_id=3541>.

536 Howell, Carla. "Mitt Romney: Champion of Big Government." *LewRockwell.com*. 31 May 2007. Web. 03 Sept. 2010. <http://www.lewrockwell.com/orig4/howell5.html>.

537 Howell, Carla. "Mitt Romney: Champion of Big Government." *LewRockwell.com*. 31 May 2007. Web. 03 Sept. 2010. <http://www.lewrockwell.com/orig4/howell5.html>.

538 Szep, Jason. "Mitt Romney's Economic Record Questioned| Reuters." *Reuters.com*. 20 Jan. 2008. Web. 24 Nov. 2009. <http://www.reuters.com/article/idUSN2033704120080120>.

539 Mooney, Brian C., Stephanie Ebbert, and Scott Helman. "Ambitious Goals; Shifting Stances." *Boston.com. Boston Globe*, 30 June 2007. Web. 15 Mar. 2010. <http://www.boston.com/news/politics/2008/specials/romney/articles/part7_main/>.

540 Strassel, Kimberley A. "Massachusetts' Other GOP Winner." *WSJ.com*. Wall Street Journal, 21 Jan. 2010. Web. 24 Aug. 2010. <http://sroblog.com/2010/01/22/kim-strassel-massachusetts-other-gop-winner-wsj-com/>.

541 Strassel, Kimberley A. "Massachusetts' Other GOP Winner." *WSJ.com*. Wall Street Journal, 21 Jan. 2010. Web. 24 Aug. 2010. <http://sroblog.com/2010/01/22/kim-strassel-massachusetts-other-gop-winner-wsj-com/>.

542 Bernstein, David S. "New and Improved Romney." *ThePhoenix.com*. 12 Feb. 2010. Web. 24 Aug. 2010. <http://thephoenix.com/boston/news/96976-new-and-improved-romney/>.

543 Strassel, Kimberley A. "Massachusetts' Other GOP Winner." *WSJ.com*. Wall Street Journal, 21 Jan. 2010. Web. 24 Aug. 2010. <http://sroblog.com/2010/01/22/kim-strassel-massachusetts-other-gop-winner-wsj-com/>.

544 Romney for US Senate. Romney for US Senate, 1994. *Politico.com*. Web. 14 Oct. 2010. <http://www.politico.com/pdf/wmr_1994_senate_flier_side_1.pdf>.

545 Gross, Daniel. "Mitt Romney for Health Czar." *Newsweek.com*. Newsweek, 29 Mar. 2010. Web. 15 Oct. 2010. <http://www.newsweek.com/2010/03/28/mitt-romney-for-health-czar.html>.

546 Romney, Mitt. "A Campaign Begins Today." Editorial. *NationalReview.com*. National Review Online, 22 Mar. 2010. Web. 15 Oct. 2010. <http://www.nationalreview.com/corner/196718/campaign-begins-today/mitt-romney>.

547 Strassel, Kimberley A. "Massachusetts' Other GOP Winner." *WSJ.com*. Wall Street Journal, 21 Jan. 2010. Web. 24 Aug. 2010. <http://sroblog.com/2010/01/22/kim-strassel-massachusetts-other-gop-winner-wsj-com/>.

548 Strassel, Kimberley A. "Massachusetts' Other GOP Winner." *WSJ.com*. Wall Street Journal, 21 Jan. 2010. Web. 24 Aug. 2010. <http://sroblog.com/2010/01/22/kim-strassel-massachusetts-other-gop-winner-wsj-com/>.

549 "RomneyCare Revisited." Editorial. *Wall Street Journal* Jan. 2010, Review & Outlook sec. *WSJ.com*. 21 Jan. 2010. Web. 30 Nov. 2009. <http://online.wsj.com/article/SB10001424052748703837004575013080421218008.html>.

550 Cheplick, Thomas, and Joe Emanuel. "Massachusetts Slashes Funding, Rations Care - by Thomas Cheplick and Joe Emanuel - Health Care News." *Health Care News* 6 Aug. 2009. *The Heartland Institute*. Web. 30 Nov. 2009. <http://www.heartland.org/publications/health care/article/25810/Massachusetts_Slashes_Funding_Rations_Care.html>.

551 Robinson, Peter. "Mitt Romney's Big-Government Health Care Plan - Forbes.com." Editorial. *Forbes*. *Forbes.com*. 7 Aug. 2009. Web. 30 Nov. 2009. <http://www.forbes.com/2009/08/06/mitt-romney-health-care-gop-opinions-columnists-peter-robinson.html>.

552 Goldstein, Aaron. "Archives: Week of April 11, 2010." Editorial. *Spectator.org*. The American Spectator, 13 Apr. 2010. Web. 24 Aug. 2010. <http://spectator.org/archives/weekly/2010–04–11>.

553 Goldstein, Aaron. "Archives: Week of April 11, 2010." Editorial. *Spectator.org*. The American Spectator, 13 Apr. 2010. Web. 24 Aug. 2010. <http://spectator.org/archives/weekly/2010–04–11>.

554 Bernstein, David S. "New and Improved Romney." *ThePhoenix.com*. 12 Feb. 2010. Web. 24 Aug. 2010. <http://thephoenix.com/boston/news/96976-new-and-improved-romney/>.

555 Bernstein, David S. "New and Improved Romney." *ThePhoenix.com*. 12 Feb. 2010. Web. 24 Aug. 2010. <http://thephoenix.com/boston/news/96976-new-and-improved-romney/>.

556 Issenberg, Sasha. "Romney Road Trip May Set Stage for White House Bid." *Boston.com*. *Boston Globe*, 24 Aug. 2010. Web. 24 July 2010. <http://www.boston.com/news/nation/washington/articles/2010/08/24/romney_road_trip_may_set_stage_for_white_house_bid/>.

557 Issenberg, Sasha. "Romney Road Trip May Set Stage for White House Bid." *Boston.com*. *Boston Globe*, 24 Aug. 2010. Web. 24 July 2010. <http://www.boston.com/news/nation/washington/articles/2010/08/24/romney_road_trip_may_set_stage_for_white_house_bid/>.

558 Press, Associated. "Romney Sports Beat-up Pickup Truck at NH Political Fundraiser." *BostonHerald.com*. Boston Herald, 06 Aug. 2010. Web. 24 Aug. 2010. <http://www.bostonherald.com/news/politics/view/20100806romney_sports_beat-up_pickup_truck_at_nh_political_fundraiser/srvc=home&position=recent>.

559 Issenberg, Sasha. "Romney Road Trip May Set Stage for White House Bid." *Boston.com*. *Boston Globe*, 24 Aug. 2010. Web. 24 July 2010. <http://www.boston.com/news/nation/washington/articles/2010/08/24/romney_road_trip_may_set_stage_for_white_house_bid/>.

560 Issenberg, Sasha. "Romney Road Trip May Set Stage for White House Bid." *Boston.com*. *Boston Globe*, 24 Aug. 2010. Web. 24 July 2010. <http://www.boston.com/news/nation/washington/articles/2010/08/24/romney_road_trip_may_set_stage_for_white_house_bid/>.

561 Issenberg, Sasha. "Romney Road Trip May Set Stage for White House Bid." *Boston.com. Boston Globe*, 24 Aug. 2010. Web. 24 July 2010. <http://www.boston.com/news/nation/washington/articles/2010/08/24/romney_road_trip_may_set_stage_for_white_house_bid/>.

562 Cummings, Jeanne, and Andy Barr. "End Run: Romney's Crafty Financing." *POLITICO.com*. 18 Aug. 2010. Web. 24 Aug. 2010. <http://www.politico.com/news/stories/0810/41228.html>.

563 Cummings, Jeanne, and Andy Barr. "End Run: Romney's Crafty Financing." *POLITICO.com*. 18 Aug. 2010. Web. 24 Aug. 2010. <http://www.politico.com/news/stories/0810/41228.html>.

564 Cummings, Jeanne, and Andy Barr. "End Run: Romney's Crafty Financing." *POLITICO.com*. 18 Aug. 2010. Web. 24 Aug. 2010. <http://www.politico.com/news/stories/0810/41228.html>.

565 Cummings, Jeanne. "Minding Business Pays off for Romney." *POLITICO.com*. 25 Oct. 2007. Web. 28 Mar. 2010. <http://www.politico.com/news/stories/1007/6535.html>.

566 Cummings, Jeanne, and Andy Barr. "End Run: Romney's Crafty Financing." *POLITICO.com*. 18 Aug. 2010. Web. 24 Aug. 2010. <http://www.politico.com/news/stories/0810/41228.html>.

567 Cummings, Jeanne, and Andy Barr. "End Run: Romney's Crafty Financing." *POLITICO.com*. 18 Aug. 2010. Web. 24 Aug. 2010. <http://www.politico.com/news/stories/0810/41228.html>.

568 Martin, Jonathan. "Early Signs of 2012 Power." *POLITICO.com*. 16 July 2010. Web. 24 Aug. 2010. <http://www.politico.com/news/stories/0710/39832.html>.

569 Miller, Sean J. "Romney Breaks from the Pack." *TheHill.com*. News Communications, Inc., 16 July 2010. Web. 24 Aug. 2010. <http://thehill.com/campaign/109173-romney-breaks-from-the-pack?ttmpl=comp…>.

570 Martin, Jonathan. "Early Signs of 2012 Power." *POLITICO.com*. 16 July 2010. Web. 24 Aug. 2010. <http://www.politico.com/news/stories/0710/39832.html>.

571 Miller, Sean J. "Romney Breaks from the Pack." *TheHill.com*. News Communications, Inc., 16 July 2010. Web. 24 Aug. 2010. <http://thehill.com/campaign/109173-romney-breaks-from-the-pack?ttmpl=comp...>.